Political Philosophy

Nate Poor

THE OPEN YALE COURSES SERIES is designed to bring the depth and breadth of a Yale education to a wide variety of readers. Based on Yale's Open Yale Courses program (http://oyc.yale.edu), these books bring outstanding lectures by Yale faculty to the curious reader, whether student or adult. Covering a wide variety of topics across disciplines in the social sciences, physical sciences, and humanities, Open Yale Courses books offer accessible introductions at affordable prices.

The production of Open Yale Courses for the Internet was made possible by a grant from the William and Flora Hewlett Foundation.

RECENT TITLES
Paul H. Fry, *Theory of Literature*
Christine Hayes, *Introduction to the Bible*
Shelly Kagan, *Death*
Dale B. Martin, *New Testament History and Literature*
Douglas W. Rae, *Capitalism: Success, Crisis, and Reform*
Ian Shapiro, *The Moral Foundations of Politics*
Steven B. Smith, *Political Philosophy*

Political Philosophy

STEVEN B. SMITH

Yale
UNIVERSITY PRESS
New Haven and London

Published with assistance from the foundation established in memory of
Amasa Stone Mather of the Class of 1907, Yale College.

Yale University Press books may be purchased in quantity for
educational, business, or promotional use. For information, please e-mail
sales.press@yale.edu (U.S. office) or sales@yaleup.co.uk (U.K. office).

Set in Minion type by Westchester Book Group.
Printed in the United States of America.

Library of Congress Cataloging-in-Publication Data

Smith, Steven B., 1951–
    Political philosophy / Steven B. Smith.
        p. cm. — (The open Yale courses series)
    Includes bibliographical references and index.
    ISBN 978-0-300-18180-7 (pbk. : alk. paper)   1. Political science—
Philosophy—History.   I. Title.
    JA71.S498 2012
    320.01—dc23

                                                                    2012016209

A catalogue record for this book is available from the British Library.

This paper meets the requirements of ANSI/NISO Z39.48–1992
(Permanence of Paper).
                    10   9   8   7   6   5   4   3   2   1

To Dylan, Geoff, Mari, Rebecca, Rek, Yedidya, Yishai,
and the memory of the Sunday Club

If you will it, it is no dream.

THEODOR HERZL, *ALTNEULAND*

Contents

Preface

This book grew out of an introductory lecture course on political philosophy that I have taught at Yale for many years. It was a pleasure for me to be able to edit and revise these lectures for Yale University Press's book series.

I have written this book as an introduction to political philosophy rather than the more conventional history of political thought. What I understand by political philosophy is treated in the first chapter. Suffice it to say that political philosophy is a rare and distinctive form of thinking and is not to be confused either with the study of political language in general or with the dry and desiccated form of "concept analysis" so prominent in the 1950s and '60s. Political philosophy is the investigation of the permanent problems of political life—problems like "Who ought to govern?" "How ought conflict to be managed?" "How should a citizen and a statesman be educated?"—that every society must confront.

The texts and authors considered here have been chosen because they help to illuminate the permanent problems of political life rather than the particular problems of the times in which they were written. I have not tried to adapt Plato or Machiavelli or Tocqueville to fit our concerns but have aimed to show how our concerns are intelligible only when viewed through the lenses of the most serious thinkers of the past. The problems we confront today, to the extent that they remain political problems, are precisely the same as those confronted in fifth-century Athens, fifteenth-century Florence, or seventeenth-century England. It would be a mistake to think otherwise.

This book is intended for readers who believe, as do I, that we still have something to learn from the great thinkers of the past. This may seem obvious, but it is hotly disputed within the current political science profession. There are those who believe that political science is or should aspire to be a discipline like physics or chemistry or certain precincts of economics and psychology that pay little attention to their own histories. It is to resist this kind of academic amnesia that I have devoted my teaching and writing. My ideal audience is a general readership with no other specialization than a desire to learn.

In writing this book I make no claim to novelty. Most of what I have said is but a reflection on some previous reflection or on a well-known text. Nevertheless, I have put these lectures together in my own way, and they bear my own stamp. I have tried to retain the informal, even conversational, style of the lecture and to avoid the minutiae of academic controversy. I have also kept footnotes and other scholarly references to a minimum, while at the same time I have freely acknowledged my debts to other scholars, teachers, and colleagues from whom I have learned so much over the years.

I have no doubt that I have learned more from writing and rewriting these lectures than have the undergraduates upon whom they have been inflicted. I can only say that it has been an honor and a privilege to have had so many wonderful students who have sat through these classes and expressed an interest in my subject. I would like to give special thanks to a former student, Justin Zaremby, for reading an earlier version of these lectures and for making many helpful comments.

Texts

Aristotle, *The Politics,* trans. Carnes Lord (Chicago: University of Chicago Press, 1984); references are to the Bekker numbers provided in the margin of the text.

Hobbes, Thomas, *Leviathan,* ed. Edwin Curley (Indianapolis: Hackett, 1994); references are to chapter and section number.

Locke, John, *Second Treatise of Government,* in *Two Treatises of Government,* ed. Peter Laslett (Cambridge: Cambridge University Press, 1991); references are to chapter and section number.

Machiavelli, Niccolò, *The Prince,* trans. Harvey C. Mansfield (Chicago: University of Chicago Press, 1985); references are to chapter and page number.

Machiavelli, Niccolò, *The Discourses of Niccolò Machiavelli,* trans. Leslie J. Waker, S.J. (London: Routledge and Kegan Paul, 1975); references are to book, chapter, and page number.

The New Oxford Annotated Bible, ed. Herbert G. May and Bruce M. Metzger (New York: Oxford University Press, 1977); references are to chapter and verse number.

Plato, *The Republic,* trans. Allan Bloom (New York: Basic Books, 1968); references are to the Stephanus numbers provided in the margin of the text.

Plato, *Apology of Socrates* and *Crito,* in *Plato and Aristophanes: Four Texts on Socrates,* trans. Thomas G. and Grace Starry West (Ithaca: Cornell University Press, 1984); citations are to the Stephanus numbers provided in the margin of the text.

Rousseau, Jean-Jacques, *The Discourses and Other Early Political Writings,* trans. Victor Gourevitch (Cambridge: Cambridge University Press, 1997); references are to page number.

Rousseau, Jean-Jacques, *The Social Contract and Other Later Political Writings,* trans. Victor Gourevitch (Cambridge: Cambridge University Press, 1997); references are to book and chapter number.

Sophocles, *Antigone,* trans. Elizabeth Wyckoff (Chicago: University of Chicago Press, 1954); references are to line number.

Tocqueville, Alexis de, *Democracy in America,* trans. Harvey C. Mansfield and Delba Winthrop (Chicago: University of Chicago Press, 2000); references are to volume, part, chapter, and page number in brackets.

CHAPTER 1

Why Political Philosophy?

Custom dictates that I say something about the subject matter of political philosophy at the outset of our course. This may be a case of putting the cart before the horse—or before the course—because how is it possible to say what political philosophy is in advance of having studied it? Nevertheless I will try to say something useful.

In one sense political philosophy is simply a branch or a "subfield" of political science. It exists alongside other areas of political inquiry like American government, comparative politics, and international relations. Yet in another sense political philosophy is the oldest and most fundamental part of political science. Political philosophy *is* political science in its oldest or classic sense. Its purpose is to lay bare the fundamental problems, the fundamental concepts and categories, which frame the study of politics. In this sense it is less a branch of political science than the very foundation and root of the discipline.

The study of political philosophy today often begins with the study of the great books of our discipline. Political science is the oldest of the social sciences—older than economics, psychology, or sociology—and it can boast a wealth of heavy hitters from Plato and Aristotle to Machiavelli and Hobbes to Hegel, Tocqueville, Nietzsche, Hannah Arendt, and Leo Strauss. The best way to find out what political philosophy is, is simply to study the works and ideas of those who are regarded as its master practitioners. How better to learn than to read with care and attentiveness those who have shaped the field?

Such an approach is not without its dangers. Let me just list a few. What makes a book or thinker great? Who is to say? Why study just these thinkers and not others? Isn't any list of so-called great thinkers or texts likely to be arbitrary and tell us more from what such a list excludes than what it includes? Furthermore, the study of the great books and the great thinkers of the past can easily degenerate into a kind of pedantry or antiquarianism. We may find ourselves easily intimidated by a list of famous names and we end up not thinking for ourselves. Doesn't the study of old books—often *very* old books—risk overlooking the issues facing us today? What can Aristotle and Hobbes tell us today about the world of globalization, terrorism, and ethnic conflict? Hasn't political science made any progress over the preceding centuries? After all, economists no longer study Adam Smith; psychologists no longer read Freud. Why should political science continue to study Aristotle and Rousseau? These are all serious questions. Let me try to respond.

One very widely held view among political scientists is that the study of politics is a progressive field very much like the natural sciences. Just as a modern particle physicist does not feel compelled to study the history of physics, so political science has now outgrown its earlier prehistory. The methods and techniques of experimental and behavioral social science—it is often argued—have doomed to oblivion the earlier and immature speculations of an Aristotle, a Machiavelli, or a Rousseau. To the extent that we study these thinkers at all, it would be more as a curator or an archivist who is only interested in their contributions to the collective edifice of modern social scientific knowledge.

This progressive or scientific model of political science is often combined with another, that of the historicist or the relativist. According to this view, all political ideas are a product of their own time, place, and circumstance. We should not expect ideas written for an audience in fifteenth-century Florence, seventeenth-century England, or eighteenth-century Paris to provide any lessons for readers in twenty-first-century America. All thinking is bound by its own time and place, and the attempt to extract enduring wisdom or lessons from writers or texts of the past is a mistake. This belief—widely held by many people of today—is almost literally self-refuting. If all ideas are limited to their own time and place, then this must also be true for the idea that all ideas are limited to their own time and place. Relativism or historicism, as it is sometimes called, insists, however, that it alone is true, that it alone is eternally valid, while at the same time condemning all other ideas to their historical circumstances. One does not need to be a profound logician to understand that relativism is incoherent even in its own terms.

The historicist manner of reading denies the claim that there is a single tradition linking the works of Plato and Aristotle to Machiavelli, Hobbes, Rousseau, and beyond. This has been contemptuously dismissed as an exercise in "myth-making." In the name of seeking greater historical accuracy, historicism has resulted in the deliberate parochialization of the great works, confining them to their purely local contexts and interests. The historicist thesis often regards ideas as no more than "rationalizations" or "ideologies" expressing different preexisting social interests. The fact is, however, that ideas have a causal power of their own. Ideas not only have consequences, their consequences often stretch far beyond their immediate context and environment. Constitutional theories like those of John Locke's that were developed in England under one set of circumstances often take on a life of their own when they are transplanted to other places such as the North American continent. The history of the twentieth century with its clash of ideologies—communism, fascism, democracy—testifies to the power of ideas to shape the world. Ironically it took no less an authority than the economist John Maynard Keynes to bring out the limitations of a purely economic theory of history: "The ideas of economists and political philosophers," he wrote, "both when they are right and when they are wrong, are more powerful than is commonly understood. Indeed the world is ruled by little else. Practical men, who believe themselves to be quite exempt from any intellectual influences, are usually the slaves of some defunct economist. Madmen in authority, who hear voices in the air, are distilling their frenzy from some academic scribbler of a few years back."[1]

The study of political philosophy is not simply some kind of historical appendage attached to the trunk of political science; nor does it perform some kind of custodial or curatorial function—keeping alive the great glories of earlier ages like mummified remains in a natural history museum. Political philosophy is the study of the deepest, most intractable, and most enduring problems of political life. The number of such problems is by no means infinite and is probably quite small. The study of political philosophy has always revolved around such questions as "Why should I obey the law?" "What is a citizen and how should he or she be educated?" "Who is a lawgiver?" "What is the relation between freedom and authority?" "How should politics and theology be related?" and perhaps a few of others.

The thinkers that we will be reading provide the basic frameworks— the constitutive concepts and categories—through which we can begin to think about politics. They provide the forms of analysis that make possible the work of later and lesser thinkers who work within their orbit. We continue to ask the same questions about law, about authority, about justice and freedom asked by Plato, Machiavelli, and Hobbes even if we do not always answer them in the same way. We may not accept all of their answers, but their questions are often put with unrivaled clarity and insight. These questions do not simply go away. They constitute the core problems of the study of politics. The fact is that there are still people who describe themselves as Aristotelians, Thomists, Lockeans, Kantians, Marxists, and Heideggerians. These doctrines have by no means been refuted or surpassed, consigned to the dustbin of history as have so many defunct or discredited scientific or cosmological theories. They remain constitutive of our most basic outlooks and attitudes that are still alive and very much with us.

One thing you will quickly discover is that there are no permanent answers in the study of political philosophy, only permanent questions. Among the great thinkers there is often profound disagreement over the answers to even the most basic questions regarding justice, rights, freedom, the proper scope of authority, and so on. Contrary to popular wisdom, apparently all great minds do *not* necessarily think alike. But there is some advantage to this. The fact that there is disagreement among the great thinkers allows us to enter into their conversation, to listen first, to reason about their differences, and then judge for ourselves. I will admit that I am not a great thinker, but neither—I should add straight away—are any of the professors you are likely to encounter at Yale or any other university. Most of the people who call themselves philosophers are in fact only professors of philosophy. What is the difference?

The true philosopher is rare; one would be fortunate to encounter such a person maybe once in a lifetime, maybe once in a century. But here is where philosophy differs from other fields. One can be, say, a mediocre historian or a mediocre chemist and still function quite effectively. But a mediocre philosopher is a contradiction in terms. A mediocre philosopher is not a philosopher at all. But those of us who are not great thinkers can at least try to be competent scholars. While the scholar is trained to be careful and methodical, the great thinkers are bold, they go, in the words of *Star Trek*, where no man has gone before. The scholar remains dependent on the work of the great thinkers and does not rise to their inaccessible heights. The scholar is made possible by listening to the conversation of the greatest thinkers and staying alive to their differences. I do at least have one advantage over the great thinkers of the past. Aristotle and Hobbes were great thinkers, but Aristotle and Hobbes are long dead. With me you at least have the advantage that I am alive.

But where should one enter this conversation, with which questions or which thinkers? Where should we begin? As with any enterprise, it is always best to begin at the beginning. The proper subject of political philosophy is political action. All action aims at either preservation or change. When we seek to bring about change we do so to make something better; when we seek to preserve we do so to prevent something from becoming worse. Even the decision not to act, to stand pat, is a kind of action. It follows, then, that all action presupposes some judgment of better and worse. But we cannot think about better and worse without at some point thinking about the good. When we act we do so to advance some idea or opinion of the good and when we act politically we do so to advance some idea of the political good or the common good. The term by which political philosophers have designated the common good has gone under various names, sometimes the good society or the just society or sometimes simply the best regime. The oldest, the most fundamental, of all questions of political life is "What is the best regime?"

The concept of the regime is an ancient one, yet the term is familiar. We often hear even today about shaping regimes or changing regimes, but what exactly is a regime? How many kinds are there? How are they defined? What holds them together and causes them to fall apart? Is there a single best kind of regime? The term goes back to Plato and even before him. In fact the title of the book we know as Plato's *Republic* is actually a translation of the Greek word *politeia,* meaning constitution or regime. But it was above all Aristotle who made the regime the central theme of the study of politics. Broadly speaking, the regime indicates a form of government, whether it is ruled by one, few, or many or whether it is some mixture or combination of these three ruling elements. The regime is identified in the first instance by how a people are governed, how public offices are distributed—by election, by birth, by outstanding personal qualities—and what constitute a people's rights and responsibilities. The regime refers, above all, to the form of government. The political world does not present an infinite variety. It is structured and ordered into a few basic regime types: monarchies, aristocracies, democracies, tyrannies. This is one of the most important propositions of political science.

But a regime is more than a set of formal political structures. It consists of the entire way of life—moral and religious practices, habits, customs, and sentiments—that make a people what they are. The regime constitutes what Aristotle called an *ethos,* that is, a distinctive character that nurtures distinctive human types. Every regime shapes a distinctive human character with distinctive human traits and qualities. The study of regimes is, therefore, in part the study of the distinctive character types that constitute the citizen body. So when Tocqueville studied the American regime in *Democracy in America* he started first with our formal political institutions as enumerated in the Constitution, the separation of powers, the division between state and federal authority, but then went on to look at such informal practices as American manners and morals, our tendency to form small civic associations, our materialism and restiveness as well as our peculiar defensiveness about democracy. All of these help to constitute the democratic regime. In this respect the regime describes the character or tone of society, what a society finds most worthy of admiration, what it looks up to.

There is a corollary to this insight. The regime is always something particular. It stands in a relation of opposition to other regime types. As a consequence the possibility of conflict, tension, and war is built into the very structure of politics. Regimes are necessarily partisan. They instill certain loyalties and passions in the same way that one may feel partisanship toward the New York Yankees or the Boston Red Sox, Yale or Harvard. These passionate attachments are not merely something that takes place between different regimes, they take place within them as different parties, factions, and groups with different loyalties and attachments contend for power, for honor, and for interest, the three great motives of human action. Today it is the hope of many both here and abroad that we might some day overcome the basic structure of regime politics and organize our world around global norms of justice and international law. Is such a hope possible? It cannot be entirely ruled out, but such a world—a world administered by international courts of law, by judges and judicial tribunals—would no longer be a political world. Politics is only possible within the structure of the regime.

This raises a further question, namely, how are regimes founded? What brings them into being and sustains them over time? For thinkers like Tocqueville, regimes are embedded in deep structures of human history that have evolved over long centuries and determined our political institutions and the way we think about them. Yet other voices—Plato, Machiavelli, Rousseau—believe that regimes can be self-consciously founded through the deliberate acts of great statesmen or "founding fathers" as we might call them. These statesmen—Machiavelli refers to Romulus, Moses, Cyrus in the way we might think of Washington, Jefferson, Adams—are the shapers of peoples and institutions. The very first of the *Federalist Papers* by Alexander Hamilton begins by posing this question in the starkest of terms: "It has been frequently remarked," Hamilton writes, "that it seems to have been reserved to the people of this country, by their conduct and example, to decide the important question, whether societies of men are really capable or not of establishing good government from reflection and choice, or whether they are forever destined to depend for their political constitutions on accident and force."[2] Hamilton leaves the question open, but he clearly believes that the founding of regimes can be an act of deliberate statecraft.

The idea that regimes may be founded by acts of deliberate statecraft raises another question related to the regime, namely, who is a statesman? In its oldest sense political science meant the science of statecraft. It was addressed to statesmen or potential statesmen charged with steering the ship of state. What are the qualities necessary for a good statesman? How does statecraft differ from other activities? Must the good statesman be a philosopher versed in mathematics and metaphysics as Plato argues? Or is statesmanship a purely practical skill requiring judgment based on deliberation and experience as Aristotle suggests? Is a streak of cruelty and a willingness to act immorally necessary for great leaders as Machiavelli argues? Must the legislator be capable of literally transforming human nature as Rousseau maintains or is the sovereign a more or less faceless authority much like an umpire or a referee as Hobbes and Locke believe? All of our texts, the *Republic,* the *Politics, The Prince, The Social Contract*, and so on, offer different views on the qualities necessary to found and maintain states.

This practical side of political philosophy was expressed by all of our authors. None of them was a cloistered scholar or university professor detached from the real world of politics. Plato undertook three long and dangerous voyages in order to advise the tyrants of Sicily; Aristotle was famously a tutor to Alexander the Great; Machiavelli spent a large part of his career in the foreign service of his native Florence and wrote as an adviser to the Medici; Hobbes was the tutor to a royal household who joined the court in exile during the English Civil War; Locke was associated with the Shaftsbury circle and was also forced into exile after being accused of plotting against another English king; Rousseau had no official political connections, but he signed his name "Citizen of Geneva" and was approached to write constitutions for Poland and the island of Corsica; and Tocqueville was a member of the French National Assembly whose experience of American democracy deeply affected the way he saw the future of Europe. The great political philosophers were all engaged in the politics of their times and provide us with models of how to think about ours.

The study of the regime either implicitly or explicitly raises a question that goes beyond the boundary of any given or existing society. A regime constitutes a people's way of life, what makes it worth living—and perhaps dying—for. Although we are most familiar with our own democratic regime, the study of political philosophy reveals to us that there is a variety of regime types, each with its own distinctive set of claims or principles, each vying with and potentially in conflict with the others. Underlying this cacophony of voices is the question of which of the regimes is best, which has, or ought to have, a claim on our loyalty and rational consent. Political philosophy is always guided by the question of the best regime.

But what is the best regime? Is the best regime, as the ancients believed, an aristocratic republic, one in which only the few best habitually rule? Or is the best regime, as the moderns believe, a democratic republic, where in principle political office is open to all by virtue of their membership in society alone? Will the best regime be a small closed society that through generations has made a supreme effort toward human perfection? Or will it be a large cosmopolitan society embracing all human beings, a universal league of nations with each nation consisting of free and equal men and women? Whatever form the best regime takes, it will necessarily favor a certain type of human being with a certain set of character traits. Is that type the common man as in democracies, those of acquired taste and money as in aristocracies, the warrior, or even the priest as in a theocracy? No question could be more fundamental.

And this finally raises the question of the relation between the best regime and actually existing regimes. What function does the best regime play in political science, and how does it guide our actions here and now? This issue received its most famous formulation in Aristotle's treatment of the difference between the good human being and the good citizen. For the good citizen, patriotism is enough, to uphold and defend the laws of your own country simply because they are your own is both necessary and sufficient. Such a view of citizen virtue runs into the obvious objection that the good citizen of one regime will not be the good citizen of another. A good citizen of contemporary Iran will not be the same as the good citizen of contemporary America.

But the good citizen is not the same as the good human being. While the good citizen is relative to his or her regime—regime specific, we might say—the good human being is good anywhere. The good human being loves what is good simply, not because it is his or hers, but because it *is* good. Lincoln once said of Henry Clay: "He loved his country *partly* because it was his own country, but *mostly* because it was a free country."[3] Clay exhibited here, at least on Lincoln's telling, something of the philosopher. What he loved was an idea, the idea of freedom, and this idea was not the property of America in particular, but of any good society. The good human being, it would seem, is a philosopher who may only be truly at home in the best regime. But the best regime, so far as we know, lacks actuality. The best regime, therefore, embodies a supreme paradox: it is superior to all actual regimes but has no concrete existence. This makes it difficult for the philosopher to be a good citizen of any actual regime; the philosopher will never feel truly at home, never truly be loyal, to any regime but the best.

This tension between the best regime and any actual regime is the space that makes political philosophy possible. In the best regime political philosophy would be unnecessary or redundant; it would wither away. Karl Marx famously believed that in the ideal socialist society of the future philosophy would no longer be necessary, presumably because society would at last become transparent to those living under it. Similarly, it is not clear in Plato's *kallipolis*, his ideal city, what function philosophy would continue to have once philosophers ruled as kings and kings became philosophers. In such a world philosophy would cease to exercise its critical function and become merely descriptive of the way things are. What is wrong with this, you might well ask. The acceptance of continued social injustice seems a high price to pay just to make political philosophy possible. Political philosophy exists—and can only exist—in this zone of indeterminacy between the Is and the Ought, between the actual and the ideal. Philosophy presupposes a less-than-perfect society, a world that requires interpretation and, perforce, political criticism. This is why philosophy is always potentially a disruptive undertaking. Those of you who embark on the quest for knowledge of the best regime may not return the same people you were before. You may return with very different loyalties and allegiances. There is at least some small compensation for this. The Greeks had a beautiful word for this quest, for this desire for knowledge of the best regime. They called it eros or love. Philosophy was understood as an erotic activity. The study of political philosophy may be the highest tribute paid to love.

CHAPTER 2

Antigone and the Politics of Conflict

*Antigone, Daughter of Oedipus and His Mother, Jocasta. Greek Tragedy and
Play by Sophocles.* Photo credit: Chris Hellier / Alamy

The problem of conflict—what it is, what its causes are, how to control and
contain it—is one of the oldest issues of political life. As America's greatest
political scientist, James Madison, wrote: "But what is government itself but
the greatest of all reflections on human nature? If men were angels, no government would be necessary."[1]

Madison's point is that if cooperation and agreement came naturally to us, we would not need the instrumentalities of law, the state, and political institutions to impose order. That we are beings whose natural condition is one of competition, envy, disagreement, and conflict is a point we will see reiterated very forcefully in the work of Thomas Hobbes.

That we live in a world pervaded by deep and intractable conflict is an insight that goes back to the Greeks. The so-called pre-Socratic philosophers saw the human world—even the cosmos as a whole—as pervaded by constant and continual flux. Order and stability were largely fragile and uncertain, man-made creations to hold back the all-pervasive chaos with which the human things were threatened. Among the pre-Socratics it was a man named Heraclitus who came closest to grasping this insight that everything is flux. It was this deep sense of chaos and the fragility of life to which the Greek tragedians especially gave profound voice.

For Sophocles, in particular, conflict between fundamental values and ways of life was something built into the very fabric of human nature. The idea of a world like Plato's *Republic,* Rousseau's *Social Contract,* or Marx's classless society where conflict had been banished would have been literally unthinkable. To be human was to live in a world of conflict torn by the necessity to make difficult and even dangerous choices between conflicting goals and loyalties. It is this awareness of the role of the intractable conflict between competing goods—their incommensurable quality, as we would say today—that brings us to the heart of Sophocles's *Antigone.*

The *Antigone* is by some accounts the greatest specimen of ancient tragic drama. What concerns us, however, is not so much the place of *Antigone* within the dramatic canon as what it reveals about the nature of political life. The *Antigone* is a play about conflict and its role in politics. Moreover, it is a play about conflict at several different levels: between the household (*oikos*) and the city (*polis*), between men and women, between nature and convention.

What is more, the play is a study of the role of reason in political life. Is creative human reason or speech—*logos*—sufficient to govern public life and conquer the natural world, as Creon believes? Or must human practical reason take a back seat to the unwritten and unspoken laws of kinship and religious obligation whose origins lie beyond reason? The *Antigone* is perhaps the first work to appeal to a higher law that precedes man-made or positive law (449–60). Like the great philosophers, Sophocles was concerned with the nature, limits, and power of human rationality and its role in human affairs. He was a philosopher as well as a playwright.[2]

The *Antigone* deals at once with the oldest and most enduring conflict of political life. This tension between human reason and ancestral piety, between the city and the gods, is an expression of what the great twentieth-century political philosopher Leo Strauss called the "theologico-political dilemma."[3] This problem deals with the greatest and most important issue, namely, what is the ultimate source of authority. Does authority derive from the city and those appointed as its governors or does authority descend from God or the gods and those appointed as priests and interpreters? This is a problem which continues to strike at the heart of politics today and to which our modern conception of the separation of church and state is one, but only one, answer.

The highest expression of this theologico-political dilemma is revealed in the conflict between what can metaphorically be called Jerusalem and Athens, the city of faith and the city of philosophy. Whereas for Jerusalem fear of God is the deepest human experience, for Athens it is intellectual curiosity and a confidence in the powers of our own reason that speaks to the highest human possibilities. Which of these is right? We might concede that every attempt to settle this question is ultimately an act of faith. If so, have we not decided in favor of Jerusalem? But perhaps we do not know the answer and are willing to listen to the claims of each. By saying we wish to listen first and then judge, haven't we decided in favor of Athens? In either case this problem constitutes the nerve or core of the West. Although reflection on this problem reached its height with the great medieval political philosophers—Maimonides, Al-Farabi, and Thomas Aquinas—it was given its first and perhaps most memorable expression in the writings of the Greek tragedians and philosophers who struggled with the problem of religious piety and the limits of reason.

The outline of the *Antigone* is relatively simple. Antigone, a daughter of Oedipus, has buried her brother Polynices, a traitor to Thebes, against the express orders of the king, Creon. Antigone disobeys Creon's edict in the name of the sacred ancestral law of family with its ties of blood and kinship. Creon in turn orders Antigone to be buried alive as punishment for her disobedience. But before the order is carried out Antigone kills herself, and Haemon, Creon's son, takes his own life in protest against his father's cruelty. Finally, Creon's wife commits suicide when she learns of the death of her son.

For readers today, it is difficult to imagine a world where the claims of family and blood relations took such powerful form. "The claims of blood relationship are not so strong for us," the classicist Bernard Knox has written. "We have no fresh history of conflict between family and state."[4] Rather, for contemporary readers it is necessary to try to imagine a world where family obligations represented the absolute and primordial form of loyalty. One example that comes to mind is the flashback scene at the very end of *The Godfather, Part II* when Michael tells his brothers he has joined the Marines after the Japanese attack on Pearl Harbor. His older brother, Sonny, is furious and shouts that he has no right to risk his life for anybody not in the family ("What, did you go to college to get stupid?"). At the end of the scene we see the members of the Corleone family united in celebration of the patriarch's birthday, but Michael remains alone. What is he thinking? Perhaps he is reflecting on the tension between himself as a member of the Corleone family and as an American. Which will have a greater pull: the ties of blood and family or the ties of national identity? This is a conflict that Sophocles would have readily understood.

There are further obstacles to understanding the world of *Antigone*. When we read the play today we are more apt to see it as representing a conflict between the individual and the power of the state. This is the way the play was often put on during the past century. There are modern adaptations of the play that depict Creon as a kind of fascistic dictator using political power to crush all expressions of opposition and individual free expression. This is surely not the way that Sophocles intended the play to be read.

There is another more recent tendency to regard *Antigone* as a feminist drama depicting the conflict between Creon and Antigone as expressing the female struggle against repressive patriarchy. There is an important respect in which male and female archetypes are used throughout the play to express certain primordial conflicts, but to read the play through the moralistic lenses of contemporary feminist theory is no less true than seeing it through the simplistic dualism of the sensitive individual sacrificed on the altar of the totalitarian state.

The desire to reduce the play to moralistic categories of good and evil fails to do justice to Sophocles's sense of the true nature of tragic conflict. The clash between Antigone and Creon is more than a simplistic clash of good and evil. It is a clash between two valid yet conflicting sets of social morality, each of which is equally binding. The power of the *Antigone* to move us even today is not because it sets right against wrong but because it pits one morally justified set of claims against another. It is a conflict between two contending moralities that is the essence of tragic drama.

The best statement of this point of view ever written occurs in Hegel's treatment of Greek tragedy from his *Lectures on the Philosophy of Religion*. Excuse me if I quote the passage at length:

> The collision between the two highest moral powers is enacted in that absolute exemplar of tragedy *Antigone*. Here, familial love, the holy, the inward, belonging to inner feeling, and therefore known also as the law of the gods, collides with the right of the state. Creon is not in the wrong. He maintains that the law of the state, the authority of the government, must be held in respect, and that infraction of the law must be followed by punishment. Each of these two sides actualizes only one of the ethical powers and has only one as its content. This is their one-sidedness. The meaning of eternal justice is made manifest thus: both attain injustice because they are one-sided, but both also attain justice.[5]

This passage is difficult, but Hegel's general point is not hard to grasp. The standpoints of Antigone and Creon represent conflicting moral points of view. If they did not—if one were simply right and the other simply wrong—the situation would not be tragic. If Creon were simply a tyrant, he would not be worthy of Antigone's challenge, nor would his defeat represent a tragic spectacle. Rather, Creon represents the voice of public legal authority. Creon is no mere tyrant; rather, he is the voice of the polity, of public life, and its claim to supremacy over all matters affecting public behavior. His is the mind devoted exclusively to civic safety and well-being. For Creon, the welfare of the city is the highest ethical obligation.

This becomes evident when we examine Creon's use of moral concepts, such as good and bad, noble and base, to justify his conduct. In his first speech he indicates that the categories of friend and enemy are distinguished by their usefulness to the city (162–210). The good are those who promote the public well-being, while the bad detract from the city's welfare. The quality of being *agathos* (a good man or person) is inseparable from one's value to the city. Thus, to give honorable burial to Polynices, a traitor, would be to confer equal benefits on the good and the bad alike. For Creon, the city and its rules transcend the natural ties of family and kinship. The city is even seen to become like a family honoring those who honor it. "Never shall I, myself," Creon says, "honor the wicked and reject the just. The man who is well-minded to the city from me in death and life shall have his honor" (207–10).

For Creon, then, the city with its man-made rules of justice represents the highest order of things. Underlying this standpoint is the deeper and more profound conviction that reason alone is a sufficient tool for governing human affairs. One of Creon's favorite metaphors is the image of reason setting things right or straight. In his first speech he uses that image three times (163, 167, 190); the third time he refers to the city as that which "saves us, sailing straight," for "only so can we have friends at all."

Not only is human reason capable of creating public rules for our safety and welfare, Creon goes on to praise reason as a source of technological mastery capable of harnessing and controlling nature, making it serve human purposes. There is a kind of rationalistic humanism underlying Creon's early views that is echoed in the Chorus's early praise of the incomparable resourcefulness and ingenuity of man, the rational animal. Consider the lines of the famous Choral Ode:

> Many the wonders but nothing walks stranger than man. This thing crosses the sea in the winter's storm, making his path through the roaring waves. And she, the greatest of gods, the earth—ageless she is, and unwearied—he wears her away as the ploughs go up and down from year to year. . . .
>
> Language, and thought like the wind and the feelings that make the town, he has taught himself, and shelter against the cold, refuge from rain. He can always help himself. He faces no future helpless. There's only death that he cannot find an escape from. He has contrived refuge from illnesses once beyond all cure.
>
> Clever beyond all dreams the inventive craft that he has which may drive him one time or another to well or ill. (332–68)

This famous ode validates a certain moral attitude toward politics and the natural world that is at the center of Creon's vision. Risking extreme anachronism we could call it the attitude of the Enlightenment, which regards the world as basically amenable to human technique or artfulness. On this view, the polis along with the rules of law and justice are human creations and a crucial step in exerting our control over a hostile and indifferent environment. Any step away from this order threatens a return to the primordial chaos of nature. It is a view that we will see expressed in various ways in the works of Descartes, Hobbes, and many of the great advocates of the Enlightenment.[6]

This position of Enlightenment humanism was given powerful expression in the works of Protagoras and other Greek sophists in a phrase that will be familiar: "Man is the measure of all things." This famous statement expresses the view that our rational human agency is the standard by which we try to seek mastery and control over nature. Only when we attain to rational mastery do we truly become the masters of our own fate. We become, in a word, self-determining. Underlying the Choral Ode is an attitude that will be central to the modern Enlightenment's doctrine of progress, namely, through the self-conscious application of rational techniques and planning we will be able to attain complete control over nature and ensure our own creativity, autonomy, and self-determination.

In contrast to this view of enlightened humanism stands Antigone. She is the representative of the world of the household and the family. Note here and throughout that Antigone does not see herself as an individual expressing a personal moral code and finding herself thwarted by an intolerant public authority. When she invokes the "unwritten law" (459–60) some see this as a fragile imitation of the later humanistic ideals of the inner conscience thwarted by the conservative norms of the polis. This view of Antigone is false.

Antigone does not regard herself as an individual; she is first and foremost a daughter, a sister, a member of a family with specific ethical obligations to her dead brother. The family and one's obligation to it are at the core of her being. Antigone, you could even say, is a conservative: she believes that the core of morality is to be found in the nuclear family; she devotes herself to defending the priority and sanctity of the family and opposing Creon's rationalistic innovations.

Not only is Antigone's morality a morality of family ties, the tie between the household and religion is central to her moral experience. The household is the natural home for the gods. This is not the time or place to discuss the role of religion in the world of the Greek cities except to note that religion was understood as an exclusively household affair. This has been brought out brilliantly by the nineteenth-century French classicist and anthropologist Fustel de Coulanges in his book *The Ancient City*, stressing the ties between family and religion: "The members of the ancient family were united by something more powerful than birth, affection, or physical strength; this was the religion of the sacred fire and of dead ancestors. This caused the family to form a single body, both in this life and in the next. . . . Religion, it is true, did not create the family; but certainly it gave the family its rules; and hence it comes that the constitution of the ancient family was so different from what it would have been if it had owed its foundation to natural affections."[7]

Fustel saw in a way that few can understand today how the Greek polis was not a secular democracy—although you could easily get this impression by reading many modern interpreters—but a community where religion, law, and government were inseparable, one where "religion was absolute master both in public and private life": "Where the state was a religious community, the king a pontiff, the magistrate a priest, and the law a sacred formula; where patriotism was piety, and exile excommunication; where individual liberty was unknown; where man was enslaved to the state through his soul, his body, and his property; where the notions of law and of duty, of justice and of affection, were bounded within the limits of the city; where human association was necessarily confined within a certain circumference around a prytaneum; and where men saw no possibility of founding larger societies."[8]

This conception of the polis as a theologico-political institution is entirely consistent with Antigone's view. She regards her actions as dictated not by some man-made law of reason but by a higher law the origins of which she admits are unknown (449–60). Her appeal to what is beyond human doing or making shows her to be the reverse side of Creon's emphasis on the creative power of human rationality. Antigone's world is not the sphere of public reason but the private world of nature, cult, and mystery. It is just this world that Creon, the public figure, cannot understand. Creon would deny the ties of kinship and family in order to celebrate the civic bonding of the polis. But Antigone's views are equally exclusionary. She would deny the power of public law over obligations to the family. Her position is prepolitical or even subpolitical.

While Creon values persons only insofar as they contribute to the public life, Antigone takes the fact of blood and kinship to be more fundamental because they are more natural. Underlying her view is the idea that the family is a deeper source of moral attachment because it is older than the city, because it has always existed; that although the family can exist without the city, the city cannot exist without the family. Further, while the city exists only as a contrivance, by an act of will, the family exists by nature, by the higher law.

The conflict portrayed in the *Antigone* goes beyond that of two social institutions—the city and the family—and addresses the underlying gender differences that these institutions express. As Sophocles portrays it, the city as represented by Creon expresses the virtues of maleness: reason, order, self-rule, and autonomy. The family expresses the virtues of the female: piety, obedience, tradition, and respect for the ancestors. The play reveals an enduring, permanent tension between the authority of divinely sanctioned law and human statesmanship's need for autonomous flexibility and practical judgment. The point of the play, to express it succinctly, is that tragedy ensues when people try to live by their own self-made laws without acknowledging the divine order or sense of cosmic justice to which everything is subject.

Like every great tragedian, Sophocles was a cultural conservative trying to show that human misery is caused by our attempts to impose our own rational designs upon the world and thus deny the claims that nature, family, and religion have upon us. It is the purpose of the tragic drama to illustrate the limits of human rationality.

But if Creon represents maleness and its drive for domination and setting things straight, Antigone represents a kind of denial of all creativity and change. Her world is that of the family; it represents the natural cycle of birth, growth, and decay. Her attitude toward the family is best captured as one of piety where piety means obedience to the sacred or ancestral order of things. Because this order of things was established by the gods, it is strictly forbidden to submit this order to critical questioning. The world of family piety is one of unquestioning obedience or submission to the ancestral or traditional way of life.

The two positions that the play stakes out are, then, strictly opposed to one another; in fact they are paralyzing. Is there a way out? At the end of the play Creon belatedly admits, "It's best to hold the laws of old tradition to the end of life" (1113). If this is true, he would seem to have come round, somewhat belatedly, to Antigone's position. The play would conclude with a vindication of Antigone. This might be in keeping with a standard view of Greek tragedy that sees the tragic situation as brought on by excessive pride or *hubris,* in this case Creon's desire to exert control over nature and the family at the expense of the higher law. But I think this will not do justice to Sophocles's play.

Sophocles tries to bring out the inherent tension between a politics of pure reason—the sophistic claim that man is the measure of all things—and the attitude of sacred awe and piety before those things that reason cannot control. Sophocles's *Antigone* is about the limitations of human reason. There is inherent in reason a leveling and reductive tendency: a belief that reason is the measure—the only measure—for evaluating and adjudicating between conflicts of goods and the view that all conflicts between competing goods must have some rational solution or some one overriding good to which all lesser goals are subordinate. The tragedians were not irrationalists; they did not celebrate the limitations of reason. Rather, they saw profound dangers in reason's tendency to reduce the multiplicity of things to some underlying unity and order. This tendency not just to seek but to impose uniformity is a sign of tyranny. The critique of reason is at bottom a political critique. In seeking to reduce the many to the one—diversity to some underlying unity—we end by distorting the meaning of things. A politics based on reason alone will be a politics indifferent to difference, to the natural differences between men and women, between family and polis, between public life and private life. In trying to find a simple, uniform standard to "set things straight," we necessarily lose sight of the complexity of experience. It is the purpose of tragic drama to bring out and reveal the danger of reason's imagined potency and creativity.

CHAPTER 3

Socrates and the Examined Life

Jacques-Louis David (1748–1825). *The Death of Socrates.* 1787. Oil on canvas.
Photo credit: World History Archive / Alamy

Plato was an Athenian. He was born around the year 427/28 B.C.E. He was a young man during the waning years of the great war between the Athenians and the Spartans known as the Peloponnesian War. He was born around the same year as the death of the great Athenian statesman Pericles. So he lived at the very end of what has been considered the golden age of

Athens. It was during his teens or early twenties—around the age of a college undergraduate—that he made the acquaintance of Socrates. Plato came from a leading family of Athens. He must have been like one of those young men depicted in many Platonic dialogues who found themselves bewitched and enchanted by this remarkable teacher. He was in his late twenties at the time of Socrates's death in the year 399.[1]

Plato went on to establish something like the first university, named by him the Academy. People came from all over the Greek and Mediterranean world to study there, among them a young man from the north of Greece named Aristotle (more about him later). Plato later engaged in three long and dangerous voyages to Sicily to serve there—unsuccessfully, as it turned out—as an adviser to two Sicilian tyrants, both named Dionysius, after which he withdrew from political life to engage, we suppose, in writing, teaching, and administering his Academy. He died in Athens at the age of about eighty.

Plato was a prolific author who wrote thirty-five works, all in the form of dialogues. These works range from just a few pages to several hundred pages in length. If just one of you were to develop a passion for Plato—I do not mean just a passing enjoyment but a passion that would develop into a lifelong interest—I would consider this course an enormous success.

Plato's *Apology of Socrates* is the best introduction to political philosophy known to me, for two reasons. First, it shows Socrates—the reputed founder of political philosophy—explaining himself and his way of life before a jury of his peers. It is the only Platonic dialogue that shows Socrates speaking in a public forum defending the social utility of philosophy for political life. And second, the *Apology* demonstrates the vulnerability of political philosophy—genuinely free thought—in relation to the city. Philosophy meant for Socrates not simply the name for an academic discipline, as it is often understood today, but the life of free investigation and the active pursuit of truth. The *Apology* put on trial not just a particular individual, Socrates, but the very idea of philosophy. From its origins, philosophy and the city have stood in tension with one another. Socrates was charged by the city of Athens with corrupting the youth and impiety toward the gods—in other words, treason. No other work of which I am aware better illustrates the conflict—the inevitable conflict—between the demands of the life of the mind and the requirements of political life.

For generations the trial of Socrates has stood out as a symbol of the violation of freedom of expression, the case that sets the individual committed to the "examined life" over and against the bigoted and prejudiced multitude. The clearest statement of this reading is to be found in John Stuart Mill's famous tract *On Liberty* where he writes: "Mankind can hardly be too often reminded that there was once a man named Socrates between whom and the legal authorities of his time there took place a memorable collision."[2] Over and over again Socrates has been described as a "martyr for freedom of speech." He has been compared at different times to Jesus, Galileo, and Sir Thomas More and has been used as a role model for thinkers and political activists from Henry David Thoreau to Gandhi to Martin Luther King Jr.

This reading of the *Apology* as a brief for freedom of expression and a warning against the dangers of censorship and persecution has been enormously influential, but is it in fact the reading that Plato intended? Note that Socrates does not defend himself by reference to the doctrine of unlimited free speech. Rather, he maintains that the "examined life" alone is worth living. Only those engaged in the continual struggle to clarify their thinking and remove all sources of confusion and incoherence can be said to live free and worthwhile lives. "The unexamined life is not worth living," Socrates confidently asserts (38a). Nothing else matters. His seems to be a highly personal, highly individual quest for self-perfection and not a doctrine about the value of free expression as such.

But there is also something deeply political about the *Apology*. At the heart of Socrates's quarrel with his accusers is the question—perhaps never stated directly—over who has the right to educate future citizens and statesmen of the city of Athens. Socrates's defense speech, like all Platonic dialogues, is ultimately a speech about education and who has the right to educate the next generation of political leaders. It is ultimately a quarrel over that oldest of all political questions, "Who governs?" or better "Who should govern?" Remember that the city that brought Socrates to trial was not just any city. It was a particular kind of city: it was Athens, and Athens was until only fairly recent times the most famous democracy that ever existed. The speech of Socrates before the jury of Athens is Plato's attempt to put democracy itself on trial. Not only does the *Apology* force Socrates to defend himself and his way of life before the city of Athens, Socrates puts the city of Athens on trial and makes it defend itself before the high court of philosophy. The ensuing debate can be read as a struggle over whether the people, the *demos,* or Socrates, the philosopher-king, should be vested with ultimate political authority.

The Political Context

The trial of Socrates took place in the year 399 B.C.E., which, as some of you may know, followed almost immediately on the heels of the Peloponnesian War. The story of this war was related by the Athenian historian Thucydides, Socrates's great and slightly older contemporary. The war took place between the two greatest powers of the Greek world, the Spartans and the Athenians. The Athens that fought in this war was an Athens at the height of its power. Under the leadership of its first citizen, Pericles, Athens had built the Acropolis, established a mighty naval force, expanded its empire, and created an unprecedented artistic and cultural life. Athens was also something completely unprecedented in the ancient world: a democracy. "Our constitution," Pericles boasted to his audience, "does not copy the laws of neighboring states; we are rather a pattern to others than imitators ourselves."[3]

Even today the expression "Athenian democracy" conveys an ideal of the most complete form of democratic government ever to have existed. "The freedom which we enjoy in our government extends also to our ordinary life," Pericles continues. "At Athens we live exactly as we please." Rather than exercising a jealous surveillance over its citizens, the Athenians live with an unprecedented openness: "We throw open our city to the world and never exclude foreigners from any opportunity of learning or observing even though the eyes of an enemy may profit from our liberality."[4] The Athenians, Pericles maintains, are "the school of Hellas": "We cultivate refinement without extravagance and knowledge without effeminacy; wealth we employ more for use than for show, and place the real disgrace of poverty not in owning to the fact but in declining the struggle against it. Our public men have, besides politics, their private affairs to attend to, and our ordinary citizens, though occupied with the pursuits of industry, are still fair judges of public matters; for unlike any other nation, regarding him who takes no part in these duties not as unambitious but as useless."[5]

The question asked by so many for so long is how could the world's freest and most open society sentence to death a man who spoke freely about his own ignorance and who professed to care for nothing so much as virtue and human excellence?

At the outbreak of the Peloponnesian War Socrates was about forty years old, and we learn from the *Apology* that he fulfilled his military service. The war was fought over an almost thirty-year period and concluded in the year 404 with the defeat of Athens and the installation of a pro-Spartan oligarchy known as the Thirty Tyrants. Among those implicated in the tyranny was a former associate of Socrates's named Critias and an uncle of Plato's named Charmides (both of whom have Platonic dialogues named after them). According to Aristotle, fifteen hundred people were executed by the Thirty, and many more sympathetic to the democracy were driven into exile.[6] In the year 401 the oligarchs were driven out and a democratic government was reestablished in Athens. Just two years later, three men—Anytus, Meletus, and Lycos—all of whom had fought in the democratic resistance movement against the Thirty—brought charges against Socrates, for corrupting the young and not believing in the gods that the city believes in (24b).

The charges brought against Socrates by these three men did not grow out of thin air. As the old expression has it, "no smoke without fire." Perhaps the question should be rephrased: not why did the Athenians bring Socrates to trial but why did they permit him to carry on his practice of challenging the laws and their authority for as long as they did? Add to this the fact that when Socrates was brought to trial not only had the democracy been recently reestablished but Socrates had many friends, former students as it were, who were implicated in the rule of the Thirty Tyrants. Socrates was certainly not above suspicion. He had himself been a close associate of Alcibiades, the man who engineered the disastrous Sicilian Expedition and ended as a defector to Sparta and later to Persia. Alcibiades was the leading Athenian politician in the generation after Pericles. His complex relation with Socrates is recounted vividly in his drunken speech given in the Platonic dialogue called the *Symposium*. The trial of Socrates thus takes place in the shadow of military defeat, conspiracy, and betrayal.

The Two Accusations

Early on in his defense speech Socrates claims that his current accusers who have brought charges against him are themselves the descendents of an earlier generation of accusers who were responsible for creating an unfavorable prejudice against him. The charges are not new, and Socrates alludes to the fact that many members of the jury will have heard unfavorable opinions about him. He alludes to the earlier accuser as a "comic poet," an unequivocal reference to the comic playwright Aristophanes (18d).

This allusion to Aristophanes is a part of what Socrates will call in the *Republic* "the old quarrel between philosophy and poetry." This quarrel is a staple of Plato's dialogues. It is a central theme of his dialogue the *Sympo-*

sium, in which Aristophanes is actually present, and is a key feature of the *Republic,* where Socrates offers a proposal for the censorship and control of poetry if it is to be made compatible with the just city. In fact you cannot properly understand the *Republic* until you understand the poetic backdrop to it and Socrates's long-standing engagement with the poetic tradition.

The core of this quarrel is not just aesthetic but political. It gets to the essence of the question of who is best equipped to educate future citizens and civic leaders—are philosophers or poets the true legislators for mankind? At the time of Socrates, the Greeks already had a centuries-long poetic tradition going back to the time of Homer and Hesiod that set out certain exemplary models of civic virtue and heroic action. The Homeric and Hesiodic epics were to the Greek world what the Bible is—or used to be—to ours, the ultimate authority regarding the ways of the gods, their relation to the human world, and the types of virtue appropriate to men at war. The virtues endorsed by the poetic tradition were the virtues of a warrior culture and warlike peoples. These were the qualities that guided the Greeks for centuries and contributed to their rise to power and greatness and enabled them to achieve a level of artistic, intellectual, and political accomplishment akin to that of Renaissance Florence, Elizabethan England, and Goethe's Weimar.

What is at stake in this quarrel between Socrates and the poets? First, Socrates's manner of teaching is markedly different from that of the poets. "Sing goddess, the wrath of Achilles" is the opening line of the *Iliad.* The poets are oracular. They call on gods and goddesses to inspire them with song, to fill them with inspiration, and to tell stories of people with almost superhuman strength and courage. By contrast, the method of Socrates is conversational or "dialectical." He makes arguments and wants others to engage with him to discover which argument can best withstand the test of rational scrutiny and debate. He makes continual and critical questioning—not the telling of stories or the recitation of verse—the essence of this new civic education.

Second, Homer and the poets sing the virtues of men at war. Socrates wants to replace the warrior citizen with a new type of citizen who has a whole new set of citizen virtues. The new Socratic citizen may have some of the features of the older Homeric warrior but will replace military combat with a new kind of verbal combat in which the person with the best argument will be declared victorious. The famed "Socratic method" of argument is all that remains of the older agonistic culture of struggle and combat. The Socratic citizen-statesman is to be trained in the art of dialectic. We will see a little later just what the qualities are that Socrates ascribes to this new kind of citizen.

It is as a challenge to the poetic tradition that Socrates asserts himself. The *Apology* presents him as a new kind of hero seeking to replace the older poetic models. Socrates's challenge to the poetic tradition provides the crucial basis for the resentment built up against him by Aristophanes and his early accusers. In fact so seriously was Socrates taken that Aristophanes devoted an entire play called the *Clouds* to debunking and ridiculing Socrates's professions of learning. Aristophanes's play is the clearest example we have of just how seriously Socrates was taken by his greatest contemporaries. Mockery remains one of the sincerest forms of flattery.

The *Clouds* is a play that in some editions is included alongside the *Apology.* Here Aristophanes presents Socrates as the head of a kind of early think tank dubbed the Phrontisterion, literally, the "thinkery," where fathers bring their sons to be indoctrinated into the secrets of Socratic wisdom. In the play Socrates is depicted as hanging over the stage in a basket in order to better gaze at the clouds—symbolizing his indifference to the ordinary affairs that concern his fellow citizens. Socrates is shown not only mocking the gods but also teaching that incest and the beating of one's parents are permissible. To make a long story short, the play concludes with Socrates's think tank being burned to the ground by a disgruntled disciple.

How accurate is Aristophanes's portrait of Socrates? The *Clouds* was written and first performed in 423 when Socrates was in his mid-forties. The Aristophanic Socrates is essentially a natural philosopher—a scientist as we would say today—investigating the things aloft and below the earth (18b). But this seems quite removed from the Socrates who is brought up on charges of corrupting the young and impiety in the *Apology.* In order to respond to Aristophanes's story, Socrates tells a story of his own—provides an intellectual autobiography, as it were—of an incident that occurred long before the trial and that set him on a new and very different path. A friend of his named Charephon (who appears again in the *Gorgias*) asked the oracle at Delphi if there was anyone wiser than Socrates, and the pythia concurred that there was no one wiser. Socrates took this as a challenge. He set out to disprove the oracle's veracity. In order to prove the oracle mistaken he tells of a quest—a lifelong quest—to find someone wiser than himself, in the course of which he interrogated politicians, poets, craftsmen, all people reputed to be knowledgeable. His conversations led him to ask not about natural scientific phenomena but rather the human question, the question, who can teach the virtues of a human being and a citizen (20b)?

This is the famous "Socratic turn"—Socrates's "second sailing" as it is sometimes called. It represents the moment of his turn away from the study of natural phenomena to the investigation of human and political things. The Delphic story, for what it is worth, marks a major turning point in the intellectual biography of Socrates, the move from the younger "pre-Socratic" Socrates, who investigated the basic elements of nature to the more familiar Platonic Socrates, who is the founder of political science, who seeks out the virtues of moral and political life, justice, and the best regime. Socrates's account of this turn leaves many questions unanswered. Why did he turn away from the investigation of natural phenomena to the study of human and political things? The Delphic oracle is interpreted by Socrates to command engaging with others in philosophical conversation. Why does this seem the proper interpretation, and why did he not have such conversations before? It is this Socrates, the Platonic Socrates, who is brought up on charges of corruption and impiety. What is the nature of Socrates's crime? Whom did he corrupt, and what is meant by impiety? To try and answer these questions, let us turn to the nature of the new Socratic citizen.

Socratic Citizenship

The new charges brought against Socrates by Anytus and Meletus are those of impiety and corruption. What exactly do these mean? What is impiety, and why should it be considered a crime? What would impiety have meant to an ancient Athenian? At a minimum impiety suggests disrespect of the gods. Impiety need not connote atheism, although Meletus confuses the two, but it does suggest irreverence, even blasphemy, toward the things that society most deeply cares about. When people today refer to burning the American flag as "desecration," they are speaking the language of impiety. Meletus—whose name actually means "care" in Greek—accuses Socrates of not properly caring about the things that his fellow Athenians care about.

Every society operates within the medium of belief or faith. Our founding document, the Declaration of Independence, declares that all men are created equal, that we are endowed with unalienable rights, and that all legitimate government grows out of the consent of the governed. These beliefs form something like our national creed, what it means to be an American. Yet how many people could give a reasoned account of what makes these beliefs true? Are they true? Most of us, most of the time, hold these as matters of belief, or because we have learned these from childhood, or because they were written by Thomas Jefferson. Piety or faith is, then, the natural condition of the citizen. Every society, no matter what kind, requires this kind of faith in its ruling principles.

But philosophy cannot rest content with mere belief. Philosophy grows out of the passionate desire—the restless and intransigent desire—to replace opinion with knowledge, to replace belief with true principles. For philosophy, it is not enough to hold a belief on faith; one must be able to give reasons or arguments for one's beliefs. Its goal is to replace faith or belief with reason or truth. Philosophy therefore necessarily stands at odds with faith. This much is axiomatic. The citizen may accept certain beliefs on faith because he or she is attached to a particular political order or regime, or because this or that is what we have been brought up to believe; the philosopher, on the other hand, seeks to judge in terms of true standards, in the light of what is true always and everywhere. As a quest for knowledge, there is a necessary and inevitable tension between philosophy and belief or, put another way, between the philosopher and the city.

From this point of view, was Socrates guilty of impiety? On the face of it, the charge seems justified. Socrates does not care about the same things that his fellow citizens care about or he does not care about them in the same way. His opening words to the jury—"I am simply foreign to the manner of speech here" (17d)—is a statement expressing his lack of care or his disaffection from the ways and concerns of the Athenians. Yet it certainly does not seem correct to say that Socrates does not care at all. He claims to care deeply, perhaps more deeply, than any of those around him. Among the things he cares deeply about is his calling to "do nothing but persuade you, both younger and older, not to care for bodies and money, but how your soul will be in the best possible condition" (30b).

This concern with the state of the soul, both his own and those around him, Socrates tells the jury, has led him not only to impoverish himself and neglect his family but also to turn away from the business of public life, from the things of concern to the city, to the pursuit of private life. Here are his actual words:

> This is what opposes my political activity, and its opposition seems to me altogether noble. For know well, men of Athens, if I had long ago attempted to be politically active, I would long ago have perished, and I would have benefited neither you nor myself. Now do not be vexed with me when I speak the truth. For there is no human being who will preserve his life if he genuinely opposes either you or any other multitude and prevents many

unjust and unlawful things from happening in the city. Rather, if someone who really fights for the just is going to preserve himself even for a short time, it is necessary for him to lead a private rather than a public life. (31d–e)

How are we to understand this very peculiar Socratic claim that the pursuit of justice requires one to turn away from public to private life? What is this new and strange kind of Socratic citizen?

The Great Abstainer

Socrates's insistence that he has led a private life cannot strictly be true. His investigations carried out on behalf of the Delphic oracle have been undertaken in public. He interrogates politicians, poets, and other public figures. What Socrates means when he claims to have led a purely private life is that he appeals only to his listeners' powers of reason and self-examination. Not only does he counsel radical independence from all traditional sources of authority, he encourages what might be called a *principled abstinence* from political life. Only by abstaining from participation in the collective actions of the city can the new Socratic citizen avoid complicity in injustice. His motto seems to be: "Just say no."[7]

Socrates gives two examples of his principled abstinence to the jury. The first concerns his refusal to join in the judgment to condemn and execute the ten Athenian generals who had failed to collect the bodies of the men lost in a battle. Here he refuses to engage in any ascriptions of collective guilt.[8] Second, he reminds the jury of his refusal to follow the order to arrest Leon of Salamis, who he knew would be executed without a trial (32c). Both of these were actual historical events, attested by other authors, and either of which could have cost Socrates his life. In both cases, Socrates makes his own individual moral integrity a litmus test for whether to engage or disengage from political life. "I was the sort of man," he reminds the jury, "who never conceded anything to anyone contrary to what is just" (33a).

The question is whether this kind of principled disobedience to the law—something like Thoreau's model of civil disobedience—vindicates or indicts Socrates of the charge of corruption and impiety. Can a citizen put his own conscience above the law? What would a community of Socratic citizens look like? Can we pick and choose which laws to obey or which authority to follow? Socrates is so concerned with his moral integrity that he says he will not dirty his hands with the Assembly or the courts. What kind of citizen is it who teaches abstinence from—maybe even rejection of—political life?

Socrates tries to avoid these charges by showing that his policy of abstinence actually carries a social benefit to Athens. In a famous passage from the *Apology* he defines himself as a gadfly who improves the quality of the city:

> So I, men of Athens, am now far from making a defense speech on my own behalf. I do it rather on your behalf, so that you do not do something wrong concerning the gift of the god to you by voting to condemn me. For if you kill me, you will not easily discover another of my sort, who—even if it is rather ridiculous to say—has simply been set upon the city by the god, as though upon a great and well-born horse who is rather sluggish because of his great size and needs to be awakened by some gadfly. Just so, in fact, the god seems to me to have set me upon the city as someone of this sort: I awaken and persuade and reproach each one of you, and I do not stop settling down everywhere upon you the whole day. (30d–e)

Socrates suggests here that he is providing a public benefit in his role as social critic. It is not for his behalf but for his fellow citizens that he does what he does. You may not like me, he tells the jury, but I am good for you. Furthermore, he claims in quasi-religious language that he has no choice in the matter. He is a "gift of the god" and is merely following what has been commanded. "Men of Athens," he says, "I will obey the god rather than you; and as long as I breathe and am able to, I will certainly not stop philosophizing" (29d).

What are we to make of the religious language in which Socrates envelopes this idea of citizenship? Is he sincere, or is he being ironical? He is, after all, on trial for his life. Would he not try to rebut the charge by describing his refusal to cease philosophizing in the kind of religious language that would resonate with the jury? Socrates could be speaking ironically here— and also provocatively—in describing himself as a gift of the god. In a sense, what could be more ludicrous?

But Socrates also seems to take his divine calling very seriously. It was only when the Delphic oracle replied to Charephon that no one was wiser than Socrates that he undertook his "second sailing," his turn toward problems of moral virtue and justice. He repeatedly maintains that the path he has taken was not of his own choosing but the result of divine command. It is precisely his devotion to the god that has led him to neglect worldly affairs and the well-being of his family, as well as suffer the abuse and prejudice directed against him. He presents himself as a man of unparalleled piety and devotion who will risk death rather than quit the post commanded by the god.

Do we believe Socrates? Is he being sincere? What is this peculiar piety that he claims to practice? In replying to the jury's verdict and request that he simply cease from public philosophizing, he explains himself as follows: "It is hardest of all to persuade some of you about this. For if I say that this is to disobey the god and because of this it is impossible to keep quiet, you will not be persuaded by me on the ground that I am being ironic. And on the other hand, if I say that this even happens to be a very great good for a human being—to make speeches every day about virtue . . . and that the unexamined life is not worth living for a human being, you will be persuaded by me still less" (37e–38a).

Socrates recognizes here that he is on the horns of a dilemma. On the one hand, his reference to a divine mission will be taken by members of his audience to be ironical. On the other, he recognizes that trying to persuade people on rational grounds that only the examined life is worthwhile will be exceedingly difficult. So what is a Socratic citizen to do?

Should Socrates Be Tolerated?

The question asked by the *Apology* is how far freedom of speech—speech that may verge into civic impiety—can or should be tolerated. It has been an assumption of readers of Plato over the years that there ought to exist the fullest liberty or freedom of thought and discussion and that Plato demonstrates the clearest argument against the attempt to stifle or prevent free inquiry. But is this right? Is this Plato's teaching?

The *Apology* presents the most intransigent case for the philosopher as a radical critic or questioner. Socrates demands not this or that change in the Athenian polity but nothing less than a drastic, even revolutionary, change in Athenian civic life. He tells his co-citizens that their lives are "not worth living." Even when presented with the option to cease his constant criticism, he refuses on the ground that he is acting under a divine command and cannot do otherwise. Is Plato asking us to regard Socrates as a man of principle, standing up for what he believes in the face of death, or as a revolutionary agitator who cannot and should not be tolerated by society whose basic laws and values he will not accept? One is inclined to say both.

The answer to this question is provided in the *Crito,* the companion piece to the *Apology.* The *Crito* gets far less attention than the *Apology* in part, I suspect, because it presents the city's case against Socrates. If the *Apology* presents the philosopher's case against the city, the *Crito* presents the city's case against the philosopher. Here Socrates makes the case against himself, and makes it far better than his own accusers did in the *Apology.* The speech between Socrates and the Laws that forms the central action of the dialogue presents the case that Meletus and Socrates's accusers should have brought against him. While the *Apology* denigrates the political life as requiring complicity in injustice, the *Crito* makes the case for the dignity or majesty of the laws that sustain the city. While the *Apology* defends a position of principled abstinence from politics, the *Crito* makes the most complete and far-reaching case for obligation and obedience to the law ever made.

The two dialogues differ both in content and in dramatic context. Consider some of the following: the *Apology* is a speech given before a large and largely anonymous audience of more than five hundred persons; the *Crito* is a conversation between Socrates and a single individual. The *Apology* takes place in the court of Athens, the most public of settings, while the *Crito* occurs within the darkness and confinement of a prison cell. The *Apology* presents Socrates defending himself and his way of life as a "gift of the god" that most truly benefits the city, while in the *Crito* we see him bow down to the authority of the laws that he had previously rejected. And finally, if the *Apology* presents Socrates as the first martyr for philosophy, the *Crito* shows Socrates's trial and sentence as a case of justice delivered. These contrasts clearly force us to ask what Plato is doing. What is his point in presenting two such sharply contrasting points of view?

The *Crito* is named for a friend and disciple of Socrates's who at the outset of the work is sitting as a watchful guardian. He urges Socrates to allow him to help him escape. The jailers have been bribed, and escape would be easy. Rather than try to convince Crito directly, Socrates creates a dialogue—a dialogue within the larger dialogue—between himself and the Laws where he puts forward the case against escape (50a–d). The argument runs roughly as follows: no state can exist without rules; the first rule, as it were, is that citizens are not free to set aside the rules, to choose which ones to obey and disobey; to engage in civil disobedience of any kind is to call into question not this or that rule but the very nature of law; to question or disobey the law is tantamount to destroying the authority of the state. The breaking of so much as a single law would constitute the essence of anarchy.

But Socrates goes further. The citizen owes his or her very existence to the laws. The laws "begat" the citizen, brought him or her into being (50d–e). They exercise paternal or tutelary authority over us insofar as we are made by the communities of which we are a part. We owe to the law a reverence or piety of the kind that we owe to the oldest things, the ancestors, the founding fathers, as we would say. Socrates seems to accept entirely the authority of the law. He does not offer arguments for noncompliance or dissent as he did in the *Apology*. Where is Socrates the apostle of civil disobedience? He accepts the covenant that every citizen has with the laws that binds him to absolute obedience. The question is, why does Socrates exhibit such proud defiance and independence of the laws in the *Apology* and such total, even mouselike, acquiescence to the laws in the *Crito*?

Plato's answer to this dilemma might be something like the following: the *Apology* and the *Crito* represent a tension—in fact a conflict—between two more or less permanent and irreconcilable moral codes. The one represented by Socrates regards reason—the sovereign reason of the individual—as the highest authority. It is precisely the philosopher's reliance on his or her own reason that frees him or her from the dangerous authority of the state and safeguards the individual from complicity in the injustice and evil that are a necessary part of political life. The other moral code is represented by the speech of the Laws in the *Crito,* where it is the law or *nomos* of the community—its oldest and deepest customs and institutions—that are obligatory. The one point of view takes the philosophic life, the examined life, to be the life most worth living; the other takes the political life, the life of the citizen engaged in the business of deliberating, legislating, making war and peace as the highest calling. These two constitute fundamentally irreconcilable alternatives, two different callings, and any attempt to reconcile or synthesize the two can only lead to doing an injustice to each. Plato's point seems to be that each of us must choose one or the other of the two contenders for the most serious and worthwhile life.

And yet this may not be Plato's last word. After all, why does Socrates choose to stay and drink the hemlock? Why not allow Crito to help him escape and go to Crete, where he can enjoy his old age (which is precisely what we see him doing in Plato's *Laws*)? Are the reasons Socrates gives Crito for refusing to escape—the reasons he puts in the mouth of the Laws of Athens—his true reasons, or are these merely a fiction he invents for the sake of relieving his friend of the responsibility he evidently feels for being unable to help Socrates?

In refusing Crito's offer of help Socrates once again demonstrates his superiority to the laws of Athens, first by defying the city to put him to death and then by expressing indifference to death until the very end. Socrates very much remains a law unto himself while at the same time providing Crito (and those like him) an example of rational and dignified obedience to the laws. The death of Socrates is not a tragedy. Far from it. His death at the age of seventy was intended by him as an act of philosophical martyrdom that would allow future philosophy to be favorably regarded as a source of courage and justice. In one of his letters Plato refers to his attempt to render Socrates "young and beautiful," that is, he consciously set out to idealize Socrates, presenting a picture of a man fearless before death, refusing to participate in any act of injustice, and dispensing wisdom to all those who will listen. We do not know the "real" Socrates; all we can go by is Plato's— and Aristophanes's—sketches of him. Plato's Socrates is necessarily poles apart from Aristophanes's depiction of him as a kind of sophist who makes the weaker argument the stronger. Plato's dialogues are in the broadest sense of the term his answer to the charge of Aristophanes.

Socrates and Us

What is there for us today to learn from the trial of Socrates? Most of us will find ourselves instinctively taking the side of Socrates against the city of Athens. We will accept Plato's depiction of Socrates as a just man sentenced to death by an intolerant and ignorant crowd. We will blame the Athenians for not being sufficiently democratic. We will overlook a number of inconvenient facts, namely, Socrates's hostility to democracy, his claim that the lives of his fellow citizens are not worth living, and his claim that his way of life has been commanded by a deity that no one else has ever heard or seen. None of these will make any difference—and yet they all should.

Given Socrates's claims, ask yourselves, what should a responsible body of citizens have done? One answer might be to extend greater toleration to civil dissidents like Socrates, individuals of heterodox beliefs but with views that may stimulate others to question and think for themselves. But is this to do Socrates justice? The one thing Plato does not argue is that Socrates should be tolerated. To tolerate his teaching is to trivialize it; it is to render it harmless. The Athenians pay Socrates the tribute of taking him seriously, which is exactly why he is on trial. The Athenians refuse to tolerate Socrates precisely because they know he is not harmless, that he poses a challenge—a fundamental challenge—to their way of life that they believe to be noble and worthwhile. Socrates is not harmless because of his ability to attract followers, a few today, a few more tomorrow. To tolerate Socrates would be to say to him that we care so little for our way of life that we are willing to let you challenge and impugn it every day.

The trial of Socrates forces us to consider the limits of toleration. What views, if any, do we find intolerable? Is a healthy society one that is open to every point of view? To be sure, freedom of speech is a cherished good, but is it the supreme good that should trump all others? Or does toleration reach a point when it ceases to be toleration and becomes instead a kind of soft nihilism that can extend liberty to everything precisely because it takes nothing seriously? Is this really tolerance, or is it a form of decadence that has simply grown tired of the search for truth and true standards of judgment? There is the danger that endless toleration can lead to intellectual passivity and the uncritical acceptance of all points of view, however squalid, base, or insane.

This leaves us with a perplexity: Is the lesson of the *Apology* and the *Crito* about the dangers of persecution and intolerance, or is it about the limits of toleration? Would a healthy society have acquitted Socrates, or was justice done? Plato deliberately leaves these questions unanswered. Why? Because he wants us to think about them for ourselves. My own view is that the Athenians did not do an injustice to Socrates. Far from it. They gave him that which he most truly desired, namely, the chance to die for his beliefs and to serve as the first martyr for philosophy.

The entire philosophical tradition has lived under the long shadow cast by the trial of Socrates. It set in motion the problem that every philosopher after him has had to confront: how to manage the slippery slope between the search for truth and the best regime, on the one hand, and loyalty to the laws and rules of the very imperfect societies in which we all live and act, on the other. The tension between philosophy and society is a permanent fact of life and a precondition for philosophy itself. Ancient societies recognized no intrinsic right to philosophize, and even in modern times the absolute right of freedom of inquiry has been the exception rather than the rule. For this reason philosophers have almost everywhere developed strategies of evasion and concealment precisely to avoid persecution. This persecution has ranged from outright suppression of thought and opinion to the gentler forms of shunning and social ostracism. Consider how even to-day the expression of views deemed to be "politically incorrect" can result in attempts to isolate and shame the offender.

Beginning with Plato, philosophers developed strategies of dissimulation, evasion, and concealment to protect their true views from public condemnation and possible persecution. To avoid suffering the fate of Socrates, philosophers began to promulgate two teachings, one *public,* intended for their audience at large, the other *private,* intended for other philosophers and students of philosophy. This dual strategy or "double truth" as it came to be called was a means of avoiding persecution but also of displaying public responsibility, to show that philosophy could be a trustworthy ally of society. Such strategies of concealment have been used at all times but especially during periods of censorship and persecution when philosophy has been endangered from sources of intolerance, though whenever the teachings of philosophy are at odds with the requirements of social order. Until such time as the gap between the real and the ideal has been bridged, the trial of Socrates will remain an object lesson for the future of philosophy.

CHAPTER 4

Plato on Justice and the Human Good

Marble bust of Plato, 428–348 B.C.E. Photo credit: The Art Archive /
Capitoline Museums, Rome / Collection Dagli Orti / Art Resource, NY

The *Republic* is the book that started it all. Every other work of philosophy is a reply to the *Republic*, beginning with Aristotle's *Politics* and extending up to our own day with John Rawls's *A Theory of Justice*. The first and most obvious thing to note about the *Republic* is that it is a long book, not Plato's longest work, but long enough. It will not reveal its meaning on a first reading, perhaps not even on a tenth reading unless it is approached in the proper manner with the proper questions. So we must ask, what is the *Republic* about?[1]

This is a question that has divided readers of the *Republic* almost from the beginning. Is it a book about justice as the subtitle of the work suggests? Is it a book about moral psychology and the right ordering of the human soul? Is it a book about the power of poetry and myth? Or is it about metaphysics and the ultimate structure of Being? It is about all of these things—and some others as well—but at least at the beginning we should stay at the surface. The surface of the *Republic* reveals that it is a dialogue, a conversation. We should approach the book not as we would an analytical treatise but as we might approach a work of literature. It is a work comparable in scope to other literary masterworks, like *Hamlet, Don Quixote, War and Peace.* As a conversation, it is something that the author wants us to join, to take part in. We are invited to become not passive onlookers but active participants in the conversation that takes place in the book over the course of a single evening. Perhaps the best way to approach the book is to read it aloud as you might a play to yourself or with your friends.

The republic that Plato presents is a utopia (a word not coined until much later by Sir Thomas More). Plato was an extremist. He presents an extreme vision of the polis. The guiding thread of the book is the correspondence between the parts of the city and the parts of the soul. Discord both within the city and within the soul is regarded as the greatest evil. The aim of the *Republic* is to establish a harmonious city based on a conception of justice that harmonizes the individual and society. The best city will necessarily be one that seeks to produce the best or highest type of individual. Plato's famous answer to this question is that the city—any city—will never be free from factional discord until kings become philosophers and philosophers, kings (473d).

Many of the debates about the *Republic* return to the idea of the philosopher-king. Is it intended as a serious proposal for political reform, or did it represent a satire on political radicalism?[2] Fortunately, Plato provides a partial solution to this puzzle. In his old age, approximately fifty years after the trial of Socrates and after his abortive Syracusan expeditions, Plato wrote a letter describing at considerable length his disillusionment with politics and returning to the idea of the philosopher-king that he had formed many years before. Here is what he says in the famous *Seventh Letter:*

> When I was a young man I had the same ambition as many others: I thought of entering public life as soon as I came of age. And certain happenings in public affairs favored me, as follows. The constitution we then had, being anathema to many, was overthrown; and a new government was set up consisting of fifty-one men . . . with absolute powers. Some of these men happened to be relatives and acquaintances of mine, and they invited me to join them at once in what seemed to be a proper undertaking. My attitude toward them is not surprising because I was young. I thought that they were going to lead the city out of the unjust life she had been living and establish her in the path of justice, so that I watched them eagerly to see what they would do. But as I watched them they showed in a short time they made the previous democracy seem like a golden age.
>
> The more I reflected upon what was happening, upon what kind of men were active in politics, and upon the state of our laws and customs, and the older I grew, the more I realized how difficult it is to manage a city's affairs rightly. For I saw it was impossible to do anything without friends and loyal followers; and to find such men ready to hand would be a piece of sheer good luck, since our city was no longer guided by the customs and practices of our fathers, while to train up new ones was anything but easy. And the corruption of our written laws and our customs was proceeding at such amazing speed that whereas at first I had been full of zeal for public life, when I noted these changes and saw how unstable everything was, I became in the end dizzy. . . . At last I came to the conclusion that all existing states are badly governed and the condition of their laws practically incurable, without some miraculous remedy and the assistance of fortune; and I was forced to say, in praise of true philosophy, that from her height alone was it possible to discern what the nature of justice is, either in the state or in the individual, and that the ills of the human race would never end until

either those who are sincerely and truly lovers of wisdom come
into political power, or the rulers of our cities, by the grace of
God, learn true philosophy.[3]

This autobiography provides a kind of introduction to the *Republic*.
Here we have in Plato's own words the way he viewed politics and his reasons for his political philosophy. Yet if the older Plato looked back with a
kind of comprehensive despair and disillusionment with the prospects of reform, the *Republic* recalls an earlier and happier moment in Plato's life and
the life of his city. The action of the dialogue takes place long before the defeat
of Athens, before the rise of the Thirty, and the execution of Socrates, but in
the period that Plato refers to in the letter as a "golden age" where perhaps
many things seemed possible.

The *Republic* asks us to consider seriously what would be the look or
form of a city ruled both by and for philosophers. In this respect it is the
perfect bookend to Plato's *Apology*. While the *Apology* viewed the dangers posed to philosophy and the philosophical life from the city, the *Republic* asks what a city would look like ruled by philosophy. What would
it be like for philosophers to rule? Such a city would require—so Socrates
tells us—the severe censorship of poetry and theology, the abolition of
private property and the family, at least among the guards, and the use of
selected lies and myths—what today would be called "ideology"—as tools
of political rule.

Much of modern political philosophy is directed against Plato's legacy.
The modern state is based on the separation of civil society—the entire domain of private life—from the state. Plato's *Republic* recognizes no such independent private sphere and for this reason has been thought by some readers
to be a harbinger of totalitarianism or fascism. A famous professor at a distant university used to begin his lectures on the *Republic* by saying, "Now we
will consider Plato the fascist." This was the view of perhaps the most influential book written about Plato during the last century: Karl Popper's *The Open
Society and Its Enemies,* which accused Plato of establishing a totalitarian
dictatorship along the lines of Stalin's Russia and Hitler's Germany.[4]

But Plato's *Republic* is a republic of a special kind. It is not a regime
like ours, devoted to maximizing individual liberties, but one that holds the
education of its members as its highest duty. His *Republic,* like the Greek
polis itself, was a tutelary association, and its principal good was the education of citizens for positions of public leadership and high statesmanship.

Plato, it is good to remember, was a teacher. He was the founder of the first university in the Western world, the Academy. This in turn spawned other philosophical schools throughout the Greek and later the Roman worlds. With the demise of Rome in the early Christian centuries, the philosophical academies were transformed into the medieval monasteries, and these in turn became the basis of the first universities in places like Bologna, Paris, and Oxford. When these were transplanted to the New World to places like Cambridge and New Haven, we can say today without doubt that we are literally the inheritors of the Platonic *Republic*. We are the heirs of Plato. Without him, no Yale.

And in fact the institutional and educational requirements of the *Republic* share many features with a place like Yale. In both places men and women are selected from a relatively early age because of their capacities for leadership, courage, self-discipline, and responsibility; they spend several years living together, eating in common mess halls, exercising, and studying far from the oversight of their parents. The best of them are winnowed out to pursue further study and eventually assume positions of high public authority. Throughout, they are subjected to a course of rigorous study and physical training that will lead them to adopt prominent positions in the military and other branches of public service. Does this sound at all familiar? It should. If Plato is a fascist, I would ask, what then are you?

Plato is an extremist, and he often pushes some of these ideas to their most radical conclusion, but he is defining a kind of school. He regards the *politeia* or republic as a school whose chief goal is preparing students for the guidance and leadership of a community. No less an authority than Jean-Jacques Rousseau understood this in its deepest sense: "Do you want to get an idea of public education?" Rousseau wrote in his *Emile*. "Read Plato's *Republic*. It is not at all a political work, as think those who judge books only by their titles. It is the most beautiful educational treatise ever written."[5]

"I went down to the Piraeus"

"I went down" or in Greek, *katēben*. These first words of the *Republic* are not merely incidental. I heard a story that when the German philosopher Martin Heidegger taught the *Republic* he never got beyond the opening lines. Socrates's descent to the Piraeus is a *katabasis*, a going down, modeled on Odysseus's descent to Hades in the *Odyssey*. The work is a kind of philosophical *Odyssey* that both imitates Homer and anticipates other odysseys of the mind, like those of Cervantes or Joyce. The book is full of a number of descents and corresponding ascents, like the climb up the Divided Line to the world of the imperishable Forms late in the book, only to return to the underworld in the Myth of Er at the very end. The work is written not only as a timeless philosophical treatise but as a dramatic dialogue with a setting, a cast of characters, and a firm location in time and place.

The action of the dialogue begins at the Piraeus, the port of Athens, sometime around 421 B.C.E. during the so-called Peace of Nicias when there was a truce in the war between Athens and Sparta. At the beginning we see Socrates and his friend Glaucon trolling the waterfront, so to speak. What are they doing? Why are they together? What do they see in one another? These are questions that immediately come to mind. We learn shortly after that they had gone down to the Piraeus to view a festival where a new goddess was being introduced. The suggestion is that it is the Athenians—not Socrates—who introduce new deities. Socrates's remark that the Thracians put on quite a show suggests that his own perspective is not bound by his own city. It suggests a loftiness and impartiality characteristic of a philosopher, but not of a citizen.

On their way back to town they are accosted by a slave who has been sent on by Polemarchus and his friends, who order Socrates and Glaucon to wait up. "Polemarchus orders you to wait," the slave says. "He is coming up behind you," he continues, "just wait." "Of course we'll wait," Glaucon replies. When Polemarchus and his friends arrive—friends who include Adeimantus, the brother of Glaucon, and Niceratus, the son of the famous general Nicias, whose brokered peace they are now enjoying—they challenge Socrates to stay with them or prove stronger. "Could we not persuade you?" Socrates asks. Not if we won't listen, Polemarchus replies. Instead a compromise is reached. Let Socrates and Glaucon come with Polemarchus and the others to the home of Polemarchus's father, where a dinner will be provided, and later return to the festival, where a horserace will take place. "It seems we must stay," Glaucon acquiesces, and Socrates concurs (328b).

This opening gambit sets the stage for much of what is to follow. The issue is, who has title to rule? Is it Polemarchus and his friends, who claim to rule by the strength of numbers alone, or Socrates and Glaucon, who hope to rule by the powers of reasoned speech and persuasion? Can democracy, which expresses the will of the majority, be rendered compatible with the needs of philosophy that claims to respect only reason and the better argument? Or can a compromise between the two be reached? Is the just city a combination of the two, of force and persuasion?

The Faces of Justice

The first book of the *Republic* is a preamble for what follows. Here we see Socrates carry on a number of conversations, no doubt of the kind for which he became famous and for which he was subsequently tried and executed. As in any Platonic dialogue it is important to look not just at what is said but at what Plato chooses to reveal about the particular individuals with whom Socrates speaks. It is not only the words but also the action of the dialogue that counts. Who are Socrates's interlocutors? What do they represent? There is Cephalus, the venerable father of the family, Polemarchus his son, a solid patriot who defends not only his father's honor but also that of his friends and fellow citizens, and Thrasymachus, a cynical intellectual who rivals Socrates as an educator of future leaders and statesmen.

There is in the dialogue a distinct hierarchy of characters who, we see later on, express certain distinctive features of both the soul and the city. Cephalus, we learn, has spent his life in the acquisitive arts, concerned with satisfying the needs of his body; he represents the appetitive soul. Polemarchus—whose name means War Lord—is preoccupied with questions of honor and loyalty; he represents the spirited part of the soul. And Thrasymachus, a visiting sophist, seeks to teach and educate, anticipating what the *Republic* calls the rational soul. Each of these characters serves to prefigure the relatively superior natures of those who come later in the dialogue. The two brothers, the hedonistic and pleasure-seeking Adeimantus, the fierce and warlike Glaucon, and of course the philosophically minded Socrates each embody one of the key components of the soul—appetite, spiritedness, and reason. Together these figures form a kind of microcosm of humanity. Each of the participants in the dialogue represents one of the specific classes or groups that will eventually occupy the just city, to which Socrates will give the name Kallipolis.

We do not need to interrogate at length the arguments that Socrates makes against each of his interlocutors. Most important is what they stand for. Cephalus represents the claims of age, tradition, and the family. At the beginning of the dialogue, he has just returned from performing certain ritual sacrifices to the gods. His place as head of the household supported by wealth and the authority that wealth confers makes him the natural lead-off batter. Cephalus initially expresses great joy at seeing Socrates but is abruptly challenged by him with the question what it is like to be so old, to which Socrates then adds insult to injury by asking whether Cephalus's reputation for justice is not merely a consequence of his great wealth. Cephalus then tells Socrates how his advanced age has freed him from the erotic passions that had occupied his youth, that when he was not engaged in or thinking about sex, he devoted his life to increasing his fortune. He recalls a line from Sophocles, who was asked whether he could still enjoy sex in his old age. "Silence, man," the poet replied. "Most joyfully did I escape it as though I had run away from a kind of frenzied and savage master" (329c). Now in the twilight of his years he is able to turn his attention to justice, that is, performing sacrifices commanded by the gods. Why does Plato begin here?

Cephalus is the very embodiment of the conventional. He is not a bad man, but a thoroughly unreflective one. In attacking Cephalus, Socrates attacks the embodiment of the conventional opinions supporting the city. Note that Socrates turns Cephalus's statement that the pious man practices justice by sacrificing to the gods into the proposition that justice means paying one's debts and returning what is owed. This sleight of hand, which Socrates then turns against Cephalus—What do you think about returning a borrowed weapon to a madman?—has the effect of pushing Cephalus out of the conversation for good. Socrates achieves his desired effect. He banishes the natural head of the household in the same way that he will later try to abolish the family and property from Kallipolis. Socrates asserts his claim to rule over and above the claims of traditional authority.

Socrates next pursues the conversation with Polemarchus, the self-professed "heir" of the argument as well as to the family fortune. Polemarchus is what the Greeks would call a gentleman or *Kalosgathos*—a person willing to stand up for and defend his family and friends. Unlike his father, who shows himself concerned with the needs of the body (wealth and sex), Polemarchus is concerned to defend the honor and safety of the polis. He accepts the view of justice as giving to each what is owed, but interprets this to mean doing good to your friends and harm to enemies. Justice is, then, a kind of loyalty that we feel to family, members of a team, fellow students of a residential college, or to Yale as opposed to all other places. It is the kind of patriotic sentiment that citizens of one country feel for one another in opposition to all other places. Justice is a devotion to the good of one's own family, friends, and citizens.

Socrates challenges Polemarchus on the grounds that loyalty to a group cannot be a virtue in itself. Do we ever make mistakes? he asks Polemarchus. Isn't the distinction between friend and enemy based on a kind of knowledge? If so, haven't we ever mistaken friend for enemy? How can we say that justice means helping friends and harming enemies when we may not even know with certainty who our friends and enemies really are? Why should the citizens of one state, namely our own, have any moral priority over the citizens of another state? Isn't such an unreflective attachment to our own bound to result in injustice to others? Once again we see Socrates dissolving the bonds of the familiar. At no other point in the *Republic* do we see so clearly the tension between philosophical reflectiveness and the sense of comaraderie, mutuality, and esprit de corps necessary for political life.

Polemarchus appears to believe that a polity can only survive with a vivid sense of what it is and what it stands for and an equally vivid sense of what it is not and who its enemies are. Socrates challenges the very possibility of political life by questioning our ability to distinguish friend from enemy. Although Polemarchus is reduced to silence, it is notable that his argument is not defeated. Later in the *Republic* Socrates will argue that while the best city will be characterized by peace and harmony, this will never be the case in relations between cities. This is why even the best city, even Kallipolis, will require a warrior class. War and the preparation for war will be an intrinsic part of the just city. Even the Platonically just city will have to cultivate a "noble lie" to convince its citizens that there is a difference in nature between them and citizens of other states (414c–415d).

Thrasymachus presents the most difficult challenge to Socrates, in part because he is Socrates's alter ego. Thrasymachus is a rival to Socrates as an educator and teacher. Unlike the others, he claims to have knowledge of what justice is and is willing to teach it for a price. His teaching is presented in the language of hard-boiled realism—he professes disgust at Polemarchus's and Socrates's lofty discussions of loyalty, friendship, and conferring benefits on others. Justice, he claims, is the interest of the stronger. Every polity, he argues, is based upon a distinction between the rulers and the ruled. Justice consists of the rules that are made for the benefit of the ruling class. It is nothing more—and nothing less—than the self-interest of the stronger party (338c).

Thrasymachus is the kind of "intellectual" who enjoys bringing the harsh and unremitting facts about human nature to light. No matter how much we might dislike Thrasymachus, we all feel there is more than a grain of truth in what he says. He contends that man is a being who is first and foremost dominated by a desire for power. This is what distinguishes the true man or the real man from the slave. Power and domination are what we care about most. What is true of individuals is also true for states. Every polity seeks its own advantage against others, making relations between states an unremitting war of all against all. Politics, in the language of modern game theory, is a zero-sum game. There are winners and losers. The rules of justice are simply the laws set up by the winners to protect their own interests.

Socrates challenges Thrasymachus with a version of the argument that he used against Polemarchus. Do we ever make mistakes? he asks. That is, if justice is the interest of the stronger, doesn't it require some kind of knowledge to know what it is in our interest to do? Interests are not brute facts but require reflection. We frequently distinguish our true or long-term interests ("enlightened self-interest") from short-term gains and immediate gratification. What it is in our interest to do or to be is not always self-evident. Do we ever mistake what is in our interests? Of course we do, Thrasymachus cannot help but admit. So justice cannot be simply power, it is power in conjunction with knowledge. We are close to the famous Platonic thesis that all virtue is knowledge.

Most of the exchange with Thrasymachus turns on the problem of what kind of knowledge justice involves. Thrasymachus contends that justice consists in the art of convincing people to obey rules that are really in the interests of the rulers. Justice is based on a kind of elaborate deception. We obey the rules of justice because we fear the consequences of injustice. The true man or real man would be the one with the courage to act unjustly for his own interests. The true ruler is one who treats his subjects like a shepherd treats his flock, that is, not for the good of the sheep but for the good of the shepherd. All rule, like all justice, is based on self-interest. Is Thrasymachus wrong to believe this?

Socrates wins his argument with a sleight of hand. Both he and Thrasymachus believe that justice is a virtue, but what kind of virtue can it be to deceive and fleece people? Thrasymachus is forced to admit that the just person is a fool for obeying laws that are not beneficial to him, while the best life is one of perfect injustice, doing whatever you want whenever you want. With this realization Thrasymachus begins to blush with embarrassment (350d). Why does Thrasymachus blush? Why should he be embarrassed to defend the unjust life? Apparently, he is not as tough as he thinks. He reveals himself to be far more conventional than his bold and ruthless words would seem to admit.

Book 1 ends in uncertainty with the three arguments of Cephalus, Polemarchus, and Thrasymachus having been silenced, but as yet no clear alternative to put in their place. It is only now that the real action of the dialogue can begin.

Glaucon and Adeimantus

Book 1 is a kind of warm-up for what follows in the rest of the *Republic*. In the first book we see Socrates refute—or appear to refute—a number of views of justice, yet we have no better idea of what justice is than we did at the beginning. Until we know this, there is little reason for us to abandon our previous ideas. It is here where Glaucon intervenes.

Glaucon tells Socrates that he is dissatisfied with his refutation of Thrasymachus—and so should we be. Thrasymachus has been shamed (he blushes), but not refuted. Glaucon tells Socrates that it is not enough to show that injustice is wrong; what we need is to hear the case for why justice is good or, more precisely, he wants to hear justice praised "for itself." "Is there in your opinion," he challenges Socrates, "a kind of good that we would choose because we delight in it *for its own sake?*" (358a). This is where the rubber hits the road.

Before addressing Glaucon's challenge we might ask who he is. Glaucon and his brother, Adeimantus, are the brothers of Plato. Other than their appearance in the *Republic* there is no historical record left of either of them, but Plato has given us enough. In the first place, they are young aristocrats, and Glaucon's desire to hear justice praised "for its own sake" indicates his scale of values. It would be vulgar to speak of justice or any virtue in terms of material rewards or consequences. Glaucon does not need to hear justice praised for its benefits. Rather, he complains that he has never heard justice defended the way it ought to be. The brothers' desire to hear justice praised for itself alone is expressive of their freedom from utilitarian or mercenary motives; it reveals a kind of idealism and loftiness of soul not present in any of the previous interlocutors.

Certainly the brothers are not slouches. Although their role later in the dialogue may be reduced to repeating "Yes, Socrates" and "No, Socrates," their early challenges show them to be potential philosophers, the kind of persons who might one day rule the city. Of the two, Glaucon is clearly the superior. He is described as "most courageous," which in the context means most manly and virile. Later Socrates admits that he has "always been full of wonder at the nature" of the brothers and goes on to cite a line of poetry written about them after they had distinguished themselves in battle (368a).

They are also highly competitive super-achievers—something like yourselves. There is quite a bit of jousting between them that one needs to be attentive to. Each proposes to Socrates a test that he will have to pass in order to prove the value of justice and the just life. Glaucon goes on to rehabilitate Thrasymachus's argument about the unjust life, but presents it more vividly than Thrasymachus could do himself. Glaucon tells the story of Gyges, who possessed a magic ring that conferred on him the power of invisibility.[6] Who has not wondered what we would do if we had this power? Gyges murders the king and sleeps with his wife. What would you do? In any case, Glaucon wants to hear why a man with the power of Gyges should wish to be just. If we could commit any crime, indulge any vice, commit any outrage and be sure that we could get away with it, why would we want to be just? That is the challenge Glaucon poses to Socrates. Why would someone with absolute power and complete immunity from the law prefer justice to injustice? If justice is something truly worthy, then Socrates should be able to convince Gyges that it is in his interest to be just. This is certainly a tall order.

Now Adeimantus chimes in. He has heard parents and poets praise justice for its benefits in this life and the next. He takes this to mean that justice is a virtue for the weak, lame, and unadventurous, that is, justice is presented as good because of the consequences that will attend it. A real man does not fear the consequences of injustice. His concern, Adeimantus tells us in a revealing image, is with self-guardianship or self-control: "each would be his own guard" (367a). In other words we should not care what people say about us but instead we should be prepared to develop qualities of self-containment, autonomy, and independence from the influence that others can exercise over us. If justice is worth pursuing, then it is worth pursuing for its sake alone, not for some putative advantages or disadvantages that might follow.

The two brothers' desire to hear justice praised for itself (Glaucon) and to live freely and independently (Adeimantus) shows to some degree their distance from their own society. To put the case slightly anachronistically: these two are sons of the aristocracy who feel degraded by the mendacity and hypocrisy of the world around them. What person with any sensitivity has not felt this way at one time or another? The two are open to persuasion to consider alternatives—perhaps radical alternatives—to the society that nurtured them. They are potential revolutionaries. The remainder of the *Republic* is addressed to them and people like them.

City and Soul

With the speeches of Glaucon and Adeimantus, the circle around Socrates has effectively closed. Socrates knows that he will not be returning to Athens that evening. He proposes instead a kind of thought experiment that he hopes will work magic on the two brothers. Let us, he proposes, "watch a city coming into being in speech" (369a). Rather than considering justice microscopically in an individual through a magnifying glass, let us view justice in a city in order to help us better understand what justice is in an individual.

This idea that the city is essentially analogous to the soul is the central metaphor around which the entire *Republic* turns. It is introduced quite innocuously, and no one in the dialogue objects, yet everything else follows from this idea that the city is in its essential aspects like an individual, and vice versa. What is Socrates trying to do here, and what function does the city-soul analogy serve?

To state the obvious: Socrates introduces the analogy to help the brothers better understand what justice is in an individual or in the soul, to use the proper Platonic term. The governance of the soul—Adeimantus's standard of self-control—must be like the governance of the city in some decisive respects. But how is a city like a soul, and in what respect is self-governance like governing a collective entity like a polis?

Consider what we mean when we say that someone is "typically American" or that someone else is "typically French." We take it to mean that their character and behavior expresses certain traits that we have come to regard as representative of a cross-section of their countrymen. Is this a useful way to think and speak? More specifically, what does it mean to say that an individual can be seen as magnified in his or her country or that one's country is simply the collective expression of certain individual character traits?

One way of thinking about this thesis is to regard it as a particular causal hypothesis about the formation of both individual character and political institutions. This reading of the city-soul analogy grows out of the view that, as individuals, we live in societies that both shape us and that we help to shape in turn. The city-soul analogy is an attempt to understand how societies reproduce themselves and shape citizens who in turn help the society in question to function.

This is helpful, but it still makes us think. In what ways are cities like individuals? Does it mean that something like the presidency, the Congress, and the Supreme Court can be discerned within the soul of every American citizen? This would clearly be absurd. Or does it mean that American democracy helps to produce a particular kind of democratic soul, just as the old regime in France tended to produce a certain kind of aristocratic character. Every regime will produce a distinctive kind of individual, and this individual will come to embody the dominant traits of character of the regime.

The remainder of the *Republic* is devoted to crafting a regime that will produce a certain distinctive character type. This is why Plato's republic is properly called a utopia. There has never been a regime in history that was so single-mindedly devoted to this end, to produce this rarest and most difficult species of humanity, namely, the philosopher.

The Reform of Poetry

Socrates's "city in speech" proceeds through various stages. The first stage, proposed by Adeimantus, is the simple city, the "city of utmost necessity," that is, a city limited to the satisfaction of certain basic needs. This primitive or simple city expresses the nature of Adeimantus's soul. There is a kind of noble simplicity that treats its subjects as pure bodies or creatures of limited appetites. The simple city is little more than a combination of households designed for the purpose of securing existence.

At this point Glaucon retorts that it seems as if his brother has created a "city of pigs" (372d). Where are the luxuries? Where are the "relishes," he asks? Where are the things that make up a city? Glaucon's city in turn expresses his soul. The warlike Glaucon would preside over a "feverish city," as it is called, one that institutionalizes honors, competition, and above all war. If Adeimantus expresses the appetitive part of the soul, Glaucon represents spiritedness, or what Plato calls *thymos*. Thymos is the central psychological category of the *Republic*. Spiritedness is that quality of soul that is most closely associated with the desire for honor, fame, and prestige. It is what seeks distinction, the desire to be first in the race of life, to lead and dominate others. It is the quality we associate with the alpha male. The issue for Socrates is how to channel thymos from a wild and untamed passion into support for the city and the common good. Can this be done? How would one begin the domestication of the thymotic soul? The entire thrust of the book is devoted to the taming of spiritedness.

It is here where Socrates turns to his first and one of his most controversial proposals. The creation of a just city—and not merely Glaucon's luxurious city—can only begin with the control of poetry and music. It is from this that the image of Plato as educator derives. The first order of business for the founder of a city is the oversight of education. It is the principal task of a lawgiver to control what kinds of stories, histories, drama, poetry, and music people are permitted to hear and see. His proposals for the reform of poetry, especially Homeric poetry, represent a radical departure from Greek educational practices and beliefs. Why is this so important?

In the first place, it is from the poets in the broadest sense of the term— mythmakers, storytellers, artists, and musicians—that we receive our earliest and most vivid impressions of heroes and villains, gods and the afterlife. These stories shape us for the rest of our lives. The Homeric epics were to the Greek world what the Bible has been for ours. The names of Achilles, Priam, Hector, Odysseus, and Ajax would have been as familiar to the Greeks as the names and stories of Abraham, Isaac, Joshua, and Jesus are to us.

Plato's critique of Homeric poetry is twofold: theological and political. The theological critique is that Homer depicts his gods as fickle and inconstant; such beings cannot be worthy of true worship. But more important, the Homeric heroes are said to be simply bad role models. They are shown to be intemperate in sex and unduly fond of money. To these vices Socrates adds excessive cruelty and disregard for the dead bodies of one's opponents. The Homeric heroes are ignorant and passionate men, full of blind anger and the furious desire for retribution. How could such figures possibly serve as positive models for the future citizens of Kallipolis?

Socrates's answer is, of course, the complete purgation of poetry and the arts. He wants to deprive the poets of their power to enchant and bewitch, something to which Socrates admits later he has always been susceptible (607c). In place of the pedagogical power of poetry, Socrates proposes to install philosophy. Consequently, the poets will have to be expelled from the just city.

Is Socrates's censorship of poetry and the arts an indication of his totalitarian impulse? This is the part of the *Republic* most likely to call up our First Amendment instincts. Who are you, Socrates, we want to ask, to tell us what we can read, hear, and listen to? Furthermore, Socrates is not saying that Kallipolis would have no poetry and music; it would simply have to be Socratic poetry and music. But what would such Socratically purified poetry and music look or sound like? I do not have an answer to this. Perhaps the *Republic* as a whole is a piece of Socratic poetry.

It is important to remember that the question of education is introduced in the context of taming the warlike passions of Glaucon and others like him, whom Socrates refers to as the Auxiliaries of the city. The question of censorship and telling of lies is introduced not as an aesthetic matter but as a matter of military necessity. Nothing at all is said about the education of farmers, artisans, merchants, and laborers. To speak bluntly, Socrates does not care about them. Nor has he said anything yet about the education of the philosopher. His interest here is in the creation of a tight and highly disciplined cadre of young warriors who will protect the city much as watchdogs protect their homes (376a). Such individuals will subordinate their own desires and satisfactions to the group and live by a strict code of honor.

Are Socrates's proposals unrealistic? Undesirable? Not if you believe, as he does, that even the best city must make provisions for war and therefore a warrior class. Such a life—the soldier's life—requires harsh privations in terms of material rewards and benefits as well as a willingness to die for others, fellow citizens to be sure, but people whom they will not even know. Far more unrealistic would be those who believe that we can one day abolish war and the passions that give rise to it. So far as the passionate or spirited aspect of human nature remains strong, Plato believes, so long will it be necessary to attend to the warriors of society.

The Soul of the Guards

The great theme of the *Republic*—at least one of the great themes—is the control of the passions. Of course, this is the theme of every great moralist from Spinoza to Kant to Freud. How do we control the passions? Every moralist has a strategy for helping us to submit our passions to the control of reason or some kind of supervening moral power. Recall that this is the problem raised at the beginning of book 2 by Adeimantus, who puts forward an idea of self-control or self-guardianship that essentially entails protecting ourselves from the passion for injustice. Independence means not only freedom from control by others but also an image of self-control, control over our most powerful passions and inclinations.

The most powerful passion is designated by Socrates as thymos. This we have seen is the political passion par excellence. It is the kind of fiery desire for fame and love of distinction that leads men (and women) of a certain type to pursue their ambitions in public life. It is connected to the capacity for heroism and self-sacrifice, but it is also related to the exercise of domination and tyranny over others. The quality of thymos is possessed by every great statesman, but also by every tyrant who has ever lived. The question posed by the *Republic* is whether this thymotic quality can be controlled, and if it can, can it be put into the service of the public good?

Socrates introduces the problem of thymos with a story. In book 4 he tells a story that he says he has heard and believes: "Leontius, the son of Aglaion, was proceeding up from the Piraeus outside the North wall when he perceived corpses lying near the public executioner. At the same time, he desired to see them and, to the contrary, he felt disgust and turned himself away; and for a while he battled with himself and hid his face. But eventually overpowered by desire he forced his eyes open and rushing toward the corpses said, 'See you damned wretches! Take your fill of the beautiful sight'" (439e).

The story that Socrates tells here is not one of reason controlling the passions but one of intense internal conflict. Leontius is torn by conflicting emotions, both to see and not to see; he is at war with himself. Who has not experienced this situation? Is it not the same emotion we feel when passing a car wreck on a highway? There is something shameful about slowing down to look to see if there is a body on the road, and yet our eyes are compelled to look, often despite ourselves. Think about it. The result is that Leontius becomes angry with himself for wanting to look on something he knows to be shameful. It is his thymos that is the cause of this anger.

The thymos of Leontius is connected to the fact that he is a certain kind of man: proud, independent, someone who wants to be in control of himself (and yet can't be). His is a soul at war with itself and potentially at war with others. The *Republic* tries to offer a strategy—perhaps we might even call it a therapy—for dealing with thymos, for submitting it to the control of reason and allowing us to achieve a level of balance, self-control, and moderation. These qualities, taken together, Plato calls justice, which can only be achieved when reason is in control of our appetites and desires. Can such an ideal of justice ever be achieved? Can reason soften and moderate our conflicting emotions and desires? Can the soul of the guardian serve the cause of justice? These questions are addressed by Socrates with his construction of Kallipolis.

The Three Waves

The construction of Kallipolis proceeds through what Socrates calls "three waves." These waves are, first, the restriction of private property, second, the abolition of the family, and, third, the establishment of the philosopher-king.

Each of these waves is regarded as necessary for the proper construction of the just city. I will say something here about the proposals for coeducation of men and women that are a part of Socrates's plan for the abolition of the family.

The core of Socrates's proposal is the equal education of men and women, a proposal that in context he presents as laughable knowing it will certainly seem that way to Glaucon and Adeimantus. There is no job, Socrates states, that cannot be performed equally well by both men and women. Gender differences are no more relevant when it comes to positions of rule than is the distinction between the bald and the hairy (454c–d). Socrates is saying not that men and women are the same in every respect but that they are equal with respect to competing for any job at all. There will be no glass ceilings in Kallipolis. Socrates is perhaps the first champion of the emancipation of women from the household.

The proposal for a level playing field demands equal access to education. Here Socrates insists that if education is to be equal, both men and women should be submitted to the same regimen, meaning that they will exercise in the nude among one another in coed gymnasia. Moreover, marriage and procreation are to be for the sake of the city. Accordingly, there must be strict oversight of sexual contact between men and women. There is to be nothing like "romantic love" among the members of the guardian class. Sexual relations are intended strictly for the sake of reproduction, with unwanted fetuses aborted. The only exception to this prohibition is for members of the guardian class who are beyond the age of reproduction; they may have sex with anyone they want (a version of "recreational sex") as a reward for a lifetime of self-control. Child bearing may be inevitable for the woman, but rearing the child will be the responsibility of the community or at least the class of guardians in common day-care centers. In the language of Hillary Clinton, "It takes a village." No children should know their biological parents and no parents, their children. The purpose of this scheme is to eliminate the pronouns "me" and "mine," which should be replaced by "ours."

The Platonic community is to be one where men and women are rendered as alike as possible, "a community of pleasure and pain" (464a). I am reminded of the story told by the French feminist philosopher Simone de Beauvoir, who expressed a similar point of view about creating a community where the "I" would literally become a "We." What if I have a pain in my foot, someone objected. "No," she replied, "we will have a pain in your foot."[7]

The objections to Socrates's—and Beauvoir's—proposals are obvious. Aristotle was only the first to complain that common ownership, whether of children or property, leads to common neglect. We truly care only about what is ours; the community will never replace the individual as the ultimate locus of our love and concern. This is an old story, but again it is worth remembering that Socrates advances his prescriptions not to create happy or satisfied individuals, but for the sake of creating a unified guardian class capable of protecting and defending the city. The purpose of marriage is, to put it bluntly, to create soldiers.

It is in the same context of his treatment of men and women that, it often goes unnoticed, Socrates proceeds to rewrite the laws of war. In the first place children will be taught the art of war; "this must be the beginning [of their education]," Socrates notes, "making the children spectators of war" (467c). Not only is expulsion from the ranks of the guardians the penalty for cowardice, Socrates suggests that there should be erotic rewards for those who excel in bravery. Consider the following remarkable proposal:

SOCRATES: "But I suppose," I said, "you wouldn't go so far as to accept this further opinion."

GLAUCON: "What?"

SOCRATES: "That he kiss and be kissed by each."

GLAUCON: "Most of all," he said. "And I add to the law [of war] that as long as they are on that campaign no one whom he wants to kiss be permitted to refuse, so that if a man happens to love someone, either male or female, he would be more eager to win the rewards of valor."

SOCRATES: "Fine," I said. (468b–c)

A rather prudish twentieth-century translator of Plato, Paul Shorey, notes of this proposal: "This is almost the only passage in Plato that one would wish to blot."[8] But just imagine what an incentive such as this might do for military recruitment today!

Justice as Harmony

At long last we are able to come to the theme of the *Republic:* justice. Recall that the Platonic idea of justice concerns harmony, both harmony in the city and harmony in the soul. We learn that the two are structurally homologous.

Justice is variously defined as "what binds [the city] together and makes it one" (426b) and as "minding one's own business" (433a). Put another way, it consists of everyone and everything performing those functions for which they are best equipped. "Each of the other citizens," Socrates says, "must be brought to that which naturally suits him—one man, one job—so that each man practicing his own, which is one, will not become many but one, thus, you see, the whole city will naturally grow up to be one" (423d).

At the very least, these passages indicate that it was not Adam Smith but Plato who discovered the division of labor. But while Smith saw how the increased specialization of functions—his famous example was a pin factory—contributed to the overall "wealth of nations," he was also cognizant of how the division of labor contributed to the narrowing and moral enervation of the worker. The paradox was that while the division of labor contributed to increased prosperity for society, it could also lead to the stultification of the individual. But Plato raises no such objection. For him, the division of labor leads to a concentration of the mind on the one or few activities that give life a sense of wholeness, gravity, and purpose.

The idea here is that justice consists in following a strict division of labor, everyone working at the job or task that naturally fits or suits him or her. One can, of course, raise several objections to this view of justice. Again Aristotle took the lead: Plato's excessive emphasis on unity destroys the natural diversity of human beings that make up a city. Is there one and only one thing that each person does best and, if so, who is to decide what it is? Will such a plan of justice not be unduly coercive in forcing people into predefined social roles? Shouldn't individuals be free to choose for themselves their own plans of life wherever these might take them?

However this may be, Plato believes he has found in the formula of the division of labor—one person, one job—a foundation for justice. That is to say, if the three parts of the city—craftsmen, auxiliaries, and guardians—all work together by each attending to his or her own tasks, doing his or her own job, peace and harmony will prevail. And since the city is simply the soul writ large, the three social classes merely express the three parts of the soul. The soul is a just soul when appetite, spiritedness, and reason cooperate, with reason ruling spirit and appetite, just as in the polis the philosopher-king rules the warriors and the craftsmen. The result is a perfect balance of the parts of the whole. The city and the soul each appear as a pyramid rising from a broad and flat base to a peak of perfection something like the following:

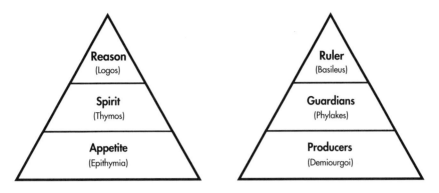

But this is to return us to Socrates's initial proposal. Are the structure of the city and the structure of the soul really identical? Maybe not. For example, every individual necessarily consists of three parts of the soul—appetite, spirit, and reason—yet each of us will be confined to one and only one task in the social hierarchy. Why should a multifaceted being be confined to one social role? I assume what Socrates means is that although every person will embody to some degree all three of these features, only one of them will be the dominant trait in each of us. Some of us are dominantly appetitive, others spirited, and so on. But does even this make sense? The capacity to make money requires not just the appetites but also the powers of foresight and calculation, and a willingness to take risk. The capacity for war requires more than thymos alone; it requires the ability to conceive strategy, to pursue tactics, and to exhibit qualities of leadership and command. To confine the individual to one, and only one, sphere of life seems an injustice to the internal moral and psychological complexity that makes of us who we are.

There are further discrepancies in this analogy between city and soul. Justice in the city consists of each member fulfilling his or her task in the social division of labor. But this is a very far cry from justice in the soul that consists in a kind of rational autonomy or self-control, where reason directs the appetites. In point of fact, very few citizens will live a life of rational mastery and self-control. Most will be consigned to remedial tasks where they will live under the tutelary control of the guards of Kallipolis. The irony is that while the vast majority of citizens may live in a Platonically just city, very few of them will lead Platonically just lives. The only truly just individuals will be the philosophers who live according to reason and who control their passions and appetites. But what of the rest? The harmony and self-discipline of the city will not be due to each of its members; social justice will be the result of a functionally mandated division of labor that will be controlled by the selective use of lies, myths, and various other deceptions. How can a city be just if very few of its citizens are permitted to live just lives?

This question is raised in the *Republic* by Adeimantus, who at the beginning of book 4 asks Socrates: "What would your apology be Socrates if it were objected that you're hardly making these men happy?" (419a). Adeimantus is concerned here that Socrates is being unfair to the Guards, giving them all the responsibilities but none of the rewards of political rule. How can a citizen of Kallipolis live a just or a happy life if he or she is deprived of the goods or pleasures that most of us seek? "In founding the city," Socrates replies, "we are not looking to the exceptional happiness of any one group among us, but that of the city as a whole" (420b). Socrates deliberately suppresses here the definition of justice as self-guardianship or independence for the political definition of justice as collective well-being or collective harmony. Why does he do this? Is such an answer satisfactory? What does such an answer tell us about Socrates?

The fact that neither Adeimantus nor Glaucon disputes Socrates's answer suggests that they share a common belief that the justice or collective well-being of the city must take precedence over the happiness of the individual. They are not natural ascetics; they desire pleasure, but in the case of a conflict between the happiness of the individual and the happiness of the city they agree that their own interests and desires must take a back seat. But the idea of a conflict between the individual and the city suggests that Kallipolis is not complete. The city-soul analogy proposed in book 2 suggested that a just city would be one where city and soul were in perfect accord, where conflict between the private good of the individual and the public welfare of the city were one and the same. At the least, the task of founding the city is incomplete. It will only be complete, and we will only see justice "coming into being," with the introduction of the philosopher-king.

The Philosopher

The Platonic republic is not complete until the third and final wave of paradox with the proposal for a philosopher-king. "Unless the philosophers rule as kings or those now called kings and chiefs genuinely philosophize,"

Socrates asserts, "there will be no rest from ills for the cities" (473d). Socrates presents this proposal as outlandish. He says that he expects to be "drowned in laughter." This has led some readers to suggest that Socrates's proposal for philosopher-kings is ironical, that it is intended as a kind of joke to discredit the idea of a just city or at least to indicate its extreme implausibility. The question is why Socrates regards philosopher-kingship as a requirement for a just polity.

I am by no means sure that Plato did regard the idea of the philosopher-king as an impossibility, much less an absurdity. Plato himself took three arduous trips to Sicily to serve as an adviser to two different kings. Although his mission to turn these Syracusan tyrants into Platonic philosophers failed and as a result Plato later retired from politics, the ambition to unite philosophy and politics has been a recurring dream of political philosophy ever since. What may have appeared as laughable to Socrates and his companions might appear very different in other times and places. The idea of a philosophically educated statesman—the later model of the enlightened despot—has resonated throughout the modern era where philosophers—one thinks of names like Machiavelli, Hobbes, Rousseau—all sought the ear of political leaders or those who could help to convert their political ideas into practice.

Most of the objections to Plato's philosopher-king have centered on the practicability of the idea. Beyond this, however, there is a problem with the very cogency of the concept. Can philosophy and politics actually be united? The needs of philosophy seem quite different from the needs of political rule. Can one imagine Socrates willingly giving up one of his conversations for the tedious business of legislation and administration? The philosopher as described by Plato is someone with knowledge of the eternal Forms lying behind (or beyond) the many particulars. But just how does this kind of knowledge help us deal with the constant change and flux of political life? Plato does not say. It is not enough that the philosopher have knowledge of the Forms; this knowledge must be supplemented by experience, judgment, and a sort of practical rationality. On top of this, there is the question of the potential abuse of political power by the philosopher. Philosophers are not thinking machines but human beings composed of reason, spiritedness, and appetite. Will not even philosophers offered the possibility of absolute political power be tempted to abuse their positions?

The question we have to ask ourselves, then, is to what problem is the philosopher-king intended as the answer. Plato seems to draw our attention to the fact that political power is the deepest aspiration of philosophy. The

Republic as a whole is a surrogate for Socrates's failed ambition to rule Athens and Plato's failed attempt to serve as an adviser to a king in Sicily. There are at least two implications that follow from this reading. The first is the view that Plato is the true founder of the revolutionary tradition, one that seeks to unite theory and practice, reason and reality, that reaches its culmination in the doctrines of Hegel and Marx. Plato, on this reading, is the founder of the view that politics is an activity guided by intellectuals, theoreticians, or philosopher-priests. It is this view of politics that has been consistently deplored by the conservatives of the philosophical tradition from Aristotle to Montesquieu to Burke, who have all been deeply suspicious of the efforts to reform politics in accordance with a plan or program of reason.

But there is another reading of the *Republic,* however, that stresses the ultimate impossibility of uniting philosophy and the city and that stresses not only the dangers to the city but also the dangers to philosophy. The effort to turn philosophy into a tool of political rule necessarily turns philosophy itself into an "ideology," a form of propaganda forced to resort to lies, distortions, and half-truths in order to ensure its hold on political power. One aspect of the *Republic* that frequently goes unmentioned is that there are no non-Platonists in the city. The effort to maintain absolute control over thought cannot help but become tyrannical. Philosophy requires a certain distance, a certain independence, from the city if it is to remain a critical activity and not simply a tool of political power. Seen from this point of view, the proposal for philosopher-kings must be adjudged a failure. It demonstrates, at least for some readers, that politics and philosophy must maintain a respectful distance from one another.

The Cave and the Sun

The relation of philosophy to political power is the explicit theme of one of Plato's most enduring images: the cave (514a–17a). Here Socrates challenges Glaucon to "make an image of our nature in its education and want of education" (514a). The image is of a cave in which from childhood its inhabitants have been shackled to one another facing a wall and have seen only the images projected on the wall from a fire burning behind them. The image is something like a modern movie theatre or a television screen where the spectators absorb the images they see in front of them. As a result the "prisoners"—for that is what they are—are never allowed to see the objects themselves that are projected on the wall, only the shadows of these objects. These persons—passive and enthralled—Socrates claims are "like us" (515a).

The objects reflected on the wall are described as "artifacts"—statues of wood and stone and the like—that are manipulated by "puppet handlers." These puppeteers are in the first instance the legislators of the city, its founders, statesmen, and legislators, the bringers of law and codes of justice. Next to them are the poets of the city, its mythologists, historians, and artists; and next to them are its craftsmen, architects, city planners, and designers. All of these form the horizon within which the collective life of the city takes place.

But then imagine, we are asked, that one of these prisoners escaped, that someone dragged him away "by force" in such a way that he could no longer see the fire projecting the shadows but was led out of the cave into the sunlight, the life-giving force, by which the cave itself was, however dimly, illuminated. Socrates describes this situation as having one's soul "turned around," the Greek word for which is *periagogē.* This kind of soul-turning is tantamount to a form of conversion moving far beyond the kind of politically useful education described earlier in the *Republic:*

SOCRATES: "Education is not what the professions of certain men assert it to be. They presumably assert that they put into the soul knowledge that isn't in it, as though they were putting sight into blind eyes."

GLAUCON: "Yes," he said, "they do indeed assert that."

SOCRATES: "But the present argument, on the other hand," I said, "indicates that this power is in the soul of each, and that the instrument with which each learns— just as an eye is not able to turn toward the light from the dark without the whole body—must be turned around from that which is *coming into being* together with the whole soul until it is able to endure looking at that which *is* and the brightest part of that which *is.*" (518 c–d)

This metaphor of the turning of the soul is the Platonic image of education. This is not a pleasant experience. It requires us to call into question all of the comfortable certainties that we had previously held to be true, good, and beautiful. It is common in the literature on Plato to think of this as some kind of religious conversion, and Plato often writes as if philosophy requires a retreat from society to the inner citadel of the soul. But this ascetic model of philosophy fails to account for the experience of the cave. Philosophy is fundamentally a social art and requires others to engage in it.

It entails a rigorous training that begins with mathematics and culminates in the comprehensive study of "dialectic," or the art of conversation. The education of the philosopher teaches not withdrawal from but participation in the world.

Socrates next asks the reader to imagine that the philosopher returns to the cave. How would he or she be greeted? Appear to the other cave dwellers? Readjust to the light or the lack of it? Such a person, Socrates admits, would cut a "graceless" figure in attempting to convey to the other troglodytes in the cave what had been seen on the outside. Such a person might become an object of innocent fun or of good-natured teasing, but more likely of envy, ridicule, or contempt. On Plato's telling, he might even find himself persecuted, harassed, and threatened with death as a dangerous enemy of the people.

The story of the cave is surely one of Plato's most pessimistic tales of the relation of philosophy to political power. The question that the story begs us to consider is, why would the philosopher, after escaping his shackles and seeing the sun, consent to return to the cave at all? Would not anyone prefer to remain aloof from politics—compared by Socrates to immigrating to a colony on the Isles of the Blessed—to the guarantee of failure and even death upon one's return? Would not compelling the philosophers to return to the cave be a manifest injustice to them, making them give up the best life? It is this question that is posed by Glaucon in the following bit of dialogue:

SOCRATES: "Then our job as founders," I said, "is to compel the best natures to go to the study which we were saying before is the greatest, to see the good and to go up that ascent; and, when they have gone up and seen sufficiently, not to permit them what is now permitted."

GLAUCON: "What's that?"

SOCRATES: "To remain there," I said, "and not be willing to go down again among those prisoners or share their labors and honors, whether they be slighter or more serious."

GLAUCON: "What?" he said. "Are we to do them an injustice and make them live a worse life when a better is possible for them?" (519 c–d)

Socrates's image seems to have worked its magic. It seems to have disenthralled Glaucon, if only temporarily, of his desire for political rule. Its point is that the city, even Kallipolis, is nothing but a cave and its inhabitants prisoners in comparison to the beauties of philosophy. As the image suggests, each of us is an inhabitant of a cave of our own; it may be better or worse, depending on the nature of its legislators, its poets, and its artists, but it can never be anything other than a cave. The prisoners facing the wall are not symbolic of a particularly bad or unenlightened community; they are the citizens of any possible community. By this time even Glaucon—the warlike Glaucon!—is complaining that it would be unjust to force the philosopher to return to rule the city.

The story of the cave reveals, more clearly than anything, the limitations of the city-soul analogy proposed by Socrates in book 2. Although the individual and the community may be like each other in some respects, Plato wants to show that at the highest level, in the crucial respect, they are fundamentally at odds. The aspiration of the soul, its erotic desire to escape the conventional and restrictive bonds of the community, remains the deepest impulse of philosophy. Even the best city will be experienced as a prison by those who have embarked on the long, soul-turning journey of education. We may never be able to live entirely outside the community, but we also cannot remain content within it. In this respect the *Republic* is not just a work of philosophy. It is the greatest bildungsroman ever written.

Plato's Democracy and Ours

How would Socrates respond to a regime such as ours and, most important, what have we to learn from this confrontation?

In one sense, the *Republic* is the most antidemocratic book ever written. Its defense of philosophic-kingship is a direct repudiation of Athenian democracy. Its conception of justice as "minding one's own business" is a rejection of the Athenian belief that any citizen has sufficient all-round knowledge to participate in the offices of government. Yet it is important to recall that Athenian democracy is not American democracy. Plato thought of democracy as rule of the many, which he associated with the unrestricted freedom to do as one likes. This is a far cry from American democracy based on a constitutional system of checks and balances, the rule of law, and a government created for the protection of individual rights. The differences between Athens and Washington could not be more striking on the surface.

Even if the institutions of American democracy are not what Plato had in mind in his rejection of democratic politics, there is still a condition of modern democratic life that comes very close to what he described. It is not only the politics but the culture of democracy that is of concern. Consider the following passage from book 8 of the *Republic:* "He [the democratic man] also lives along day by day, gratifying the desire that occurs to him, at one time drinking and listening to the flute, at another downing water and reducing; now practicing gymnastics, and again idling and neglecting everything; and sometimes spending his time as though he were occupied with philosophy. Often he engages in politics and, jumping up, says and does whatever chances to come to him; and if he ever admires any soldiers, he turns in that direction: and if it's moneymakers, in that one. And there is neither order nor necessity in his life, but calling this life sweet, free, and blessed he follows it throughout" (561c–d).

This account should be instantly recognizable when applied to the modern democratic individual, especially the references to dieting and exercise coupled with bouts of indulgence and moral neglect. What Plato (like Tocqueville centuries later) discerned in democracy was a certain type of materialism that elevated pleasure above all else and fostered an unwillingness to sacrifice for ideals. Democracy, as the passage above makes clear, fosters a sham universality by exciting all manner of strange interests and passions. It makes it exceedingly difficult to concentrate on the very few things that give life a sense of wholeness and importance.

What bothers Socrates most about democracy, however, is its tendency toward a form of moral anarchy that confuses liberty with license and authority with oppression. It is in this section of the *Republic* that Adeimantus asks: "Won't we with Aeschylus say whatever comes to our lips?" (563c). The idea of having the liberty to say "whatever comes to our lips" sounds to Plato like a kind of blasphemy, the view that nothing is shameful and everything is permitted. There is here a license that comes from the denial of any restraints on our desires or a kind of hedonistic belief that because all desires are equal, all should be permitted.

Plato's views on democracy are not all negative. After all, it was a democracy that produced Socrates and allowed him to philosophize freely until his seventieth year. This would never have been permitted in Sparta or any other city of the ancient world. Furthermore, Plato may have had reason to reconsider the democracy in Athens in the letter that he wrote near the end of this life, where he called the democracy a "golden age" in comparison to what went after it. Plato seems to agree with Winston Churchill that democracy is the worst regime—except for all the others that have been tried.

So what is the function of Kallipolis? What purpose does it serve? The philosopher-king may be an object of wish or hope, but Plato realizes that the occurrence of such a ruler is not to be expected. The philosophical city is introduced as a metaphor to help us understand the education of the soul. The reform of politics may not be within our power, but the exercise of self-control always is. The first responsibility of the individual who wishes to engage in political reform is to reform himself. This point is made near the very end of the *Republic* where Socrates speaks not of the soul "writ large" but of "the city within" (591d). The dialogue once again turns from the city to the soul:

> SOCRATES: "Yes, by the dog," I said, "he will [be engaged with] his own city [Kallipolis], very much so. However, perhaps he won't in his fatherland unless some divine chance coincidentally comes to pass."
>
> GLAUCON: "I understand," he said. "You mean he will in the city whose foundation we have now gone through, the one that has its place in speeches, since I don't suppose it exists anywhere on earth."
>
> SOCRATES: "But in heaven," I said, "perhaps, a pattern is laid up for the man who wants to see and *found a city within himself* on the basis of what he sees. It doesn't make any difference whether it is or will be somewhere. For he would mind the things of this city alone, and of no other." (592a–b; emphasis added)

This is a point that is often lost, that the *Republic* is above all a work on the reform of the soul. This is not to say that it teaches us withdrawal from political responsibilities. Not at all. Philosophy, certainly Socratic philosophy, requires friends, comrades, conversation; it is not something that can be usefully pursued in isolation. Socrates clearly understands that those who want to reform others must first reform themselves, must "found a city within himself," but many who have tried to imitate him have been less careful.

It is very easy to confuse, as many have done, the *Republic* with a recipe for tyranny. The twentieth century is littered with the corpses of those who have set themselves up as philosopher-kings: Lenin, Stalin, Hitler, Mao, Khomeini to name the most obvious. But such men are not philosophers; their pretensions to justice are just that, pretensions, expressions of their vanity and ambition. For Plato, philosophy was in the first instance a therapy for the passions, a way of setting limits to the desires. This is precisely the opposite of the tyrant, whom Plato describes as a person of limitless desires, lacking the most rudimentary kind of governance, namely, self-governance.

The difference between the philosopher and the tyrant illustrates two very different conceptions of philosophy. For some, philosophy represents a form of liberation from confusion, from unruly passions and prejudices, a therapy of the soul that brings peace and satisfaction. For others, philosophy is the source of the desire to dominate, it is the basis of all forms of tyranny and the great age of ideologies through which we have just passed. The question is, since both tendencies are at work within philosophy, how do we encourage one side but not the other? As that great philosopher Karl Marx once asked: "Who will educate the educator?" Exactly. Whom do we turn to for help?

There is no magic solution to this question, but the best answer I know of is Socrates. He showed people how to live and, just as important, how to die. He lived and died not like most people, but better, and even his most vehement critics admit that.

CHAPTER 5
Aristotle's Science of Regime Politics

Alexander the Great, 356–323 B.C.E., as a youth listening to his tutor Aristotle.
Ca. 1875. Photo credit: The Print Collector / Alamy

There is a story about the life of Aristotle the essentials of which run something like this: Aristotle was born; he spent his life philosophizing; and then he died. There is probably more to the life of Aristotle than these facts admit, but to some extent this captures the way in which he has been perceived: as the ultimate philosopher.[1]

Aristotle was born in 384 B.C.E. in Stagira in the northern part of Greece in what is now Macedonia. At the age of about seventeen—approximately the age of an undergraduate—he was sent by his father to study in Athens at the Academy established by Plato. But unlike most undergraduates, for the next twenty years Aristotle remained attached to the Academy, where he was later hired as a teacher. Is it not remarkable to consider that Plato and Aristotle, two people we think of as founders of the Western tradition, both lived and taught at the same place? We can only wonder what kinds of conversations they had over their many years together.

After the death of Plato, due perhaps to the choice of his successor at the Academy, Aristotle left Athens, first for Asia Minor and later for Macedonia, where he had been summoned by King Philip II to establish a school for the children of the Macedonian aristocracy. It was here that he first met and taught Philip's son, Alexander, who later went on to conquer the entire Greek world. Aristotle later returned to Athens and established a school of his own, the Lyceum. There is a story according to which Aristotle was himself brought up on capital charges, as was Socrates, due to another wave of politically motivated hostility to philosophy. Rather than staying to drink the hemlock, Aristotle was reported to have left Athens saying he did not wish to see the Athenians sin against philosophy a second time. This story, even if apocryphal, is revealing.

Aristotle has often been described as the first political scientist: he is dry. Unlike his intellectual godfather, Socrates, who wrote nothing but conversed endlessly, and unlike his own teacher Plato, who wrote imitations of those endless Socratic conversations, Aristotle wrote disciplined and thematic treatises on virtually everything from biology to ethics, from metaphysics to literary criticism. Aristotle, one assumes, would have received tenure in any number of departments here at Yale, while Socrates could not have applied to become a teaching assistant. Like the image of him in Raphael's famous painting *The School of Athens,* Aristotle kept his feet planted firmly on the ground: no flights of fantasy, no science fiction, no imaginary republics will enter his works.

These differences conceal others. While Plato's dialogues weave endless and fascinating problems and paradoxes, Aristotle seems never to have been bothered by bouts of skepticism or doubt. He was the first to give form and shape to the discipline of political science. He set up its fundamental terms and concepts; he elaborated its basic questions and problems; he was the first to give conceptual clarity and rigor to the vocabulary of politics. There is virtually no issue we study today that was not first identified by

Aristotle. His works like the *Politics* and the *Nicomachean Ethics* were intended as works of political education. They were designed less to recruit potential philosophers than to shape and educate citizens and future statesmen. His works were not "theoretical" in the sense of constructing abstract models of politics, but advice-giving in the sense of serving as an arbitrator over civic disputes. Unlike Socrates, who tended to denigrate political life as a cave, Aristotle took seriously the dignity of the city and showed the way that philosophy might be useful to citizens and statesmen alike.

It has sometimes been said that Aristotle's political theory is related "directly" to political life. He did not set out to undermine the political order or to exercise a radical change of orientation upon the knower, as Plato seems to have done. His goal was to know more closely, to put in better order, what it is we already know. Accordingly, there is a greater respect for the opinions—the *endoxa*—that ordinary individuals already hold about the world in which they live. This feature of Aristotle's thought has been nicely captured by an English reader: "Aristotle states clearly that moral theory must be in accord with established opinions and must explain these opinions as specifications of more general principles. An unphilosophic man of experience, who is of good character, usually reasons correctly on practical matters. Therefore Aristotle argues that acceptable moral theory will give a firm foundation to the principles that normally guide the decisions of the men whom we normally admire. Acceptable theory will not undermine established moral opinions nor bring about systematic moral conversion."[2] The claim expressed here that theory "must be in accord" with our ordinary perceptions and experience of the world is the key to Aristotle's statecraft.

Yet there is still a profound enigma surrounding Aristotle's political works. What were the politics of Aristotle's *Politics*? Aristotle lived at the cusp of the world of the autonomous city-state. Within his own lifetime he would see Athens, Sparta, and the other cities of Greece swallowed up by the great Alexandrian empire to the north—the first great wave of what would later be called "globalization." What we think of as the golden age of Greece was virtually at an end. Other Greek thinkers of his time, notably a rhetorician named Demosthenes, wrote a series of speeches, the *Philippics*, to warn his contemporaries about the danger posed to Athens from the Macedonians to the north. Yet Aristotle was completely silent on these truly epoch-making changes. What did he think of them?

Aristotle's extreme reticence is perhaps the result of his foreignness to Athens. He was not an Athenian and therefore lacked the protections of a citizen. At the same time, this reluctance may have been a response to the fate of Socrates and the politically endangered situation of philosophy. Yet for a man as notoriously secretive and reluctant as Aristotle, his works acquired canonical status. He became an authority, really *the* authority, on virtually everything. Maimonides could refer to him in the twelfth century as "the master of those who know." For Thomas Aquinas, writing in the thirteenth century, Aristotle was referred to simply as "the Philosopher." Period. There was no philosophy but Aristotle's. For centuries the authority of Aristotle went virtually unchallenged.

Naturally each of these thinkers read Aristotle through his own lens. Aquinas read him as a defender of monarchy, and Dante in his book *De Monarchia* saw Aristotle giving credence to the idea of a universal monarchy under the leadership of a Christian prince. Thomas Hobbes saw him completely differently. For Hobbes, Aristotle's *Politics* taught a dangerous doctrine of republican government that he had seen practiced during the Cromwellian period in the England of his time and that had been used to justify regicide, the murder of a king. "From the reading, I say, of such books, men have undertaken to kill their kings because the Greek and Latin writers, in their books and discourses of policy, make it lawful and laudable for any man so to do, provided, before he do it, he call him tyrant," Hobbes wrote in *Leviathan* (XIX, 14). Aristotle's doctrine that man is a "political animal," Hobbes believed, could only result in regicide. There are still echoes of Aristotle in the later writings of democratic political theorists from Tocqueville to Hannah Arendt.

This brings us back to the enigma of Aristotle. Who was this strange and elusive man, and what did he believe? The best place to start is with his views on the naturalness of the city.

Political Psychology

Perhaps the most famous doctrine found in the *Politics* is Aristotle's statement that man is by nature a political animal. What does this mean?

Aristotle's reasoning is stated succinctly on the third page of the *Politics* where he remarks that "every polis exists by nature" and goes on to infer that man is by nature the *zōon politikon,* the political animal. His reasoning is worth following here in some detail. "That man," he says, "is much more a political animal than any kind of bee or herd animal is clear. For we assert, nature does nothing in vain; and man alone among the animals has speech." While other species, he notes, may have voice that can distinguish pleasure from pain, *logos* is more than this. "But *logos* serves to reveal the advantageous and the harmful and hence also the just and the unjust. For it is peculiar to man as compared to the other animals that he alone has a perception of good and bad and just and unjust and other things" (1253a). So says Aristotle.

In what sense, though, is the city "by nature" and man a "political animal"? Aristotle appears to give two different accounts. In the opening pages he gives us something like a natural history of the polis. The polis is natural in the sense that it grows out of lesser forms of human association. First comes the family, then an association of families in a village, and then an association of villages that form a city. The city is natural in that it seems to be the most highly developed form of human association. But the city is natural in a second and more important sense. The city is said to be natural in that it allows human beings to achieve and perfect their *telos* or natural end. We are political animals because participation in the life of the polis is necessary for the achievement of human excellence. A man who is without a city, Aristotle says, must either be a beast or a god, that is, above humanity or below it (1253a). Our political nature is our essential characteristic.

When Aristotle claims, then, that man is by nature political, he is doing more than advancing a truism. He is advancing a philosophical postulate of great power and scope. In saying that man is by nature a political animal, he is not saying that there is some kind of biologically implanted desire that leads us to engage in political life. This would imply that we engage in politics as spontaneously and avidly as spiders spin webs or beavers build dams. Aristotle is not a kind of sociobiologist in the manner of E. O. Wilson.

Man is a political animal because we alone among the species are possessed of the power of speech. Speech or reason, far from limiting our behavior, gives us a latitude or freedom of choice not available to other species. It is reason, not instinct, that makes us political. But what is the connection between reason or the capacity for rationality and politics? It is reason that gives us the ability to judge, to deliberate, and to determine collective affairs such as war and peace, freedom and empire. Speech is what creates a community or, as Aristotle says, a sharing in what is just and unjust.

But to say that man is a political animal by nature is not just to say that we become fully human by participating in the life of our city. It means more. The form of association that leads to our perfection is necessarily something specific. The polis, as Aristotle conceived it, is a small society, what today might be called a "closed society." His word for such a city was *eusunoptos.* This is often translated as "easily taken in at a glance" or "well taken in at one view": "There is a certain measure of size in a city as well, just as in all other things—animals, plants, instruments: none of these things will have its own capacity if it is either overly small or excessive with respect to size. . . . Similarly with a city as well, the one that is made up of too few persons is not self-sufficient, though the city is a self-sufficient thing, while the one that is made up of too many persons is with respect to the necessary things self-sufficient like a nation, but is not a city: for it is not easy for a regime to be present. Who will be general of an overly excessive number or who will be herald, unless he has the voice of Stentor?" (1326a–b).

It is questionable if even during Aristotle's lifetime the polis could be truly regarded as easily surveyable. Attica was approximately the size of Rhode Island, and that, even though small by American standards, can scarcely be "taken in at a glance." Only a relatively closed society that is governed by face-to-face relations and can be held together by bonds of trust, of friendship, and of intimacy satisfies Aristotle's criterion for a polis. Only a city small enough to be governed by relations of trust and friendship can be political in the true sense of the term. The alternative to the city—the empire—can only be ruled despotically.

It follows that the city by nature can never be a universal state and not even the modern nation-state. The universal state or all-comprehensive society will exist on a lower level of humanity than a closed society that over time has made a supreme effort at self-perfection. The city will always exist in a world with other cities or states based on different principles that may be hostile to its own, which is to say, not even the best city can exist without a foreign policy. Being a political animal means distinguishing fellow citizens and friends from enemies. A good citizen of a democracy will not be a good citizen in another type of regime. Partisanship and loyalty to one's own way of life are required for a healthy city. Friend and enemy are thus natural and ineradicable political categories. Just as we cannot be friends with all persons, so the city cannot be friends with all other states. War and the virtues necessary for war are as natural to the city as are the virtues necessary for peace.

Note that Aristotle does not tell us—at least not yet—what kind of city or regime is best. How will such a city be governed? By the one, the few, the many, or some combination of the three? At this point we know only the most general features of the city. It must be small enough to be governed by a common language of justice or the common good. It is not enough merely to speak the same words; what shapes a city are common experiences and a common memory. The large polyglot multiethnic communities of today lack by Aristotle's standards a sufficient basis for mutual trust and friendship so necessary for human well-being.

The citizen of such a city can only reach perfection through actively participating in the offices of the city. Again, a large cosmopolitan state may allow each individual the freedom to live as he or she likes, but this is not freedom as Aristotle understands it. Freedom only comes with the exercise of political responsibility, responsibility for and oversight of the well-being of one's fellow citizens. It follows, then, that freedom does not mean simply living as we like; it must be informed by a sense of moral restraint, an awareness that not all things are permitted. The good society will be one that promotes a sense of moderation, restraint, and self-control inseparable from freedom. All of the above is suggested in Aristotle's claim that man is a political animal.

Slavery and Inequality

Whatever we may think about Aristotle's views on the naturalness of the polis, we must also confront his famous—or infamous—doctrine of the naturalness of slavery. The naturalness of slavery is said to follow from Aristotle's belief that inequality is the rule between human beings. If this is true, Aristotle's *Politics* would seem to stand condemned as one of the most antidemocratic works ever written. How, then, should we approach the book?

In the first place, we should avoid two equally unhelpful responses. The first is that we must not avert our eyes from those harsh, unappealing aspects of Aristotle's thought and pretend he never said such things. We should avoid the temptation to airbrush or sanitize Aristotle in order to make him appear more politically acceptable. But we should also resist the opposite temptation to reject Aristotle out of hand because his views do not correspond with our own. The question is, what did Aristotle mean by slavery? Who did he think was the slave by nature? Until we understand what he meant about these most basic questions, we have no basis for either accepting or rejecting his teaching.

The first point worth noting is that Aristotle did not simply assume slavery was natural because it was practiced by the Greeks. You will notice that he frames his analysis in the form of a debate. There are some, he says, who believe that slavery is natural because ruling and being ruled is a pervasive distinction; but others believe that the distinction between master and slave is not natural but grows out of long-standing tradition and custom (1253b). In other words, is slavery by nature or by convention? Even in Aristotle's time slavery was controversial and elicited different opinions.

Here is one of those moments where Aristotle seems almost maddeningly open-minded. He is willing to entertain arguments from both sides of the debate. He agrees with those who deny that slavery is justified by war or conquest. Wars, he remarks, are not always just, and so it cannot be assumed that those taken captive in war are justly enslaved. Similarly, he denies that slavery is appropriate only for non-Greeks. There are no racial or ethnic characteristics that distinguish the natural slave from the master. There is no hint of what we call "racism" in Aristotle's views. And in a stunning admission he says that while nature may intend to distinguish the free man from the slave, "the opposite often results" (1254b). Now we are confused. Earlier, he said that nature does nothing in vain, but now he says that nature sometimes misses the mark. How is that possible? How can nature be mistaken? Such complications should alert the careful reader.

At the same time, Aristotle agrees with those who defend the thesis of natural slavery. Slavery is natural because we cannot rule ourselves without restraint of the passions. He shows himself a good student of Plato. Restraint or self-control is necessary for freedom and self-government. A person who is a slave to his passions is unable to exhibit the characteristics of a free human being. And what is true of restraint over one's own passions and desires is true of restraint and control over others. Just as there is a hierarchy in the soul, with reason ruling the passions, so there is a social hierarchy, with rational persons ruling thoughtless ones. The natural hierarchy of master and slave is, then, a hierarchy of moral intelligence and the capacity for rational self-control.

But how did this come to be? Is the hierarchy of intelligence a genetic product or the result of nurture and education? If the latter, if differences of intelligence and moral character are a product of upbringing, can slavery ever be justified as natural? Is it not unjust that one person is elected to a position of privilege and education while another is fated to a life of anonymity and obscurity? Aristotle calls man the "rational animal," suggesting that all human beings have a desire for knowledge, a desire to cultivate the mind and live as free persons. The famous opening line of his *Metaphysics* reads: "All men have a desire to know" (980a). The phrase "all men" clearly suggests something universal in this desire. If all men have a desire to know, then all men have an aspiration to rationality. The best regime would seem to be an aristocracy that had widened itself into a meritocracy of talent and intellect.

Aristotle still regards education—true, liberal education—as the preserve of the few. The kind of discipline and self-restraint necessary for an educated mind is unequally divided among human beings. It follows that the regime according to nature will be some kind of aristocracy of education and training, an aristocratic republic where an educated elite governs for the good of all. Aristotle's republic is devoted to cultivating a high level of citizen virtue where this means those qualities of mind and heart necessary for self-government. These qualities, he believes, are necessarily the preserve of the few, of a small minority of citizens capable of sharing in the administration of justice and in the offices of the city. These few constitute Aristotle's ruling class.

Aristotle's conception of an educated aristocracy—something different from, but still related to, the Platonic notion of the philosopher-king—is not as far from our own experience as we might think. By education (*paideia*) Aristotle is speaking not of philosophy in any very precise sense but of a broader sense of intellectual culture (arts, literature, music). It is this sense of an aristocracy of education that Thomas Jefferson endorsed in a letter to John Adams. Jefferson distinguished between the "natural aristocracy" based on talent and intellect and the "artificial aristocracy" based on wealth and birth. "The natural aristocracy," he wrote, "I consider as the most precious gift of nature for the instruction, the trusts, and government of society. . . . May we not even say that that form of government is best which provides most effectually for a pure selection of the natural *aristoi* into the offices of government?" For Jefferson, it was representative institutions, in particular the institution of election, that was the best means of separating "the aristoi from the pseudo-aristoi, of the wheat from the chaff."[3]

For those surprised to see Jefferson put in the same company with Aristotle, consider also the case of the nineteenth century's greatest liberal mind, John Stuart Mill. In his *Considerations on Representative Government*, Mill was deeply concerned that the extension of the suffrage would result in the rise of mass democracy and the loss of influence for the educated minority. Accordingly, he embraced the scheme of voting proposed by Hare and Fawcett for its endorsement of proportional representation among different classes of voters in order to offset the disadvantages of "one man, one vote":

The natural tendency of representative government, as of modern civilization, is toward collective mediocrity; and this tendency is increased by all reductions and extensions of the franchise, their effect being to place the principal power in the hands of classes more and more below the highest level of instruction in the community. But though the superior intellects and characters will be necessarily outnumbered, it makes a great difference whether or not they are heard. . . . In the old democracies there were no means of keeping out of sight any able man: the bema was open to him; he needed nobody's consent to become a public adviser. It is not so in a representative government: and the best friend of representative democracy can hardly be without misgivings that the Themistocles or Demosthenes, whose counsels would have saved the nation, might be unable during his whole life ever to obtain a seat.[4]

Before we reject Aristotle's account of the republic as insufferably elitist and antidemocratic, we must ask ourselves a difficult question. What else is Yale but an elite institution intended to educate—morally and intellectually—potential members of a leadership class? Can anyone get into Yale? Should the doors be open to everyone? Does it not require precisely those qualities of self-control, discipline, and deferred gratification necessary to achieve success here? Is it any coincidence that graduates from Yale and a small number of other elite colleges and universities find themselves in the highest positions of government, business, law, and the academy? Is it unfair or unreasonable to describe this class as a natural aristocracy, an aristocracy based not on wealth or tradition but on talent and merit? Before we reject Aristotle as an antidemocratic elitist, take a look at yourself. So are you—or else you wouldn't be here.

Regime Politics

Aristotle's comparative anatomy of regime types occupies the central books of the *Politics*, books 3 to 6. The regime or *politeia* is the central concept of his political science. The term is in fact the word used for the title of Plato's *Republic*, the book dealing with the best regime or *kallipolis*. Aristotle uses it to capture something akin to the basic constitutional structure of a community. A regime refers to the formal institutional design of a community, but also to something closer to what we call the way of life or culture of a people, their distinctive customs, manners, and habits.

Aristotle's constitutional theorizing begins by asking: What is the identity of a regime? What gives it an enduring existence over time? One can distinguish between the *matter* and the *form* of the regime. The matter of a regime concerns the citizen body, that is, the character of those who constitute a city. He rejects the idea that a regime is defined by a group of people who inhabit a common territory. "The identity of a polis is not constituted by its walls," he remarks (1276a). In other words, physical proximity alone does not characterize a regime. Similarly, Aristotle rejects the view that a regime can be a defensive alliance to avoid invasion by others. In our terms NATO would not be a regime. Finally, he denies that a regime exists simply when a number of people establish commercial relations with one another for purposes of trade. NAFTA or the WTO does not a regime make. A regime is none of the above. "It is evident," Aristotle writes, "that the city is not a partnership in a location or for the sake of not committing injustice against each other and of transacting business" (1280b). So what is it?

We can say, then, that a regime is constituted by its citizen body. Citizens are those who share a common way of life and who may therefore participate in political rule. "The citizen in an unqualified sense," Aristotle says, "is defined by no other thing so much as sharing in decision and office" (1275a), or as he puts it later, "Whoever is entitled to participate in an office involving deliberating or decision is a citizen of the city" (1275b). A citizen is one who not only enjoys the protection of the laws but also takes a part in shaping the laws, who participates in political rule and deliberation. Aristotle even notes that his definition of the citizen is most appropriate to citizens of a democracy where in his famous formulation everyone knows how "to rule and be ruled in turn" (1277a). It is his reflection on the character of the citizen that leads Aristotle to wonder whether the good citizen is the same as the good human being. Is the best citizen necessarily the best type of person?

Aristotle's answer to this question is perhaps deliberately obscure. The good citizen, he remarks, is relative to the regime. The good citizen of a democracy will not be the same as a good citizen of a monarchy. Citizen virtue is regime relative. Only in the best regime will the good citizen and the good human being be the same. But this formula seems question begging. For what is the best regime? Is there a regime where the good human being and the good citizen are identical? Aristotle does not say—at least not yet. The point is that there are several kinds of regime and therefore several kinds of citizenship appropriate to each. Each regime is constituted not only by its matter but also by its form, that is, by a set of institutions and formal structures that give shape to its citizen body. Regimes or constitutions contain forms or formalities that determine how powers are shared or distributed within a community.

The citizens who constitute a regime, we have just seen, do more than occupy a common space or associate for the sake of mutual protection or convenience; they are held together by ties of common affection, loyalty, trust, and friendship. What does Aristotle mean by this? "This sort of thing [the political partnership]," he writes, "is the work of affection for affection is the intentional choice of living together" (1280a). *Philia* or friendship, he notes, is "the greatest of good things for cities," for when people feel affection for each other they are less likely to fall into conflict (1262b). What Aristotle calls by the Greek word *philia* has strong overtones of comradeship between people who share a common fate or destiny. Political friendships may well entail intense rivalry and competition for positions of political office and honor. Civic philia is not without a strong element of sibling rivalry in which each citizen strives to outdo the others for the sake of the civic good. Siblings—as everyone knows—may be the best of friends, but this does not exclude strong elements of competition and even conflict for the attention of the parents. Fellow citizens are like siblings, all competing with one another for the esteem, affection, and recognition of the city that serves as a kind of surrogate parent.

When Aristotle says that citizens are held together by ties of common affection, he means something quite specific. The civic bond is something more than an aggregate of mere self-interest, as it will later be claimed by Hobbes and many contemporary political scientists. One cannot account for politics simply in terms of the rational calculation of interest alone. But when Aristotle speaks of affection he does not mean the bonds of personal intimacy characteristic of private friendships. Citizens need not be intimates, but they must think of themselves as part of a common enterprise. They are part of an enterprise association, by which I mean a joint endeavor. Where this is lacking, where there is a breakdown of civic trust, people cannot be citizens in the true sense of the word. What Aristotle means when speaking of civic affection is more like the bonds of loyalty and camaraderie that hold together members of a team or a club. These are more than ties of mutual convenience; they require a kind of loyalty—what social scientists call "social capital"—and mutual recognition. It is the kind of spiritedness people feel when they say, "There is no 'I' in 'team.'" They are part of a collective that is greater than the sum of its parts. "The political partnership," Aristotle writes, "must therefore be regarded as being for the sake of noble actions not [just] for the sake of living together" (1281a).

If the matter of a regime concerns the composition of its citizen body, its form concerns the distribution of powers. Aristotle defines the strictly formal aspect of the politeia twice in the *Politics*. The first time appears in book 3, chapter 6: "The regime is an arrangement of a city with respect to its offices, particularly the one that has authority over all matters. For what has authority in the city is everywhere the governing body and the governing body is the regime" (1278b).

The second definition of appears in book 4, chapter 1: "For a regime is an arrangement in cities connected with offices, establishing the manner in which they have been distributed, what the authoritative element of the regime is, and what the end of the partnership is in each case" (1289a).

From these two definitions we learn a number of things. First, Aristotle distinguishes regimes on the basis of their ruling body or ruling class. A regime concerns the manner in which power is divided in any community. This is what Aristotle means when he says that a regime is "an arrangement of a city with respect to its offices." In other words, every regime will be based on some kind of judgment of how power should be distributed, to one person, the few, or the many. In every regime one of these groups will be dominant, will be the "ruling body" or ruling class in Aristotle's term, and this will define the nature of the regime in question. Aristotle's regime analysis is thus concerned with perhaps the oldest political question: "Who governs?"

All regimes are dominated by the one, the few, or the many. But typical of Aristotle, after distinguishing regimes into three basic forms he goes on to complicate his initial formulation. He also distinguishes between regimes that are well ordered and those that are corrupt. His regime analysis is not only empirical; it is normative. On the well-ordered side he includes monarchy, aristocracy, and polity; on the corrupt side he includes tyranny, oligarchy, and democracy. Rule of one can be either monarchic or tyrannical; rule of a few either aristocratic or oligarchic; and rule of the many either constitutional or democratic. His table or catalogue of regime types looks something like the following:

	Well-Ordered	Corrupt
One	Monarchy	Tyranny
Few	Aristocracy	Oligarchy
Many	Polity	Democracy

What criteria does Aristotle use to distinguish well-governed from corrupt regimes?

There are two features that Aristotle believed necessary for a decent constitutional order. The first is the rule of law. No polity worthy of the name should be made to suffer self-interested rule of the few over the many or of the many over the few. The rule of law, as we shall see later, may not guarantee justice, but of one thing Aristotle was sure, namely, that justice, and hence political legitimacy, was not possible outside the framework of law. Regulation by law and responsibility to its citizens were deemed by him the necessary minimal conditions for what he termed polity or constitutional government. The second feature of a well-ordered regime is stability. Aristotle is generally reluctant to condemn any regime out of hand—even the badly ordered ones—so long as they maintain some modicum of order. In fact he provides reasoned arguments for the strengths and weaknesses of various regime types and can even be found offering advice to tyrants on how to make their regimes more stable. He considers no regime so entirely devoid of goodness that its preservation is not worth some effort.

For example, we find Aristotle defending democracy on the grounds that the many may collectively contain greater wisdom than the few. This argument is frequently referred to as the "wisdom of the multitude." In book 3, chapter 11, Aristotle writes: "For because they are many, each can have a part of virtue and prudence and on their joining together, the multitude, with its many feet and hands and having many senses, becomes like a single human being, and so also with respect to character and mind" (1281b). We even hear Aristotle praising the democratic practice of ostracism, that is, exiling those individuals deemed to be preeminent in virtue or some other quality.

He makes a similar point in book 3, chapter 15, in describing the process of democratic deliberation, comparing it to a potluck dinner: "Any one of them taken singly is perhaps inferior in comparison to the best man; but the city is made up of many persons, just as a feast to which many contribute is finer than a single and simple one and on this account a crowd also judges many matters better than any single person. Furthermore, what is many is more incorruptible: like a greater amount of water, the many is more incorruptible than the few" (1286a). Here it is not so much the number as the diversity of offerings that add up to a feast.

Aristotle also can be found providing a defense of kingship and the rule of the one. In book 3, chapter 16, he considers the case of "the king who acts in all things according to his own will" (1287a). The kind of king he has in mind seems close to the Platonic idea of the philosopher-king. Aristotle calls it by the Greek word *pambasileia*, or literally a kind of universal kingship. He does not rule out the possibility of a person of "excessive excellence" who stands so far above the rest as to be their natural ruler.

How does one reconcile Aristotle's account of the pambasileia with his earlier emphasis on the wisdom of the multitude? Does his suggestion of universal kingship reveal a hidden "Alexandrian" strain in his political thinking that owes more to his native Macedonia than to his adopted Athens? Later in the *Politics* Aristotle develops the thesis that under favorable conditions the Greeks could establish a universal hegemony over all the nations. Consider a famous passage from book 7, chapter 7: "The nations in cold locations, particularly in Europe, are filled with spiritedness [*thymos*] but relatively lacking in discursive thought and art; hence they remain freer, but lack political governance. Those in Asia, on the other hand, have souls endowed with discursive thought and art, but are lacking in spiritedness; hence they remain ruled and enslaved. But the stock of the Greeks shares in both—just as it holds the middle in terms of location. For it is both spirited and endowed with discursive thought, and hence both remains free and governs itself in the best manner and at the same time is capable of ruling all should it obtain a single regime" (1327b).

This passage is of enormous importance. Just as Aristotle believes one man might exercise rule over all Greeks, so too does he consider that under the right circumstances the Greeks could exercise a universal empire over all people. He does not rule out this possibility. Aristotle is a constitutional pluralist. He regards different regimes as being suitable for different situations. There is no one-size-fits-all model of political life, but good regimes may come in a variety of forms. The task of the political scientist is not to be a cheerleader for any one regime, it is to recognize that there are many different legitimate regimes that can satisfy different circumstances.

Nonetheless, Aristotle understands that a person of such superlative virtue is not to be expected. Politics is much more a matter of dealing with less-than-best conditions. Most regimes, for all practical purposes, will be a mix of oligarchy and democracy, by which Aristotle means a mix of the rich and the poor. It was not Marx but Aristotle who discovered the fact of class struggle. But unlike Marx's, Aristotelian class struggle is not just a competition for resources or for control of the means of production but a struggle over positions of honor and status, ultimately over positions of political rule. It is, in short, political conflict, not economic incentives, that determines the regime.

It is a common misreading to think of Aristotle as stressing harmony and consensus over conflict and factional strife. This is clearly false. Every regime is a site of contestation where competing claims to justice and rule will be fought out. There is partisanship not only between regimes but within regimes where citizens are activated by often competing and incompatible understandings of justice. The members of the democratic faction, the poor, believe that because all men are equal, they should be equal in all things; the members of the oligarchic faction, the rich, believe that because men are unequal, they should be unequal in all things. Such rivalry is endemic to all politics; the attempt to remove the causes of conflict and create a community of interests would be an attempt to abolish politics. Politics is the art of the skillful management of conflict. How, then, to mediate the causes of faction before they lead to revolution and civil war?

Constitutional Government and the Rule of Law

Aristotle does propose various remedies to offset the competitive and potentially warlike struggle between the various factions. The most important of these is, again, the rule of law. Laws ensure the equal treatment of all citizens and prevent arbitrary rule at the hands of either the one, the few, or the many. Rule of law establishes a sort of impartiality, "for law," Aristotle writes, "is impartiality": "One who asks law to rule is held to be asking god and intellect alone to rule, while one who asks man, asks the beast. Desire is a thing of this sort; and spiritedness perverts rulers and the best men. Hence law is intellect without appetite" (1287a). But law is not the end of the story. It is only the beginning. Aristotle raises the question of whether the rule of law is to be preferred to the rule of men, even of the best individual. Typically, he examines the question from different points of view.

He begins by appearing to defend Plato's view about the rule of the best individual: "The best regime," he writes, "is *not* one based on written laws" (1286a). Law is a clumsy instrument of rule because laws deal only with general matters and cannot apply to particular situations. Further, the rule of law ties the hands of statesmen and legislators, who must always be prepared to respond to new and unforeseen situations.

At the same time, Aristotle makes the case for law. The judgment of an individual, no matter how wise, is subject to bias, whether due to passion, interest, or simply the fallibility of human reason. The sovereignty of the law, which is an imitation of wisdom, replaces the sovereignty of the human ruler. Further, he notes, no one person can oversee all things. This is a matter of practicability. But Aristotle also makes the case for law by claiming that no one can be trusted to be a judge in his own case. Doctors bring in other doctors when they are sick, just as trainers consult other trainers for fitness. Only a third party, in this case the law, is capable of adequately judging. The law can serve as a surrogate for the sovereignty of a single ruler.

So, should law be changed, and if so, how? Here again Aristotle presents different points of view. In book 2, chapter 8, he compares law to other arts and sciences and suggests that just as sciences such as medicine have exhibited progress and change, this is true for law, too. The antiquity of a law is no justification for its continued usage. Aristotle is not a Burkean conservative who identifies the ancestral with the good. He says as much: "In general all seek not the traditional but the good" (1269a).

Yet he recognizes that changes in law, even when the result is improvement, are dangerous: "It is a bad thing to habituate people to the reckless dissolution of laws," he writes, "for the city will not be benefited as much from changing [laws] as it will be harmed through being habituated to disobey the rulers" (1269a). Sudden or frequent changes in the law, even where such changes aim at improvement, will result in unintended consequences. Lawfulness, like all the virtues, is a habit of behavior, and the habit of disobeying even an unjust law tends to make people altogether lawless. "For law," Aristotle says, "has no strength with respect to obedience apart from habit . . . the easy alteration of existing laws in favor of new and different ones weakens the power of law itself" (1269a).

The most important remedy to the problem of faction is found in Aristotle's theory of polity discussed in book 4. *Polity* actually goes by the same generic word, politeia, used for regimes in general that might be loosely translated by our term "constitution" or "constitutional government." The essential feature of a polity or constitutional government is that it represents a mixture of the principles of oligarchy and democracy and therefore avoids the dominance of either extreme. By combining elements of the few and the many, polity is characterized by the dominance of the middle class. On this view, a polity with a middle class is more stable and more law abiding than regimes governed by the purely self-interested rule of the few or the many. The middle class is able to achieve the confidence of both extreme parties, and where it is sufficiently numerous, class conflict can be avoided: "Where the middling element is numerous factional conflicts and splits over the nature of the regimes occur least of all. And large cities are freer of factional conflict for the same reason—that the middling element is numerous" (1269a).

This passage should sound very familiar to readers of the *Federalist Papers*, who will recall James Madison's proposal not to try to abolish or outlaw factions but to let them check and control one another in a large extended republic. The advantage of constitutional government is that each faction is able to speak of the regime as either a democracy or an oligarchy. Constitutional government is democratic because there is a common system of education and "a wealthy person is in no way marked off from a poor one." It is oligarchic because political offices are determined by election and not by lot.[5] There is, in short, something for everyone, and "none of the parts of the city would wish to have another regime" (1294b). Aristotle's proposals for a mixture of both oligarchy and democracy also remind us of Madison's call for a government where powers are separated, where "ambition must be made to counteract ambition" in the language of *Federalist* No. 51—in order to avoid the extremes of both tyranny and civil war. Aristotle seems to have discovered something like the American constitution centuries before the fact!

Political Science and Political Judgment

What is Aristotle's political science? To ask this question is already to stake a claim. Does Aristotle have a political science—a science of politics—and if so, what is this science about? To begin to answer this question—even to begin just to think about it—requires that we stand back from Aristotle's text and ask some fundamental questions about it: What does Aristotle mean by the political, what is the goal or purpose of the study of politics, and what is distinctive about Aristotle's approach to the study of political things?

The core of Aristotle's political science is based on the discovery of a certain kind of knowledge that he describes as practical reason (*phronēsis*). He distinguishes practical knowledge from two other forms: scientific or theoretical reason (*epistēmē*) and technical or productive knowledge (*technē*).

Theoretical wisdom seeks out necessary or universal truths, what is true always and everywhere, such as those discovered in mathematics or logic. Technical know-how is the kind of instrumental knowledge involved in the production of useful objects. Practical knowledge, by contrast, is the knowledge of right action, where the end or aim of the action is the action itself performed well. It entails not a form of instrumental reasoning—knowing the most efficient means to produce a desired end—but is a kind of connoisseurship that involves knowing the right thing to do under the specific circumstances.

Aristotle is mainly concerned to distinguish the study of moral and political knowledge from purely theoretical pursuits such as mathematics or physics. In contrast to the theoretical sciences, the subject matter of politics admits of too much variation to yield law-like generalizations. Practical knowledge will always be provisional; it will produce truths that will hold for the most part but will always admit exceptions. What distinguishes practical judgment from both theoretical and productive knowledge is a sense of the fitting or the appropriate, an attention to the nuances or details of a particular situation. The *phronimos*—the person of practical reason—is the one able to grasp the fitting or the appropriate thing to do out of the complex arrangements that make up a situation. Above all, such a person embodies that special quality of insight and discrimination that distinguishes him or her from people of a more purely theoretical or speculative cast of mind.

Practical reason is, then, the type of knowledge appropriate to people situated in popular assemblies, courts of law, or any other place where deliberation takes place. It is neither theoretical knowledge aimed at abstract truths nor productive knowledge used in the manufacture of useful artifacts. This kind of practical wisdom entails insight and deliberation. We only deliberate over things where there is some choice. We deliberate with an eye to preservation or change. This kind of knowledge will be the art or craft of the skilled statesman concerned with what to do in a specific situation. It is less a body of true or universalizable propositions than a shrewd sense of know-how or political savvy. It is the skill possessed by the greatest statesmen—the fathers of the constitution, as it were—who create the permanent framework that allows lesser and later figures to manage change.

This Aristotelian quality of practical wisdom has been nicely developed, although without any explicit reference to Aristotle, in an essay by the English political philosopher Isaiah Berlin. In his essay entitled "Political Judgment," Berlin asks what intellectual quality successful statesmen possess and how this quality differs from other forms of knowledge and rationality: "The quality that I am attempting to describe," Berlin writes, "is that special understanding of public life (or for that matter private life) which successful statesmen have, whether they are wicked or virtuous—that which Bismarck had or Talleyrand or Franklin Roosevelt, or, for that matter, men such as Cavour or Disraeli, Gladstone, or Ataturk, in common with the great psychological novelists, something which is conspicuously lacking in men of more purely theoretical genius such as Newton or Einstein or Russell or even Freud."[6] "What are we to call this capacity?" Berlin continues: "Practical reason, perhaps a sense of what will work and what will not. It is a capacity for synthesis rather than analysis, for knowledge in the sense in which trainers know their animals, or parents their children, or conductors their orchestras, as opposed to that in which chemists know the contents of their test tubes, or mathematicians know the rules that their symbols obey. Those who lack this [quality of practical wisdom], whatever other qualities they may possess, no matter how clever, learned, imaginative, kind, noble, attractive, gifted in other ways they may be, are correctly regarded as politically inept."[7]

What is necessary for political judgment is what Berlin calls a "sense of reality." This does not mean simply knowledge of what will work and what will not, but a sense of what is possible and what is not. Judgment is not just a matter of fitting means to ends, but of knowing what is the fitting or appropriate thing to do under given circumstances. Good judgment in politics, just like the ability to judge good character in individuals, is not necessarily a matter of having more information or access to a larger body of facts, but the ability to see something before others do, knowing whom to trust and whom not to, and a willingness to accept responsibility for one's mistakes.

But who, we want to know, is the person of practical judgment? Who is this paragon of the noble who serves as the standard of right action? Is the capacity for moral judgment a product of habituation or is it more like a gift of nature or grace, like the talent to paint or the ability to learn foreign languages? Are certain people just born with these abilities, or can they be acquired through practice and habit? The fact is that our natural talents and abilities are distributed very unequally and have little to do with our merit or desert; they are to a large degree the product of luck. Why does one person have a talent for the piano while another is tone deaf? Why does one person have the knack for moneymaking while another follows one dead end after another? Nature provides the raw materials; habit and practice help to give those materials form or shape, but judgment is ultimately the acquisition of a kind of connoisseurship that allows one to distinguish the appropriate from the inappropriate, the genuine from the ersatz. Aristotle's motto could almost be: "Distinguish, always distinguish."   *criterion.*

What most distinguishes Aristotle's concept of practical judgment is that it is emphatically addressed not to other political scientists and philosophers but to citizens and statesmen. His language stays entirely within the orbit of ordinary speech. Such language does not claim to be scientifically purged of all ambiguity but rather adopts standards of proof appropriate to debate in assemblies, courts of law, and council rooms. While contemporary political science is mainly concerned with advancing the claims of science (a body of true propositions), Aristotle is more concerned with finding ways of bringing peace to conflict-ridden situations. His political science is eminently practical or, as we might say, "normative." It is the skill possessed by the most able political actors, a Themistocles or a Pericles to say nothing of a Lincoln or a Churchill. Aristotle's approach does not claim to stand above or apart from the political realm as if he were viewing human affairs from a distant planet or like an entomologist observing the behavior of ants. Aristotle's political science is civic-minded or patriotic. It seeks reasons for why political orders, even the less-than-best political orders in which we all live, are worth preserving and amending. From a present-day perspective, then, Aristotle's approach seems radically "unscientific" because it culminates not just in knowledge but in action, action whose goal is the maintenance and preservation of the political regime.

Of course, present-day political scientists are not entirely neutral. They frequently insert their own "values" into their discussion. But these values are regarded by them as purely "subjective," not a part of the science for which they speak. But this admits a problem. For if all values are subjective, that is, if no one has the right or authority to impose his or her values on another, then it follows that the only legitimate political order will be one that is "neutral" to the ways of life of its citizens, that maintains a strict wall of separation between the private sphere of values and the public sphere of law. But the political order that maintains or insists on the distinction between the public and the private, between law and morality, is a specific kind of political order. We call it a liberal regime. The question is whether any regime, even a liberal regime, can remain entirely neutral about the ways of life of its citizens. Isn't asking us to remain value neutral like asking someone to view some physical object but from no particular point of view? It is an impossibility. In the end one might well wonder which approach is more scientific: Aristotle's, which is explicitly and necessarily evaluative, which offers advice and exhortation about how to care for the political order, or contemporary political science, which claims to be neutral and nonpartisan, but which smuggles its values and preferences in through the back door.

CHAPTER 6
The Politics of the Bible

Rembrandt Harmensz van Rijn (1606–1669). *The Prophet Nathan before David.*
Pen and brown ink, wash. KdZ 5255 (Benesch 947). Photo credit: bpk, Berlin /
Kupferstichkabinett, Staatliche Museen, Berlin / Jörg P. Anders /
Art Resource, NY

Why would a course on political philosophy include a section dealing with the Bible? This question is both necessary and proper. Political philosophy is a part of the Western intellectual tradition, and this tradition is composed of two elements. One part derives from the philosophical tradition of Greece, but the other derives from the Bible, from the East. The influence of the Bible is evidence of the influence of the East on the West. We might call these two elements or two strands of thought Athens and Jerusalem. Neither of these alone is sufficient to characterize the West. The West consists of a centuries-old conversation, dialogue, and debate between these two. What exactly do these names indicate?

It has long been believed that Jerusalem—the city of faith, the holy city—and Athens—the city of philosophy—are the two polarities around which the Western tradition has revolved. The spirit of Athens has traditionally been understood as the embodiment of rationality, democracy, and science in the broadest sense of those terms. The spirit of Jerusalem represents the embodiment of love, faith, and morality, also taken in the broadest sense. For many thinkers—I think of the great German philosopher Hegel—modernity itself is predicated upon the synthesis of Jerusalem and Athens, of ethics and science. Modernity, and hence progress, is only possible with the synthesis of these two great currents of thought. But are these two compatible? Is such a synthesis possible? To ask again the question posed centuries ago by the Christian patristic Tertullian: "What has Athens to do with Jerusalem?"[1]

On the surface it would seem that Jerusalem and Athens represent two fundamentally different, even antagonistic, moral codes or ways of life. Greek philosophy elevates reason—our own human reason—as the one thing needful for life. Greek philosophy culminates in the person of Socrates, who famously said, "The unexamined life is not worth living." Only the life given over to the cultivation of autonomous human understanding is a worthy human life. The Bible, however, presents itself not as a philosophy or a science but as a code of law, an unchangeable divine law mandating unhesitating obedience. In fact the first five books of the Bible are known in the Jewish tradition as the Torah, and Torah is perhaps most literally translated as "Law." The attitude taught by the Bible is one not of self-reflection or critical examination but of obedience, faith, and trust in God. If the paradigmatic Athenian is Socrates, the paradigmatic biblical hero is Abraham, who is prepared to sacrifice his son in obedience to an unintelligible command.[2]

Faced with these two alternatives, the question is how to choose between them. Each side stakes a claim on our allegiance, but each side also seems to exclude the other. How to choose? One answer is to say that we are open to both and willing to listen first and then decide. But to suggest that we will make a choice on the basis of our own best judgment seems to decide the matter already in favor of Athens against Jerusalem. Yet on the other hand, we might say that any answer to the question "Who is right—the Greeks or the Jews?" is based on an act of faith. In this case Jerusalem seems to have triumphed over Athens. A philosophy that is based on faith is no longer a real philosophy. How, then, to decide?

In the Beginning

There are many ways to begin to read the Bible. It can be read as a book of wisdom providing timeless lessons on life's most difficult problems. It can be read as a holy book given by God to Moses and handed down by Moses to the patriarchs in a line of unbroken tradition. It can be read as a historical work providing archaeological and anthropological information about the world of the ancient Near East. Or it can be read, as I propose to do, as a political book providing a matchless account of the beginnings of humanity, the creation of the first family, the rise of civilization, and the eventual separation of humanity into distinct peoples and nations. This account continues with the specification of one particular people, the people of Israel, their emergence among competing nations, their enslavement and eventual emancipation, their laws and acquisition of a territory, their various attempts at self-government, and finally the emergence of a unified state under a single sovereign. But before considering this, let us return to the beginning.

The Bible enjoins us to return to beginnings.[3] The beginning of all beginnings is related in the opening of Genesis. The book begins with the famous words "In the beginning," or in some translations simply "In beginning." Who says this? Is it God? Possibly, but elsewhere God's statements are prefaced by the words "And God said." Did a person say it? Maybe, but then again there were presumably no people around to witness the beginning. In the beginning, God is said to have created heaven and earth. The earth is said to have been "without form and void." Does this mean that the earth in some sense existed before God's creation? At most God seems to have formed the earth like a sculptor forms a statue rather than created it out of nothing.

God is well known to have created the world and everything in it in six days. He proceeds by way of a number of divisions. On the first day are created light and darkness; on the second, the heavens; on the third, earth, water, and plants; on the fourth, the sun, moon, and stars; on the fifth, water animals and birds; on the sixth, land animals and man. What are we to make of these divisions, and what do they represent?

The most obvious difficulty is that days are introduced before the sun, which is not created until the fourth day. We keep track of days by the movements of the earth around the sun. How can there be days or nights before the sun had been created? We have all heard, of course, that the days of creation are not the same as earth days. Perhaps a creation day lasted billions of years. Nevertheless, the order of creation follows a reasonable plan. All beings created on the first four days lack the principle of self-motion. Sun, earth, and water may follow a fixed pattern but are in no way self-moving. The beings created on the last two days—water animals, land animals, and man— contain some principle of agency. There is introduced a hierarchy based on the capacity to initiate activity. This is confirmed by the fact that only man is said to be created in "God's image" and given dominion over the other beings. Furthermore, God concludes every day with the statement "and God said it was good," but only after the creation of man does God call his work "very good."

The order of creation seems to establish a hierarchy with objects like the sun, moon, stars, and earth as well as the various objects occupying the lower rungs of creation, with the various animals and finally man occupying the higher rungs. It is not an exaggeration to say that man is the pinnacle of creation. The Bible explicitly forbids the worship of the sun and moon. It is this depreciation of the heavens that is the specific feature of biblical cosmology. Man is given a kind of rudimentary dominion over the things of the earth that are left undenominated by God. These things gain their identities by being given names; naming is the prerogative of man. We are not told whether the power of language is innate or how it was developed, but it is through language that man expresses his dominion over the various objects of creation.

As is well known, the first account of creation in Genesis, given in chapter 1, is complicated by the second account, given in chapter 2. In the first account, man is created in God's image; in the second, man is formed from the dust of the earth. In the first account, man and woman are created together; in the second, man is created first and woman only later. All we know about the creation of woman is that it is not good for man to be alone.

Man is not intended to live a solitary life but to live as part of a couple or a family.

By the end of chapter 2, the stage is set for the unfolding of human history. God created man without knowledge of good and evil. Adam is told that he may eat freely of every tree or plant in the garden except the tree of knowledge of good and evil; if he eats of it he will die. It is not clear what the threat of death could have meant to a man who had as yet no experience of mortality. Nor is it clear why God wished to monopolize knowledge of good and evil. Why was this knowledge alone forbidden to man?

It is the serpent, the subtlest of creatures, that entices the woman to eat of the tree of knowledge with the promise that "you will be like God." Why did the woman disregard God's command? In the first place, remember that it was to Adam alone that God said that the tree of knowledge was off-limits; Adam obviously passed this down to Eve. It seems that it was not God's order but Adam's that Eve disobeyed. She had heard of the divine prohibition only at second hand, by way of "tradition," so to speak. Second, the woman exhibits a kind of natural curiosity that seems altogether absent in Adam. Adam is little more than a cipher. God commands, and he dumbly obeys. Eve alone shows some of the characteristics of a philosopher: she has a natural curiosity, an openness to experience, and a desire to learn. What must it be like, she wonders, to be like God? But most important, the Bible tells us that our original condition is one of simplicity without moral knowledge. This knowledge is the key to the development of human history. Moral knowledge—knowledge of good and evil—is what makes us human. Prior to their transgression, Adam and Eve lack this essential aspect of humanity. The eating of the fruit of the tree of knowledge represents the first decisive step toward the fulfillment of our humanity.

The story of our first parents is the story of the discovery of moral knowledge. Our earliest ancestors, apparently, lived without knowledge of good and evil; the acquisition of this knowledge is responsible for the wholesale transformation of humanity. This is what is meant in the biblical passage "Then the eyes of both were opened." The first thing they notice is their nakedness, and this induces a sense of shame. The sense of shame, you might say, is the first authentically human moment in Genesis. A person incapable of shame—as Adam and Eve were in the garden—cannot be a human being in the full or proper sense of the word. Only creatures with a sense of the shameful, beings capable of making moral distinctions, can be called human at all. What is often referred to in Christian theology as the "Fall" is really a misnomer. We have not fallen so much as risen to a higher level of moral self-awareness. For what is a human being without the capacity to feel shame, to distinguish good from evil, right from wrong?

This passage raises a central question that has been the subject of literally centuries of commentary. Does the eating from the tree of moral knowledge represent humankind's first act of rebellion and disobedience to the divine law, or does it represent the first tentative steps toward our own humanity? Is the serpent a tempter and destroyer or a benefactor? Why did God wish to monopolize this knowledge for himself alone? Why did he begrudge Adam and his progeny the knowledge of good and evil that is surely a distinctive feature of our humanity? Or was God, like any good teacher, providing a "teachable moment," allowing first Adam and Eve and through them the entire human race the opportunity to exercise those capacities of choice, will, and deliberation that are the signs of our mature self-understanding?

The idea that the serpent's temptation of Adam and Eve, rather than being a curse, is the first step toward our distinctive humanity was put forward nowhere more persuasively than in John Milton's *Paradise Lost*. Lucifer's motto—*non serviam* (I will not serve)—expressed a bold new spirit of adventure and restless individualism that we will see later on given similar form in the philosophies of Thomas Hobbes and John Locke. The punishment for Adam and Eve's transgression was, to be sure, exile and loss of home, but it also entailed the experience of travel and new, unforeseen opportunities. It is in a sense their graduation from a state of perpetual and carefree adolescence to one of the responsibilities of adulthood. Consider just the following lines from the very end of *Paradise Lost* read every year to Yale seniors on the occasion of their baccalaureate service:

> The world was all before them, where to choose
> Their place of rest, and Providence their guide;
> They hand in hand with wand'ring steps and slow
> Through Eden took their solitary way.[4]

The struggle between good and evil is the theme of the next great biblical drama, the story of the brothers Cain and Abel. Cain, the older brother, was a tiller of the soil; Abel, a keeper of sheep. For reasons that the text does not explain, God prefers the offerings of Abel. In his anger, Cain kills his brother and adds insult to injury by asking, "Am I my brother's keeper?" Cain's punishment is quite mild by biblical standards. He is forced to roam the earth, where he becomes the founder of the first city. It is the line of Cain that brings the invention of the tools and instruments necessary for civilized life. As with the brothers Romulus and Remus and the founding of Rome through an act of fratricide, the biblical message is clear: politics and the arts of civilization are built upon crime.

We can now begin to see a fundamentally different attitude between the biblical and Greek conceptions of moral and political life. For Aristotle, man is the political animal, intended for life in the city; his virtues are the virtues necessary for citizenship and statecraft. The Bible, by contrast, extols pious and humble men—men like Abel: shepherds and nomads—who have consciously or unconsciously rejected the lures of urban civilization. This is a theme that plays itself out throughout the Hebrew Bible. Consider the flight of Abraham, the first Jew, who leaves the Mesopotamian city of Ur in the very center of the civilized world in order to pursue a nomadic existence far from the splendors of urban life. It is to escape the corrupting influences of the city that Abraham seeks a new life for himself and his progeny.

This suspicion of cities, states, and political authority is a theme that is constantly reiterated throughout the Bible. It is repeated in the story of Moses, who leaves the pampered life of Mizriam—the Hebrew name for Egypt—to become a shepherd like his Abrahamic ancestors before his first encounter with God, who sends him back to Egypt for the purpose of ending the enslavement of his people. Moses is the archetype of the prophet who calls the ruler, Pharaoh, to account from a higher authority that transcends the state. The idea of the prophet is the most important biblical contribution to political thought. The political teaching of the Bible consists in large part of explicit indictments of governments—Jewish and non-Jewish alike—for the injustice of their laws and the moral failings of their rulers. There is no other work of ancient literature, to my knowledge, that puts the conscience of the individual over and above the authority of political rulers as clearly as the Bible.

The closest and only approximation in Greek thought to the role of the prophet is the place occupied by Socrates, who appeals to his *daimon* as a naysayer that protects him from injustice. Recall the following from the *Apology*: "Perhaps someone might say: But Socrates, if you leave us will you not be able to live quietly without talking? Now this is the most difficult point on which to convince some of you. If I say that it is impossible for me to keep quiet because that means disobeying the god, you will not believe me and will think that I am being ironical. On the other hand, if I say that it is the greatest good for a man to discuss virtue every day and those other things about which you hear me conversing and testing myself and others, for the unexamined life is not worth living, you will believe me even less" (37e–38a). Socrates's appeal here for what we would call civil disobedience is the closest the Greeks ever came to the biblical claims of the prophets to call their leaders to task.

Fundamental suspicion of institutions like the state and ruling authority constitutes the most important political legacy of the Bible. What is it about politics that the Bible finds problematic? The danger with the state and political rule is the ever-present temptation of idolatry. The commandment against idolatry is perhaps the single most important biblical teaching. Idolatry does not mean simply the worship of objects of gold or clay. Idols may take many forms. They are barometers of what a society holds dear, what it worships; this could be money, fame, health, status, or anything else. If the Bible teaches anything, it is that there is only one God, and this God alone is to be worshipped. In particular we must avoid finding god substitutes in our institutions and the people who govern us, turning them into objects of worship. It is this tendency—this very real and human tendency—to turn our rulers into gods that the Bible emphatically warns against.

The fear of idolatry is not just an ancient superstition. Idolatry remains a permanent human disposition. It is a form of fetishism, investing a person, thing, or ritual with certain superhuman powers. Idolatry pertains not only to the object invested with these powers but also to the peculiar passion from which it arises. The psychological basis of idolatry has been brilliantly explored by Emil Fackenheim, one of the twentieth century's great theologians: "The ancient idolater projects a feeling—fear, hope, pleasure, pain—upon an external object, and he then worships the object. The object, on its part, remains no mere object; the projected feeling gives it a life of its own, and there may be, or even must be, a special rite of consecration during which this life is conjured into it. There is, then, *worship* because the object is *other* and *higher* than the worshipper, and the worship is *idolatrous* because the object is *finite*—if only because it *is* an object."[5]

It is the suspicion of idolatrous worship that attends even the institution of kingship in Israel. By the time the Jews have entered Canaan, they find themselves under the rule of different prophets, first Eli—as in Eli Yale—then Samuel, and then his sons. But the prophets too can misuse their power—no one is infallible, not even prophets—and this is why the people yearn for a king so that they can be ruled "like all the nations." When the people demand a king, here is what Samuel tells them:

These will be the ways of the king who will reign over you: he will take your sons and appoint them to the chariots and to be his horsemen, and to run before his chariots; and he will appoint for himself commanders of thousands and commanders of fifties, and some to plow his ground and to reap his harvest, and to make his implements of war and the equipment of his chariots. He will take your daughters to be perfumers and cooks and bakers. He will take the best of your fields and vineyards and olive orchards and give them to his servants. He will take the tenth of your grain and your vineyards and give it to his officers and servants. He will take your menservants and maidservants, and the best of your cattle and asses and put them to his work. He will take the tenth of your flocks and you shall be his slaves. (1 Samuel 8:11)

I can think of no stronger indictment of government in any literature. The idea is simple: the institution of kingship is bad. This does not mean that the Bible embraces democracy. Rather, all the institutions of human government represent a kind of rebellion against God. One might wish for a philosopher-king, as did Socrates, but the biblical point of view is that politics—all politics—is coercion and tyranny. War and the constant preparation for war, slavery, and taxation are the price of kingship. Nevertheless, the people are not convinced and still cry out for a king, at which point God seems to give up. "Hearken to the voice of the people in all that they say to you," the Lord tells Samuel, "for they have not rejected you, but they have rejected me from being king over them" (1 Samuel 8:7). Never in human history—I would add—has a new government been attended by so little promise for its future.

Biblical Politics

For all of Samuel's indictment of kingship, the Bible offers a political teaching whose greatest representative is David.[6] The story of David comes to light in the wake of the people of Israel demanding that Samuel appoint a king instead of rule by the prophets. The wish to be governed "like all the nations" is taken by God to be a rebuke of his authority, but he nevertheless tells Samuel to give the people what they ask for. After Samuel's warning that kings will be inclined to tyranny and injustice, Saul is appointed the first king over Israel. It is against this backdrop that David emerges.

The figure of David is best remembered today for his famous battle with the Philistine warrior Goliath in the valley of Elah. David and Goliath have even become names for the struggle between the underdog and the established power. But David was more—much more—than this. David was a king and a warlord, a friend, lover, adulterer, and poet. He is a lover and a fighter. David may not be a philosopher, but he is a poet (he is the author of psalms); he is the master of both the sword and the harp. As a political leader, he stands somewhere between Plato's philosopher-king and Machiavelli's prince and has elements of both. In short the story of David is one of the most remarkable political lives ever told.

At first sight David appears like many other biblical heroes—he comes from the most humble of men. He is the eighth and youngest son of Jesse the Bethlehemite. When we first meet David, he has been sent by his father to the battle camp with some food and cheeses for his brothers in the army. David is a shepherd and spends his time tending the family flock while his brothers are fighting the Philistine enemies. We have no inkling yet of David's later military or political prowess, but we do get a sense of his self-confidence bordering on arrogance. When David offers to take on Goliath, the others are contemptuous, but they give him a shot at it. Saul offers David his own armor and helmet, but David refuses, saying, "The Lord who delivered me from the paw of the lion and from the paw of the bear will deliver me from the hand of this Philistine" (1 Samuel 17:37). He goes forth armed only with a sling, a story that we shall see Machiavelli tell somewhat differently.

David's victory over the Philistine immediately elevates him above his humble origins, although this victory is not without costs. David will incur the jealousy and anger of Saul, who comes to see him as a rival for power. This begins almost immediately when Saul is taunted by women singing "Saul has slain his thousands, and David his ten thousands" (1 Samuel 18:7). So begins a series of adventures (and misadventures) in which David seeks mainly to avoid the wrath of Saul. At various times he becomes a hunted man living in the wilderness, and later he is even forced to take refuge among the Philistines in order to protect himself. However, David's situation is aided by two figures who care deeply for him and who will figure prominently in the David narrative. These are Michal, Saul's daughter, and Jonathan, Saul's son. It is the bond forged between these three souls that will protect and defend David as he tries to evade Saul's attempts to have him killed.

What distinguishes David from so many other biblical figures is, above all, his great capacity for love and friendship. David's friendship with Jonathan is one of the greatest in any literature, rivaling that of Achilles and Patroclus in Homer's *Iliad*. And his love for Michal is only somewhat overshadowed by his even more famous love affair with Bathsheba. David is foremost a man of great heart or spirit, in Hebrew *ruah*. Ruah is perhaps the nearest Hebrew term to the Greek *thymos* or spiritedness. This indicates a passionate soul, a quality at the basis of our capacity for love and friendship as well as for anger and desire for revenge. David is one of the great lovers in history. Contrast his nature, if you will, to that of Socrates. Socrates is also a great lover. He is an erotic man. But Socrates is in love with philosophy. He is a lover of truth, of the examined life. He is in love with an idea. Can such a person ever truly love another human being? One suspects—and even more than suspects—that the answer is no. David, by contrast, is a lover of men and women as well as a lover of God. He has a passionate nature that finds its highest expression in fighting, singing, dancing, and making love.

At first David was promised in marriage to Saul's eldest daughter, but for reasons not explained we are told that she was given to another. It was Saul's second daughter, Michal, whom David married. "Now Saul's daughter Michal loved David and they told Saul and the thing pleased him," the text reads (1 Samuel 18:20). But it is the friendship of David and Jonathan that is central to the narrative. "The soul of Jonathan was knit to the soul of David," we read, "and Jonathan loved him as his own soul." What kind of friendship was this? The text describes it almost as a kind of wedding dowry: "Then Jonathan made a covenant with David, because he loved him as his own soul. And Jonathan stripped himself of the robe that was upon him and gave it to David and his amour and even his sword and his bow and his girdle. And David went out and was successful wherever Saul sent him; so that Saul set him over the men of war. And this was good in the sight of all the people and also in the sight of Saul's servants" (1 Samuel 18:3–5). Long before *Brokeback Mountain* Jonathan seems to say: "I wish I knew how to quit you."[7]

The result is that Jonathan and David became inseparable, severely straining the relation between Jonathan and his own father. David is a passionate man who excites passionate relations. Saul reproaches his son for his friendship with David: "For as long as the son of Jesse lives upon the earth, neither you nor your kingdom shall be established," he warns. But Jonathan is not convinced. "Why should he be put to death?" he asks. "What has he done?" The tone of defiance is clear. At this expression of rebellion, Saul erupts in anger: he hurls his spear, narrowly missing Jonathan. "And Jonathan rose from the table in fierce anger and ate no food the second day of the month for he was grieved for David because his father had disgraced him" (1 Samuel 31–34).

The final statement of David's deep friendship for Jonathan comes after David learns of the deaths of both Saul and Jonathan. By this time, David has become an outcast living in the wastelands and even seeking refuge among the Philistines. In a final battle with the Philistines, Saul and Jonathan are killed. When David learns of this he is devastated. "Then David took hold of his clothes and rent them and so did all the men who were with him and they mourned and wept and fasted until evening for Saul and for Jonathan his son and for the people of the Lord and for the house of Israel because they had fallen by the sword" (2 Samuel 1:11–12).

David not only weeps and fasts, he sings. He is a poet and a singer. "How are the mighty fallen in the midst of battle," he sings. "Jonathan lies slain upon thy high places. I am distressed for you, my brother Jonathan; very pleasant have you been to me; your love to me was wonderful, passing the love of a woman. How are the mighty fallen, and weapons of war perished" (2 Samuel 1:25–27).

David and Bathsheba

It is now many years after David's epic battles with Saul. He is almost thirty years old and is king over Judah. In the intervening years he has acquired many wives and many children. After Michal were Abigail and then Maacah, Haggith, Abital, and Eglah. And there were many children, among them Amnon, Chileab, Absalom, Adonijah, and of course later Solomon. But what has happened to Michal? Has she simply been discarded or forgotten? Not likely.

This is the period of David's greatest triumphs as a commander and political leader. David's reign over a united Israel lasted a total of forty years, and David himself lived to the age of seventy. As a sign of his success he decides to bring the Ark of the Covenant into his new capital city of Jerusalem in a procession that includes music, singing, and dancing. Here is the description of the scene: "So David and all the house of Israel brought up the ark of the Lord with shouting, and with the sound of the horn. As the ark of the Lord came into the city of David, Michal the daughter of Saul looked out of the window, and saw King David leaping and dancing before the Lord; and she despised him in her heart" (2 Samuel 6:15–16).

There is an unmistakable note of anger here. Michal, herself the daughter of a king, witnesses her husband leaping and dancing, acting shamelessly before the people, and she despises him for this. But David does not care. The people, he asserts, will love him for this dancing in front of the crowd:

> And David returned to bless his household. But Michal the daughter of Saul came out to meet David and said, "How the king of Israel honored himself today, uncovering himself today before the eyes of his servants, maids, as one of the vulgar fellows shamelessly uncovers himself." And David said to Michal, "It was before the Lord who chose me above your father and above all his house, to appoint me as prince over Israel, the people of the Lord—and I will make merry before the Lord. I will make myself yet more contemptible than this and I will be abased in your eyes; but by the maids of whom you have spoken, by them, I shall be held in honor." (2 Samuel 6:20)

This remarkable passage reveals something about the soul of David. It is inconceivable to imagine Aristotle's great king dancing nearly naked before the citizens of Athens. Yet David says that he does not mind making himself contemptible before the people, because they will love him for this. Is David a shameless demagogue? At the height of his greatest triumph we see him debase himself. And what was the result of David's passion? Michal was punished with sterility: "Therefore Michal the daughter of Saul had no child unto the day of her death" (2 Samuel 6:23). What to make of this?

As in every great story, great tragedy follows great triumph. David has united Israel, and, as the text tells us, he "administered justice and equity to all his people" (2 Samuel 8:15). There are still battles to be fought and wars to be won, but David sits in Jerusalem the head of a unified nation. His days as a warrior are over, and his life as a king and administrator has begun. We should recall here Samuel's warning to the people about the dangers of kings and their potential for injustice. This is the background to the story of David and Bathsheba.

One evening when he is bored and walking on the roofs of his palace, David sees a woman—a beautiful woman—bathing in a nearby home. He is smitten with the sight of her and sends his messengers to find out who she is. They return with the news that her name is Bathsheba, and that she is the wife of Uriah the Hittite. What follows is revealed in the tersest possible language: "So David sent messengers and took her; and she came to him and he lay with her. Then she returned to her house. And the woman conceived; and she sent and told David, 'I am with child'" (2 Samuel 11:4).

Now David has a problem on his hands. What to do? Consider: he already has many wives and many children. What's one more? And who is this Uriah? Can't David simply do whatever he wants? He is the king, after all. But apparently being the king is not sufficient to allow complete freedom from all restraints. David is subject to certain moral restraints that not even a king can afford to disobey.

David decides to construct an elaborate ruse to conceal Bathsheba's pregnancy. He sends for Uriah, who is away from home as a soldier in David's army, under the pretext of getting news from the front. How are things going? He sets up a party for Uriah and plies him with food and drink in hopes of getting him drunk, sending him home, and letting him sleep with his wife in order to cover up the crime. But David doesn't count on one thing. Uriah is a loyal solider and remains true to the soldier's oath of maintaining chastity during a military campaign. Instead of returning to his home, Uriah sleeps at the king's door with the servants.

Now David does a disgraceful thing to an innocent man and a loyal soldier. He tells Uriah to deliver a letter to his commander, Joab; David's letter instructs Joab to put Uriah in the front line of the battle and when the siege is to begin, to pull back the other troops and leave Uriah alone to be killed by the enemy, which is exactly what takes place (2 Samuel 11:14).

David successfully conceals his crime, but in the course of doing so has committed a greater one. He is responsible for the death of a just man who has done him no wrong whatever. To add insult to injury, he has even used Uriah as an unwitting pawn to deliver the letter that amounts to Uriah's death sentence. When David later receives the news from the front that Uriah the Hittite is dead, he sends word back to his field commander Joab, "Do not let this matter trouble you, for the sword devours now one and now another." He says in effect: don't worry about it. Uriah was collateral damage. David goes on to take Bathsheba as his wife after her mourning period is over, but we also learn that "the thing that David had done displeased the Lord" (2 Samuel 11:27).

We are now set up for one of the truly singular moments in the kingship of David, perhaps the kingship of any monarch. It is said that the Lord sent the prophet Nathan to the court of David to tell the following story: "There were two men in a certain city, the one rich and the other poor. The rich man had very many flocks and herds; but the poor man had nothing but one little ewe lamb, which he had bought. And he brought it up and it grew up with him and with his children; it used to eat of his morsel, and drink from his cup, and lie in his bosom and it was a daughter to him. Now there came a traveler to the rich man and he was unwilling to take one of his flock or herd to feed the wayfarer who had come to him, but he took the poor man's lamb and prepared it for the man who had come to him" (2 Samuel 12:1–4). After listening to this story David takes the bait: "Then David's anger was greatly kindled against the man; and he said to Nathan, 'As the Lord lives, the man who has done this deserves to die; and he shall restore the lamb fourfold because he did this thing, and because he had not pity'" (2 Samuel 12:5–6). Then Nathan adds the kicker: "*You* are the man" (2 Samuel 12:7).

The realization that David himself is in the position of the rich man who has stolen from the poor man strikes him like a thunderbolt, and it tells us something about David. Although he has committed an injustice, he has not become deaf to the appeal of justice. He correctly interprets Nathan's parable and feels shame at the wrong he has committed. In a century such as the one we have just lived through, when rulers are frequently mass murderers, how can we not be touched by David's recognition of his injustice against a single individual? "I have sinned against the Lord," David laments (2 Samuel 12:13). And David's sin will not go unpunished, for though David will live, the child will die.

Perhaps what is most interesting about this story is that David chooses to *listen* to Nathan. Can one imagine a current president or political leader actually listening to the kind of rebuke that Nathan delivers to David? For one thing, he could never even get an appointment until he had been thoroughly vetted and it had been determined what political party he belonged to! But David actually listens. The rule of prophets may have come to an end after Samuel's appointment of Saul as the first king of Israel, but the prophets have not lost their role as the conscience of the nation. This is what distinguishes the political theory of the Bible from every other work: the role extended to the prophet to act even as a chastiser of rulers and the voice of conscience. The idea that political leaders must bend to the moral law—the voice of conscience—is perhaps the most singular political teaching of the Bible. And of course even David—King David—has to listen.

David repents, recognizing that he has sinned against the Lord. But did he not sin also against Uriah? This statement of David's has given rise to a wealth of commentary. In *Leviathan*, for example, Hobbes uses the story of David and Nathan's parable in a very specific way. As the king, the lawful sovereign of his state, David did indeed sin against God, Hobbes reasons, but as the source of all authority he committed no injustice against Uriah. In other words, the sovereign can never act unjustly toward his subjects, because the sovereign is the source of all justice—so says Hobbes.

The story of David and Bathsheba ends on a note of ambiguity. While the child is sick, David fasts and sleeps on the ground for seven days to atone for his sin. Please don't take the child, he prays. But the child dies anyway. After his servants break the news to him, David gets up, bathes, puts on fresh clothes, has something to eat, and prepares for business. His servants are confused. He fasted and mortified himself while the child was alive but does not mourn after its death. Why? David's answer is decisive and pragmatic: "While the child was still alive, I fasted and wept; for I said, 'Who knows whether the Lord will be gracious to me, that the child may live?' But now that he is dead; why should I fast? Can I bring him back again? I shall go to him, but he will not return to me" (2 Samuel 12:23).

In other words: What can I do? There is work to be done. Let's move on. David may repent, but there is a toughness and pragmatism to him that is necessary for kingly rule.

David and Absalom

No account of the life of David would be complete without some recognition of his deep and abiding love for his own children. We have seen the story of David's love for Jonathan and his erotic passion for Bathsheba, and now his love for the most problematic of his offspring, Absalom. Only a parent can understand what it means to love a child the way that David loves Absalom. The story of David and Absalom is not only that of parent and child but also that of rebellion and civil war.

The story of David and Absalom has a complicated background. Absalom was David's son by Maacah, and he had a sister named Tamar. Absalom's half-brother Amnon conceived a violent passion for Tamar. But Tamar was a virgin as well as the half-sister of Amnon, and so she appeared to be off-limits. But an adviser to Amnon came up with a plan. Pretend to be sick, and when your father, David, comes by to see you, say that you would like Tamar to come to your apartment and bake you a cake. So the plan is set in motion. Tamar comes to Amnon's room to cook for him, and he rapes her. Then something almost as bad as the rape happens next: "Then Amnon hated her with very great hatred; so that the hatred with which he hated her was greater than the love with which he had loved her. And Amnon said to her, 'Arise, be gone'" (2 Samuel 13:15). Tamar has first been used and then rejected. When she returns home, Absalom knows something is up. He tells Tamar to keep quiet about it. David, who now realizes that he has been manipulated by Amnon, is very angry, yet Absalom remains silent. "But Absalom spoke to Amnon neither good nor bad for Absalom hated Amnon because he had forced his sister Tamar" (2 Samuel 13:22). In other words, Absalom was biding his time.

Two years pass, and little is said between the brothers while Absalom is plotting revenge. Then Absalom decides to throw a party for all of the king's sons, their families, and servants. Like a scene out of *The Godfather*, Absalom intends to put Amnon at ease and then kill him. Get him drunk, he tells his retainers, make him feel relaxed but be sure he does not leave the gathering alive. This is exactly what happens. When Amnon is killed, the other brothers flee in panic, and when the story is reported to David it appears at first as if Absalom has killed all of the brothers. Absalom is forced to flee, which he does for three years. "And the spirit of the king longed to go forth to Absalom," the text reads, because his father loved him (2 Samuel 13:39). But Absalom cannot return home—at least not right away.

After Absalom has spent three years in exile, Joab, David's strong-arm man and enforcer (something like Luca Brasi from *The Godfather*), contrives a way to bring him back to Jerusalem. But Absalom has still committed a crime by killing David's heir and successor, so he cannot simply be reinstated. It is agreed that if Absalom is allowed to return home, he will not be able live within the presence of David. After two more years of this internal exile, Absalom has become increasingly angry. He summons Joab, but Joab will not come. Then he does something to get Joab's attention that reveals something of his character. He sends his men to go and burn Joab's fields. This seems to work. Why have I been allowed to come home, Absalom reproaches him, if I must still live as an exile within my own country? Joab goes to David and beseeches him on Absalom's behalf. David then summons Absalom, who bows with his face touching the ground, and his father kisses him.

Absalom's sister is violated; he exacts revenge; banishment and forgiveness follow. End of story? Hardly: just the beginning. Almost immediately after being reinstated, Absalom begins planning a rebellion to overthrow his father. Absalom's name has become synonymous with rebellion and betrayal. He sets himself up with a chariot and horses and a posse of fifty men, who stand at the gate before David's palace. He begins to foment discontent by denying people access to the king while flattering them that their cases are just. "Oh that I were judge in the land" he tells them, "Then every man with a suit or a cause could come to me and I would give them justice." In this manner, it is said, "Absalom stole the hearts of the men of Israel" (2 Samuel 15:4–6).

Absalom is a man of immense pride and ambition; he has no intention of remaining a part of his father's royal retinue. On top of this, he is a man of great vanity and good looks. In a rare aside, the text pauses to describe Absalom: "Now in all Israel there was no one so much praised for his beauty as Absalom; from the sole of his foot to the crown of his head there was no blemish on him" (2 Samuel 14:25). His most notable feature is his long hair, of which he is excessively proud.

Absalom stealthily continues his wooing of the people for four years out of sight of his father, until at one point he asks David's permission to leave Jerusalem to visit his former home in Hebron. It is here that Absalom declares himself king and begins his siege of Jerusalem. At first it appears as if Absalom will be successful. A messenger comes to David with the news that "the hearts of the men of Israel have gone after Absalom" (2 Samuel 15:13). As a result David is forced to flee Jerusalem with his followers.

David may have been forced to flee his capital, but he is not yet defeated. The stage is set for a great battle between the army of Absalom and the army of David, recalling the struggle between David and Saul a generation before. David has organized his war party and is prepared to do battle, but his captains tell him that they cannot afford to lose him, that he must stay back. David accedes to this, but not before he is heard telling his captains, "Deal gently for my sake with the young man Absalom" (2 Samuel 18:4).

The battle is a decisive rout, and the armies of Absalom are scattered. Absalom himself is last seen trying to escape on a mule but gets his hair—his long beautiful hair—caught in the fork of an oak tree, where he is found dangling and is murdered by Joab in violation of David's orders. The victory that David has won has reestablished his kingship, but at the cost of fracturing his family. While the city is preparing a victory celebration, Joab is informed that the king is weeping and mourning for his son: "So the victory that day was turned into mourning for all the people; for the people heard that day, 'The king is grieving for his son.' And the people stole into the city that day as people steal in who are ashamed when they flee in battle. The king covered his face and the king cried with a loud voice, 'O my son Absalom, O Absalom, my son, my son'" (2 Samuel 19:1). It would take someone with a heart of stone to read David's lament for Absalom and not feel his enormous capacity for love.

But this is still not the end of the story. Immediately after David has uttered his famous cry ("Absalom, my son, my son"), Joab speaks bluntly to him, perhaps more bluntly than anyone has spoken to him since Nathan's rebuke: "You have today covered with shame the faces of all your servants, who have this day saved your life and the lives of your sons and your daughters, and the lives of your wives and your concubines because you love those who hate you and hate those who love you. For you have made it clear today that commanders and servants are nothing to you; for today I perceived that if Absalom were alive and all of us were dead, then you would be pleased" (2 Samuel 19:5–6).

Of course Joab is right, and David immediately recognizes this. Absalom has been David's bitter enemy, and many people have lost their lives fighting on David's behalf to ensure the defeat of Absalom. How will they react to David's mourning the death of their enemy, suggesting that he cares more for his defeated son than for those who have made sacrifices on David's behalf? As in the earlier case of Nathan the prophet, we see David listen to counsel and act accordingly. David is a man of great heart but also shrewd judgment. His own sense of political pragmatism tells him that he must put his bereavement aside if he is to reassert his authority as an effective leader. Thus the story concludes with David leaving his rooms where he has been in mourning and taking his place before the gates of the city: "And the people were told 'Behold, the king is sitting in the gate' and all the people came before the king" (2 Samuel 19:8).

Conclusion

Leo Strauss once remarked that the difference between Jerusalem and Athens represents a conflict between two fundamentally different moral codes or ways of life. The pinnacle of Greek ethics is Aristotle's *Nicomachean Ethics,* and the pinnacle of Aristotle's ethics is the virtue called *megalopsychia* or greatness of soul. Greatness of soul, as the name implies, is the virtue concerned with honor. The great-souled man is said to claim much because he deserves much. Such a person is concerned above all with how he is seen by others and, of course, to be worthy of the recognition bestowed on his acts of public service. The great-souled man is haughty in the extreme.

But contrast this, if you will, with the heroes extolled by the Bible. Such men are deeply aware of their own imperfections, their own unworthiness before God, and are haunted by a deep sense of guilt and inadequacy. The biblical heroes are typically the humblest of men. But more to the point, which of these two is more admirable: Aristotelian man's sense of his own self-worth and pride at his own accomplishments or biblical man's sense of his unworthiness and dependence on divine love?

These differences go deeper still. The god of the philosophers is Aristotle's famous unmoved mover. The unmoved mover is something like pure thought, which is the reason both Plato and Aristotle believed that the act of solitary contemplation brought us closest to the divine. *Thēoria*—pure contemplation—is the activity the Greeks believed to be most godlike. Needless to say, the Aristotelian unmoved mover, unlike the God of the Bible, is not concerned with man and his fate. The God of Aristotle, whatever else one might say, is not the God of Abraham, Isaac, and Jacob. This God, the God of the Bible, is said to have created us in his image. This means that it is not contemplation or philosophy but repentance and the ruthless demand for purity of heart that is required of us. Repentance—in Hebrew *t'shuva*—means return to an earlier state of purity and simplicity. The omnipotent God of the Bible is not a thinking substance but a being who dwells in the thick darkness, whose ways are not our ways.

And yet these distinctions seem not quite true, at least in the case of David. Like other biblical heroes, David may come from humble stock, but he is a man of tremendous resourcefulness, cunning, and intelligence. He has the soul of a poet and the heart of a warrior. And what is more, he is deeply convinced of his worthiness to rule. Much to the chagrin of his reserved and aristocratic wife, Michal, David dances with joy on the occasion of the return of the Holy Ark to Jerusalem. There is a story told about David by Machiavelli that is quite revealing. In recounting the story of David and Goliath, Machiavelli claims that when Saul sought to give David his armor, David refused, preferring to face his enemy armed only with a sling and a knife. As every reader of the Bible knows, David went to meet Goliath armed just with his sling and five stones (1 Samuel 17:38–40). Why does Machiavelli give him a knife? The biblical David had no need of a knife, for he relied on divine promises, but Machiavelli's David, skeptical of relying on the Lord's protection, takes along a knife just in case. While taking liberties with the biblical account, this story captures something of David's personality. Whatever there is of biblical humility in David is undercut by his boldness, audacity, confidence in his own powers, and unmitigated chutzpah. He is truly a man for all seasons.

CHAPTER 7

Machiavelli and the Art
of Political Founding

Portrait of Niccolò Machiavelli, 1469–1527. Palazzo Vecchio, Florence.
Photo credit: Erich Lessing / Art Resource, NY

Machiavelli was a Florentine. To know that is to know virtually everything you need to know about him. I exaggerate, of course, but the point is that Florence was a city-state—a republic—and Machiavelli spent his life in the service of the republic. Living in Florence, the center of the Renaissance at the height of the Renaissance, he hoped to do for politics what his contemporaries Leonardo da Vinci and Michelangelo had done for art and sculpture. He hoped to revive the spirit of the ancients, of antiquity, but to modify and correct it by the light of his own experience. As he puts it in the Dedication of *The Prince,* his book is the product of "long experience with modern things and a continuous reading of ancient ones" (Dedication/3).[1]

To be sure, Machiavelli was not an ordinary Florentine. He was born in 1469 and grew up under the rule of the Medici, the first family of Florence, but lived to see them deposed by a Dominican friar by the name of Savonarola. Savonarola sought to impose on Florence a kind of theocracy, a republic of Christian virtue, but the Florentines being what they were, his experiment proved short-lived. In its place, a republic was established under a man named Piero Soderini (whose name appears several times in *The Prince*), where Machiavelli occupied the office of the secretary of the Second Chancery—a diplomatic post—for fourteen years from 1498 to 1512. After the fall of the republic and the return of the Medici, Machiavelli was tortured and then exiled from Florence to a small estate that he owned on the outskirts of the city. It was here during this life of political exile that he penned his major political works, *The Prince,* the *Discourses on Livy,* and the *Art of War.*[2]

It was also here that he wrote voluminous letters to friends, seeking knowledge of political events and happenings. In one letter to his friend Francesco Vettori he describes how he came to write his most famous book. "When evening comes," he writes, "I return to my house and enter my study":

> On the threshold I take off my workday clothes, covered with mud and dirt, and put on the garments of court and palace. Fitted out appropriately, I step inside the venerable courts of the ancients, where, solicitously received by them, I nourish myself on that food that *alone* is mine and for which I was born; where I am unashamed to converse with them and to question them about the motives for their actions, and they, out of their human kindness, answer me. And for four hours at a time I feel no boredom, I forget all my troubles, I do not dread poverty, and I am

not terrified by death. I have jotted down what I have profited from in their conversation and composed a short study, *De principatibus,* in which I delve as deeply as I can into the ideas concerning this topic, discussing the definition of a princedom, the categories of princedoms, how they are acquired, how they are retained, and why they are lost.[3]

The Prince is a deceptive book. What else would we expect? It is a work that everyone has heard of and perhaps has some preconception about. It is a book that has spawned scores of imitators. There are serious books, like Carnes Lord's *The Modern Prince,* dealing with leadership issues in times of war, and James Burnham's classic study *The Machiavellians,* defending the role of elite rule in modern society. But there are also books with titles like *The Machiavellian Guide to Womanizing* (by an appropriately named Nick Casanova), *The Mafia Manager: A Guide to the Corporate Machiavelli,* and my personal favorite, *The Suit: A Machiavellian Approach to Men's Style.* We all know—or think we know—what the work is about. Machiavelli's name is synonymous with deception, treachery, cunning, and deceit. Just look at his likeness. His smile—really a smirk—seems to say, "I know something you don't know." The difficulty with reading Machiavelli is that we already think we know all there is to know and consequently do not read him with the care he deserves. But there is more—much more—to Machiavelli than this.

Machiavelli was, above all, a revolutionary. In the Preface to his *Discourses on Livy* he compares himself with Christopher Columbus for his discovery of "new modes and orders." What Columbus did for geography, Machiavelli will do for politics: discover a new continent, a new world, so to speak. Machiavelli's new world, his new modes and orders, will require the displacement of the previous one. He makes this clear in the opening to chapter 15 of *The Prince:* "I depart from the orders of others," he writes. "But since it is my intent to write something useful to whoever understands it, it has appeared to me more fitting to go directly to the effectual truth of the thing than to the imagination of it. And many have imagined republics and principalities that have never been seen or known to exist in truth; for it is so far from how one lives to how one should live that he who lets go of what is done for what should be done learns his ruin rather than his preservation" (XV/61). But what was Machiavelli's revolution about?

This passage is often taken as providing the essence of Machiavellian realism, often called realpolitik, his appeal from the ideal to the real, from the Ought to the Is.[4] Machiavelli's call is to take one's bearings from the "effectual truth of things": do not look at what people say, look at what they do. To be sure, Machiavelli focuses on key features of reality: murders, conspiracies, coups d'état. He is more interested in the actual evils that men do than in the goods to which they aspire. You might even say that Machiavelli takes delight in demonstrating, much to our chagrin, the space between our lofty intentions and the actual consequences of our deeds.

And yet there is more—far more—to Machiavelli than the term "realism" connotes. The term may be deeply misleading. Machiavelli speaks the language of political innovation, renewal, and even redemption. The book draws on the biblical language of prophecy, and Machiavelli presents himself as a prophet of liberation. In the passage cited above, he boldly announces his break with—indeed, his repudiation of—all those who have come before him. He both replaces and combines elements from both Christianity and the Roman republic to create a new form of political organization distinctly his own: the modern state. He is the architect of the modern sovereign state that is given theoretical expression in the later writings of Hobbes, Locke, and Rousseau, to say nothing of contemporary writers on both the left and the right, from Max Weber and Carl Schmitt to Antonio Gramsci, the author of a book called *The Modern Prince.*

The Form and Dedication of *The Prince*

Machiavelli was a partisan of the new. But like all pathbreakers, he often combined his novelties with conventional pieties and forms. His writings are a curious combination of boldness and caution. His often conventional exterior almost always belies an unconventional interior. Consider just the form and dedication of *The Prince.*

The Prince appears on its surface to be the most conventional of books. It presents itself as a work in the long tradition of what is known as "mirror of princes," that is, handbooks that attempt to advise a prince about how to behave, a kind of dos and don'ts of princely rule. Fair enough. The oldest work of this genre is Xenophon's *Education of Cyrus* (*Cyropaideia*), which Machiavelli both misidentifies and includes on his required reading list (XIV/60). The appearance of conventionality is further supported by the opening words of the book: "It is customary." Machiavelli wraps himself in the mantle of tradition. It is a work intended to ingratiate him to Lorenzo de Medici, the man whose name appears on the dedication page.

But look again. Consider the structure of the first three chapters. "All states, all dominions that have held and do hold empire over men, are either republics or principalities," Machiavelli declares in the opening sentence of chapter one (I/5). He then asserts that in this work he will deal only with principalities, leaving the discussion of republics for elsewhere, one assumes his *Discourses*. Having distinguished principalities and republics as the only two kinds of regime worth mentioning, he goes on to distinguish between two kinds of principality: hereditary princes like Lorenzo, who have acquired their authority through tradition and blood line, and new princes.

But then Machiavelli goes on to tell the reader that the exclusive subject of the book will be the new prince—not Lorenzo at all, but precisely the kind of prince who has achieved his authority through his own guile, force, and cunning. The true addressee of the book must necessarily be the potential prince, someone with sufficient political audacity to create his own authority. *The Prince* is addressed to a new kind of leader, one who is prepared to create his own authority *ex nihilo*. But there is literally only one creator who is able to create from scratch. Machiavelli's prince seems to be an answer to the creator described in the opening chapters of Genesis. *The Prince* describes a new kind of political leader emancipated from traditional forms of authority and virtue and endowed with a species of ambition, love of glory, and elements of prophetic authority that we today might call "charisma."

Armed and Unarmed Prophets

So what, then, is the character of this new prince, and how does he differ from more conventional models of princely authority? In one of the most famous chapters of the book, entitled "Of New Principalities That Are Acquired Through One's Own Arms and Virtue," Machiavelli discusses the character of the new prince (VI/21–25). He begins by stating, perhaps overstating, the difficulties in establishing one's authority. "A prudent man should always enter upon the paths beaten by great men, and imitate those who have been most excellent, so that if his own virtue does not reach that far, it is at least in the odor of it" (VI/22). One should do what archers do when attempting to reach a distant target, namely, aim one's bow high, knowing that gravity will force the arrow down. In other words, set your sights high, knowing that you will probably fall short. So who are "the greatest examples" of princely rule that the prudent man should imitate?

Here Machiavelli gives a list of heroic founders of peoples and states: Moses, Cyrus, Romulus, Theseus, and so on. "As one examines their actions and lives," he writes, "one does not see that they had anything else from fortune than the opportunity which gave them the matter enabling them to introduce any form they pleased" (VI/23). In short, these were founders who, like the biblical God, created *ex nihilo*, with only the occasion to act and the necessary virtues—strength of mind—to take advantage of their situation. "Such opportunities," he continues, "made these men successful and their excellent virtue enabled the opportunity to be recognized; hence their fatherlands were ennobled by it and they became prosperous" (VI/23).

It is here that Machiavelli introduces his famous distinction between armed and unarmed prophets. "All the armed prophets conquered and the unarmed ones were ruined," he concludes (VI/24). This seems to be—and is—a statement of sheer power politics. Political power grows out of the barrel of a gun, as a twentieth-century Machiavellian has said. But there is more than this. Why does Machiavelli compare the new prince to a prophet? What is a prophet? The most obvious answer is a man to whom God speaks. The biblical prophet—Nathan is a perfect example—is someone brought to chastise or rebuke rulers for their injustice and misuse of power. Machiavelli's prophets, however, come armed. They come to assume power. There is only one figure on Machiavelli's list who could qualify as a prophet in the strict sense, namely, Moses, whom he calls a "mere agent" who should be admired not for his skill "but for that grace which made him deserving of speaking with God" (VI/22).

But the prophet in Machiavelli's sense is also someone who inhabits the imagination (*fantasia*) of a people. It is not enough that a prophet be obeyed; he must be believed. An interesting case in point is the treatment of Savonarola, a near-prophet, who failed, so to speak, only when words failed him. "He was ruined in his new orders as soon as the multitude began not to believe in them and he had no mode for holding firm those who had believed nor for making unbelievers believe" (VI/24). The lesson of Savonarola cannot be repeated too often. Savonarola did not fail because he was the prototypical unarmed prophet; the source of his failure was not just a failure of arms but of words: the people had ceased to believe in him. Machiavelli's prophets may not be religious figures or the recipients of divine knowledge, but they must be persons of exceptional personal qualities that allow them to bring laws, to shape institutions, and reform the opinions that govern men's lives. Machiavelli's armed prophet is more than a gangster; he is an educator.

Although it is characteristic of Machiavelli to talk tough—armed prophets always conquer and the unarmed always lose—he clearly recognizes that there are huge exceptions to this rule. The most obvious and important exception of an unarmed prophet conquering is Jesus Christ. Jesus conquered by words alone, which helped to establish first a sect, then a religion, and eventually an empire. Words may well be a weapon as powerful as a gun. And, then, what is Machiavelli himself but an archetypal unarmed prophet? He controls no troops or territory. Yet he is clearly attempting to conquer in large part through the transformation of our understanding of good and evil, of virtue and vice. In order to make people obey, you must first make them believe. Machiavelli's prophetic prince must have many of the qualities of a philosopher and a religious reformer.

Midnight in the Garden of Good and Evil

It is often said of Machiavelli that he introduced a new kind of immoralism into politics. In his famous formula from chapter 15 he sets out to teach the prince "how not to be good." Leo Strauss, in perhaps the most important book on Machiavelli ever written, declared him to be a "teacher of evil."[5] Questions of good and bad, virtue and vice, appear on virtually every page of *The Prince*. Machiavelli is not simply a teacher of pragmatism, of how to adjust the means to fit the ends; he is offering nothing short of a comprehensive reevaluation of our basic moral vocabulary of good and evil.

In order to affect his transformation of Christian morality, in order to teach the prince "how not to be good," it is necessary to go to the source of morality. To effect the maxims that actually govern our lives, it is necessary to go to the foundation of those maxims, ones that can be found only in religion. Oddly enough, religion does *not* seem to be a major theme of *The Prince*. In a memorable passage from chapter 18, Machiavelli advises the prince to always cultivate the appearance of religion: "He should appear all mercy, all faith, all honesty, all humanity, all religion," he writes, adding that "nothing is more necessary to appear to have than this last quality" (XVIII/70–71). The point is clear: the appearance of religion—by which he means here Christianity—is good, while the actual practice of it is harmful.

Machiavelli's point is that if you want liberty, you have to learn how not to be good, at least as Christianity has defined goodness. The Christian virtues of humility, turning the other cheek, and forgiveness of sins must be rejected if you want to *do* good as opposed to just *be* good. You have to learn how to get your hands dirty. Between the innocence of the Christian and the worldliness of Machiavelli's new morality, there can be no reconciliation. These are two incompatible moral positions. But Machiavelli goes further. The safety and security enjoyed by the innocent, their freedom to live blameless lives and untroubled sleep, depends entirely upon the prince's clear-eyed and even ruthless use of power. The true statesman must be prepared to mix a love of the common good, a love of his own people, with a streak of cruelty that is often deemed essential for a great ruler in general. It is simply another example of how moral goodness grows out of and requires a context of moral evil. Machiavelli's advice is clear: if you cannot accept the responsibilities of political life, if you cannot accept the harsh necessities that may require cruelty, deceit, and even murder, then get out of the way. Do not seek to impose your own high-minded innocence—sometimes called justice—on the requirements of statecraft, because it will only lead to ruin. In our era, the presidency of Jimmy Carter is usually taken as Exhibit A of this confusion of Christian humanitarianism with *raison d'état*.

In the philosophical literature this is known as the problem of dirty hands, so called after a play, *Les Mains sales*, written by the French philosopher Jean-Paul Sartre. The problem of dirty hands refers to the conflict between the harsh requirements of politics and the equally demanding desire for moral purity, to keep the world at a distance. In Sartre's play, which takes place in a fictional eastern European country during World War II, a communist resistance fighter named Hoederer upbraids an idealistic young recruit who balks at the order to carry out a political assassination. The communists are no different from members of any other party, Hoederer explains. They will do whatever they have to do to achieve victory: "How you cling to your purity, young man! How afraid you are to soil your hands! All right, stay pure! What good will it do you? Why did you join us? Purity is an idea for a yogi or a monk. Well, I have dirty hands. Right up to the elbows. I've plunged them in filth and blood. But what do you hope? Do you think anyone can govern innocently?"[6]

Or take another example: Carol Reed's great film *The Third Man*. There an American innocent named Holly Martins comes to postwar Vienna to join his boyhood friend and idol, Harry Lime, who, Martins discovers, is deep inside a murderous black market racket. From a ferris wheel high above the bombed-out city, they look down on the people below, and Harry asks: "Would you really feel any pity if one of those dots stopped moving forever? If I offered you twenty thousand pounds for every dot that stopped, would you really, old man, tell me to keep my money, or would you calculate how many dots you could afford to spare?" As they prepare to part, Harry provides a speech that would have done Machiavelli proud: "Under the Borgias they had warfare, terror, murder, and bloodshed, but they produced Michelangelo, Leonardo da Vinci, and the Renaissance. In Switzerland they had brotherly love—they had 500 years of democracy and peace, and what did that produce? The cuckoo clock."[7]

Or take one more example: John Le Carré's splendid Cold War thriller *The Spy Who Came in from the Cold*. Here a British agent, Alec Lemas, carries on an affair with an idealistic young Englishwoman who has joined the Communist Party out of a belief in nuclear disarmament and world peace. In the course of the story, the two are used to protect an East German agent who has been turned by the English intelligence forces. After their unwitting role in the plot is made clear, Lemas explains what the world of high espionage is all about: "There's only one law in this game, the expediency of temporary alliances. What do you think spies are? Moral philosophers measuring everything against the word of God or Karl Marx? They're not! They're just a bunch of seedy squalid bastards like me: little men, drunkards, queers, henpecked husbands, civil servants playing cowboys and Indians to brighten their rotten little lives. Do you think they sit like monks in London balancing right against wrong?"[8]

These are all examples of what I would call faux Machiavellianism: intellectuals engaging in tough talk to show that they really have lost their idealism, the intellectual's equivalent of losing one's virginity. It suggests that the world is divided between the strong and the weak, between realists who see things the way they really are and the idealists who require the comfort of moral illusions.

Machiavelli does not so much reject the idea of the good as redefine it. He is continually speaking the language of virtue—actually *virtù*—a word which retains the Latin root for the word "man" and which translates into something like our term for manliness. What distinguishes Machiavelli's use of this term is that he seeks to locate it in certain extreme situations such as political foundings, changes of regimes, and wars, both domestic and foreign. What distinguishes Machiavelli from his predecessors is his attempt to take the extraordinary situation—the extreme—as the normal situation and then make morality fit the extreme. His examples are typically drawn from situations *in extremis* where the very survival or independence of society is at stake. In such situations—and only in such situations—is it permissible to violate the precepts of ordinary morality. Machiavelli takes his bearings from such extreme states of emergency and seeks to render them normal.

Machiavelli does not deny that in ordinary times—in what we might call times of normal politics—the rules of justice may prevail. He shows only that normal politics is itself dependent on extraordinary politics— periods of crisis, anarchy, and revolution—where the normal rules of the game are suspended. It is in these times when individuals of extraordinary virtue are most likely to emerge. Machiavelli's preference for the extreme situation expresses his belief that only in moments of great political crisis, when the very existence of society is at risk, does human nature most fully reveal itself. His writings convey a sense of urgency that evokes the neces- sity for the most drastic action. While the Aristotelian statesman is most likely to value stability and the means necessary to achieving it, the Ma- chiavellian prince seeks war because only in the most extreme situations can one hope to prosper.

Machiavelli's ethics are avowedly immoralist. What he wants the prince to value above all else are glory, fame, and honor. These are sought by the most "excellent men," Moses, Theseus, Cyrus, and maybe Cesare Borgia, but others like Agathocles lack them. The ethic of glory is a distinctively non- moral good. It aims not at justice, fairness, or friendship but at fostering those qualities that bring with them memorable greatness and lasting fame. These qualities Machiavelli believes are most conspicuously displayed in the world of "great politics," specifically building up the strength of one's city or na- tion for it to play a role in the game of world history. History, for Machia- velli, becomes the true court of judgment—the only final reward of virtue. Machiavelli's advice to the prince is to create monuments for your city, make something that will be remembered, whether for good or evil. He advises citizens to take pride in the glorious achievements of their country and make their own contributions to the annals of its history.

The question that animates Machiavelli's *Prince* is this. Politicians can- not serve their country unless they are prepared to dirty their hands through unscrupulous means. But how does one—how can one—preserve something like inner integrity while stooping to means—lying, character assassination, betrayal—that no decent person would employ? Machiavelli does not discuss the inner states or frames of mind of his heroes—Caesar, Hannibal, Borgia—who have chosen to get their hands dirty. What such men think of themselves, we have no idea. They perhaps have no inner life, and this is what renders them psychologically flat. Machiavelli seems to assume that the glory that comes with creating or strengthening a state is its own reward. His advice seems to be, "if you can't stand the heat, get out of the kitchen." If you don't like the kind of person you think you might become through the demands of political life, then stay at home.

The Aesthetics of Violence

The model of Machiavellian virtù is the Renaissance statesman and general Cesare Borgia. In chapter 7 of *The Prince* he gives a powerful example of Borgia's virtue in practice. Here Machiavelli tells the story of how Borgia appointed one of his lieutenants, Remirro de Orco, "a cruel and ready man," to help organize a territory not far from the outskirts of Florence. Remirro was an efficient officer and soon established order, but Borgia, to show that he was in charge, ordered Remirro to be murdered and the body and bloody knife to be displayed in the town square. "The ferocity of this spectacle," Machiavelli concludes, "left the people satisfied and stupefied [*satisfatte e stupidi*]" (VII/30).

Borgia's use of cruelty here is an example of what Machiavelli calls "cruelty well-used": "Those [cruelties] can be called well-used," he writes, adding parenthetically "(if it is permissible to speak well of evil) that are done at a stroke, out of the necessity to secure oneself and then are not persisted in but are turned to as much utility for the subjects as one can" (VIII/37–38). So Machiavelli criticizes Agathocles, the tyrant of Syracuse, whose "savage cruelty and inhumanity, together with his infinite crimes, do not allow him to be celebrated among the most excellent men" (VIII/35). There can be no clearer statement of what Sheldon Wolin has called Machiavelli's "economy of violence," that is, the need for quick, efficient, and resolute acts of cruelty that are judged in terms of their effects alone. "What he hoped to further by his economy of violence," Wolin writes, "was the 'pure' use of power, undefiled by pride, ambition, or motives of petty revenge."[9]

This is at best only partially true. The term "economy of violence" says little of interest about Machiavelli, but the term "spectacle" does. He is less interested in the economy than the aesthetics of violence. He approaches politics not as an economist calculating costs and benefits but as an aesthetician concerned with the spectacular effects that violence will achieve.

No one can read his descriptions of political assassination, conquest, and empire without sensing a deep admiration, even a celebration, of acts of creative violence. Thus can Machiavelli heap praise on Hannibal and his "inhuman cruelty that together with his infinite virtues always made him venerable and terrible in the sight of his soldiers" (XVII/67). But Machiavelli was not a sadist. He did not celebrate cruelty for its own sake. In a deeply revealing passage, he criticizes Ferdinand of Aragon for his acts of "pious cruelty" in expelling the Jews from Spain (XXI/88). He treated violence not as an unfortunate byproduct of political necessity but as a supreme political virtue through which form is imposed on matter.

Machiavelli's aesthetic of violence is connected to the belief that the great civilizations in history—the Persian, the Hebrew, the Roman—all grew out of acts of cruelty, domination, and conquest. The great political leaders past and present were not monks or moral philosophers calibrating finely tuned theories of justice but men with "dirty hands" who were prepared to use instruments of deceit, cruelty, and even murder to achieve conspicuous greatness. Machiavelli takes a perverse delight in bringing out the dependence of flourishing and successful civilizations on initial acts of fratricide, murder, and civil war.

There is an often violent and usurpatory character to what Machiavelli calls virtù. Virtù is above all the ability to take advantage of a situation—the "occasion," as Machiavelli sometimes calls it—that has been handed to us by *fortuna*. Virtù and fortuna are complementary terms for Machiavelli. There can be no virtue without a proper occasion in which to use it, and no occasion that does not create opportunities to exercise the proper human skills and abilities. Thus in the famous chapter 25, "How Much Fortune Can Do in Human Affairs," Machiavelli begins by considering the proposition that so much of human life is left to chance that there is little we can do to affect the course of events. "This opinion," he writes, with a nod to the present, "has been believed more in our times because of the great variability of things" (XXV/98).

Machiavelli considers the proposition, but rejects it. While much of what happens in politics is a matter of happenstance, luck, and sheer contingency, human intelligence, planning, and foresight still have some role to play. "In order that our free will not be eliminated," he conjectures, "I judge that it might be true that fortune is arbiter of half our actions, but also that she leaves the other half, or close to it, for us to govern" (XXV/98). The idea is that if fortuna governs half of life, virtù has some role in shaping the other half. And in a famous image he compares fortuna to a raging current or a flood, but says that virtù, using foresight, can create artificial barriers like dams to control the uncontrollable and put in order what is by nature chaotic. It follows that those who rely or depend too much on the power of luck—like those people who live in perpetual hope that they will purchase a winning lottery ticket—will come to ruin, while those who adapt themselves to the times have a greater chance of success. This seems to be a variation of the adage that fortune favors the prepared.

But Machiavelli goes further than this. Virtù is not simply a matter of adaptation and adjustment to the circumstances. It is also a matter of forcing the circumstances to adapt to you. There is a violent and aggressive aspect to Machiavelli's idea of adapting to the occasion. "I judge this indeed," he writes, "that it is better to be impetuous than cautious because fortune is a woman and it is necessary, if one wants to hold her down, to beat her and strike her down" (XXV/101). In other words, fortune responds more easily to audacity than to caution, to boldness and resoluteness than to moderation. Machiavelli's virtue is nothing if not a policy of preemption. Furthermore, Machiavelli tells the reader that such policies are more likely to find favor among the young, who he says are "less cautious, more ferocious, and command her [fortuna] with more audacity" (XXV/101).

Two Humors

What kind of government did Machiavelli think best? As he indicates at the beginning of *The Prince,* there are two kinds of regimes: principalities and republics. But each of these regimes is based on certain contrasting dispositions or what he calls "humors." "For in every city," Machiavelli writes in chapter 9, "two diverse humors are found, which arises from this: that the people desire neither to be commanded nor oppressed by the great and the great desire to command and oppress the people" (IX/39).

Machiavelli here uses a psychological, even quasi-medical term—"humors" (*umori*)—to designate the two great classes of people on which every state is based. Machiavelli's theory of the two humors is reminiscent of Plato's account of the three classes of the soul, with one vivid exception: each class in the city is bound to a "humor," but neither humor is anchored in reason. Every state is divided into two classes, the *grandi,* the rich and powerful who wish to dominate, and the *popolo,* the common people who wish merely to be left alone, who desire neither to rule nor be ruled. One might expect the author of a book entitled *The Prince* to favor the great. Are not these aristocratic goals of honor and glory precisely what Machiavelli has been advocating?

Yet Machiavelli proceeds to deprecate radically the virtues of the nobility. "The end of the people," he says, "is more decent than that of the great, since the great want to oppress and the people want not to be oppressed" (IX/39). His advice seems to be that the prince should seek to build his power base on the people rather than the nobles. Because of their ambition for power, the nobles will always be a threat to the prince, while a prince who has the people for his base can rule with greater ease and confidence. In an interesting reversal of the classical conception of politics, it is the nobles who are here said to be fickle and unreliable, while the people are more constant and stable. "The worst that a prince can expect from a hostile people is to be abandoned by it," Machiavelli writes, "but from the great, when they are hostile, he must fear not only being abandoned but also that they may move against him" (IX/39–40).

The main business of government consists, then, in knowing how to control the great because they are always a potential source of conflict. The prince must know how to chasten the ambition—to humble the pride, as it were—of the great and powerful. This, as we will see, will be a major theme in the political philosophy of Hobbes. The rule of the prince or sovereign requires the ability to control ambition and to do so through selective policies of execution, public accusations, and political trials. Remember the example of Remirro de Orco and how his execution left the people "satisfied and stupefied." Here is a perfect example of how both to control the ambitions of the nobles and to cater to the desires of the people.

Machiavelli's prince, while not exactly a democrat, recognizes the essential decency of the people and the need to keep their faith. By decency Machiavelli seems to mean their absence of ambition, the absence of the desire to dominate and command. But this decency is not the same as goodness. For there is a tendency on the part of the people to descend into what Machiavelli deems "idleness" or license. The desire not to oppress others may be decent, but at the same time the people must be taught how to defend their liberty. Fifteen hundred years of Christianity have left men weak, without the capacities to exercise political responsibility or the resources to defend themselves from attack. Just as the prince must know how to control the ambitions of the nobles, he must know how to strengthen the desires of the common people.

Some readers—even some very astute readers—of Machiavelli have thought that his prince is really a kind of democrat, and that *The Prince* is intended precisely to alert the people to the dangers of a usurping prince. Consider Spinoza's *Political Treatise:* "[Machiavelli] perhaps wished to show how careful a free people should be before entrusting its welfare to a single prince. . . . I am led to this opinion concerning that most far-seeing man because it is known that he was favorable to liberty."[10] Or, if you do not believe Spinoza, consider Rousseau's comment from *The Social Contract:* "Machiavelli was an honest man and a good citizen; but being attached to the house of Medici he was forced during the oppression of his fatherland to disguise his love of freedom."[11]

These comments are extremely revealing. Both of these great political writers take Machiavelli to be an apostle of freedom. Spinoza takes him to be offering a warning to the people about the dangers of princely rule; Rousseau takes him to have deliberately disguised his love of freedom due to the tyrannical rule of the Medici. Both regard him to be surreptitiously defending the people against the nobles.

Spinoza and Rousseau may exaggerate, but they are surely on to something. In the classical republic it is the nobility—the gentlemen possessed of wealth and leisure who are therefore capable of forming judgment—who dominate, while in Machiavelli's state it is the people who are going to be the dominant social and political power. Machiavelli wants to redirect power away from the nobles and toward the people. Why? In the first place, he judges the people to be more reliable than the great. Once the people have been taught to value their liberty, have learned to oppose encroachments on their freedom, to be fierce and vigilant watchdogs rather than humble and subservient underlings, they will serve as a reliable basis for the greatness and power of a state. With the people on his side, the prince is more likely to achieve his goals of a robust civil life for his people and eternal glory for himself.

As Machiavelli likes to say, a prince must know how to adapt to the times. What is true for princes is no less true for their advisers like Machiavelli. One must know the nature of both princes and peoples. In the Dedication Machiavelli compares himself to a landscape painter who must place himself on top of mountains to paint the valleys and in the valleys to paint the mountains (Dedication/4). In the ancient republics it may have been necessary to find restraints on the passions of the *demos,* but in the modern world, where republics have become a thing of the past, the people need to be taught to value their liberty above all else. The most excellent princes of the past were those, like Moses, who brought tablets of the law and prepared their people for self-government. It is fitting that Machiavelli concludes *The Prince* with a chapter calling upon his countrymen to emancipate themselves and to liberate Italy from foreign intruders.

Machiavelli's Utopianism

Let me conclude this analysis of *The Prince* by considering what I want to call Machiavelli's utopianism. On the face of it, this term seems to be an oxymoron. Doesn't Machiavelli exhort us to consider only "the effectual truth" of things, as opposed to imagined principalities, that is, to look at what people do, not at what they say, at the Is rather than the Ought? Yet despite his avowed rejection of ancient utopianism, Machiavelli tells readers to take as their models the greatest founders of peoples and nations, that these founders must be endowed with certain charismatic or prophetic properties, and that such people have come to power not through force alone but through their own virtù. These views provide evidence for an idealistic, even utopian, strain in Machiavelli's thought.

Nowhere is Machiavelli's idealism more on display than in the final chapter of *The Prince,* "Exhortation to Seize Italy and Free Her from the Barbarians." This chapter has probably given rise to more discussion than any other part of the book. Why at the end of what to many readers seems no more than a technical, how-to manual on politics does Machiavelli conclude with a passionate call for liberation? Some readers even believe there was a gap of several years between the composition of the first twenty-five chapters of the book, written in 1513, and the final chapter. For such readers the sections of the final chapter that speak of the liberation from the barbarians and the call for the redemption of Italy could only have been written around the year 1518.[12]

Far from an afterthought, these reflections were an obsession of Machiavelli's throughout all of his writings. His answer to the weakness and disunity of the Italian states was the myth of the prince: the figure personifying virtù, strength, and charisma whose redemptive power could point the way to a new Rome. In fact the opportunity for such a prince to exhibit real virtù is dependent on the current degradation of society, just as "it was necessary for anyone wanting to see the virtue of Moses that the people of Israel be enslaved in Egypt" (XXVI/102). The prophet and his people are linked. There is no such thing as a prophet without a people, or redemption without a redeemer. That Machiavelli expected such a redeemer-prince to emerge from the conditions of current decadence is clear from a letter to Vettori of August 26, 1513, during the time he was writing *The Prince:* "I certainly do not think that they [the Swiss] will create an empire like the Romans, but I do think they can become masters of Italy thanks to their proximity and thanks to our disarray and bad situation. And because these things appall me, I should like to remedy them . . . and now I am ready to start weeping with you over our collapse and our servitude that, if it does not come today or tomorrow, will come in our lifetime."[13]

It is precisely out of the degradation of Italy that Machiavelli believes political redemption will follow. In fact the condition of Italy's degradation is even necessary for the accomplishment of its eventual redemption. Like Moses, Machiavelli seems to be aware that he would not live to see the new promised land, that he was an unarmed prophet, who at best could show a new prince the way out of the wilderness and to a new Jerusalem. Machiavelli is aware that such a redeemer-prince may not come "in our time," that the immediate future of Italy will be one of weakness and disorder, but come he will; and when he does, he will not be the prince of peace but another Borgia, Hannibal, or Alexander. Machiavelli writes to hasten the coming of this redeemer-prince. He may well have added: "May he come quickly and in our time."

Machiavelli's *Discourses*

For serious students of Machiavelli, the *Discourses on Livy*—the full title of the book is actually *Discourses on the First Ten Books of Titus Livy*—has always been considered his most important work. In part because of its length and the organization of its subject matter, it is not read nearly so frequently as *The Prince*. In fact the relation between the two books has been something of an enigma for generations of readers.

The Prince was published in 1513, the year after Machiavelli was expelled from public office. The date of the *Discourses* is more difficult to establish. The best guess is that it was written sometime between the years 1513 and 1517, although it was not published until 1531, four years after Machiavelli's death. Even so, he seems to have been working on both books simultaneously. In the second chapter of *The Prince*, he makes what seems to be an allusion to the *Discourses*. He remarks that *The Prince* will deal only with principalities and that he has saved his discussion of republics for elsewhere. That is commonly believed to be a reference to the *Discourses*.

Machiavelli's statement here tells us something about the subject matter of the two books. *The Prince* follows the genre of the mirror of princes. It is a manual on how to achieve and maintain princely power. The *Discourses* is commonly regarded as Machiavelli's book on republics. It takes the form of a historical and political commentary on the first ten books of Livy's history of Rome, *Ab Urbe Condita*. Livy was widely regarded as the greatest of the Roman historians. He told the history of Rome from its founding—actually, its numerous foundings—to the establishment of the republic and the height of its power. He did not dwell (as he might have) on the descent of the republic into civil war and the transition from the republic to the monarchy under the emperors (although he wrote during the reign of Augustus). Livy's history was always regarded as the Bible of republican government. Machiavelli, in choosing to present his teaching by means of a commentary on the greatest Roman historian, calls the reader's attention to the greatness, the unsurpassable greatness, of Rome. Anyone who wants to understand greatness must understand Rome. Machiavelli's turn to Rome, and especially to the history of the republic, is a signal that he sides with the ancients against the moderns and the republic against princely rule.

The Two Dedications

The difference between *The Prince* and the *Discourses* is further indicated by the dedications of the two books. *The Prince* is dedicated to Lorenzo de Medici. Machiavelli begins by noting that it is customary for a man of low station to dedicate his work to a person of high station. The *Discourses* by contrast is dedicated to two young friends of Machiavelli's—Zanobi Buondelmonti and Cosimo Rucellai—who he says have "forced" him to write the book that he would never have written of his own accord. In what way, we wonder, was Machiavelli forced? These two young men were part of a literary circle to which Machiavelli belonged.[14] More important than who they were is what they represent. Sociologically, they were members of the grandi—the aristocracy—and as such the future members of the Florentine ruling class. Machiavelli's audience was composed of young men like Buondelmonti and Rucellai, cultured aristocrats who frequented the social gatherings in the great houses of the Italian cities, who gathered for discussions in the court of Lorenzo, and who attended productions of Roman and contemporary plays in the Orti Oricellari (Rucellai Gardens), which have been compared to the Platonic Academy. It was, apparently, under the trees in these gardens that Machiavelli first read sections of his tribute to republics to his Medicean audience!

Yet something seems amiss. Machiavelli is writing a book in praise of republics but dedicates it to two members of the aristocracy, who by their birth, education, and upbringing were bound to be deeply hostile to the cause of republican government. To be sure, Machiavelli's best friends were members of this class. The two best known were his friend Francesco Vettori, the Florentine ambassador to Rome with whom he shared a lengthy correspondence, and the historian Francesco Guicciardini. What was he trying to accomplish? What seems clear is that he intended the *Discourses* as a kind of educational treatise for these young aristocrats. He presents himself as a teacher, an educator. The length and academic form of the work—a commentary on an ancient historian—would presumably have appealed to the two young Florentine humanists. In any case Machiavelli knows how to flatter his readers: "I have chosen to dedicate these, my discourses, to you in preference to all others; both because, in doing so, I seem to be showing some gratitude for benefits received, and also because I seem in this to be departing from the usual practice of authors, which has always been to dedicate their works to some prince and blinded by ambition and avarice, to praise him for all his virtuous qualities when they ought to have blamed him for all manner of shameful deeds" (Dedication/201–2).

In his dedication Machiavelli seems to be engaged in an act of self-criticism, repudiating his dedication of *The Prince* to Lorenzo. "So to avoid this mistake," he continues, "I have chosen not those who are princes, but those . . . who deserve to be . . . those who know how to govern a kingdom, not those who, without knowing how, actually govern one" (Dedication/202). Machiavelli enjoys underscoring the youth of his audience. In fact book 1 of the *Discourses* ends with a reference to "very young men" who won triumphs for Rome. In the dedication and throughout the book, Machiavelli presents himself as a guide to the young.

Of course, Machiavelli exaggerates. If the young readers to whom the work is dedicated already knew how to govern a kingdom, then his act of writing the *Discourses* would appear superfluous. You don't write a book of this length to tell people what they already know. Machiavelli insinuates himself into his readers' good graces in order to gain their confidence. His purpose, I want to suggest, is to win over this class to the cause of republicanism, to show them the well-ordered republic so that they might create the republic that might yet be. The *Discourses* brings out Machiavelli's ambition and idealism. His desire is nothing less than to create a new Rome.

"New Modes and Orders"

Machiavelli hopes to whet his readers' appetite for Rome in the Preface to the *Discourses*. This is where he famously announces his discovery of "new modes and orders." He compares himself to Columbus in a search for "new seas and unknown lands" and boasts that he has entered upon "a new way as yet untrodden by anyone else" (Preface/205). But it turns out that Machiavelli's nautical image is the discovery not exactly of a wholly unknown land but rather of a forgotten land, a land that time has forgotten. This new land is Rome.

Machiavelli knows this claim will seem strange. He lives in a time—the Renaissance—and place—Florence—saturated with antiquity. The humanists of Machiavelli's time were themselves imbued with love of the ancients. In order, then, to distinguish himself, Machiavelli contrasts his approach to the ancients to the aestheticizing tendency of his contemporaries in order to return his readers to the first principles of the Roman republic. Rather than praising dilettantes who collect fragments of Roman statuary to adorn their houses and gardens, Machiavelli points his readers to the actual deeds of the Romans as related by Livy: "When I notice that what history has to say about the highly virtuous actions performed by ancient kingdoms and republics, by their kings, their generals, their citizens, their legislators, and by others who have worn themselves out in their country's service, is rather admired than imitated; nay, is so shunned by everybody in each little thing they do, that of the virtue of bygone days there remains no trace, it cannot but fill me at once with astonishment and grief" (Preface/205–6).

Machiavelli's sarcasm is obvious. What interests his contemporaries about Rome, he implies, is its artistic style—its art and architecture. In focusing on matters of what we would call art history, they forget the most vital and important lessons, that is, the political lessons. It is important to return to Rome today, Machiavelli says, because our capacity for self-government has undergone degeneration. The moderns are inferior to the ancients in precisely those qualities that contribute to freedom. Machiavelli attributes this decline in part to Christianity, but even more to a degeneration in the art of reading. His book will be a reading lesson—a very long reading lesson—addressed to those who lack "a proper appreciation of history, owing to people failing to realize the significance of what they read, and to their having no taste for the delicacies it comprises. Hence it comes about that the great bulk of those who read it take pleasure in hearing of the various incidents that are contained in it, but never think of imitating them, since they hold them to be not merely difficult but impossible of imitation, as if the heavens, the sun, the elements of man had in their motion, their order, and their potency, become different from what they used to be" (Preface/206).

Machiavelli wants to encourage his readers not just to idly and eclectically reflect on what they read but to actively imitate the great deeds of their ancient ancestors. It is this, he says, that has led him to write a commentary on Livy. Indeed, to do full justice to the *Discourses* one would need to read with constant reference to Livy and to Machiavelli's many other sources. To be sure, the *Discourses* is no ordinary commentary. Machiavelli uses Livy promiscuously, and for long stretches of time he disappears altogether from Machiavelli's text. He hopes to improve upon Livy and therefore to improve upon Rome. Machiavelli will not confine himself to the study of his ancient sources alone but will constantly be "comparing ancient with modern events" in order to draw "practical lessons" from them. Let us consider some of these lessons.

Republics Ancient and Modern

The paradox at the heart of the *Discourses* is that Machiavelli's claim to novelty—his nautical image of the discovery of new lands—is actually a recovery of ancient modes and orders. How does Machiavelli make something very old appear to be new and unprecedented? One answer is that he uses Livy—a respected and respectable authority—as a means to advocate for his own views on what constitutes a well-ordered republic. He hides behind Livy's authority in order to give himself the sheen of respectability and therefore takes full advantage of the immunity of the commentator. There are four features, I want to suggest, that constitute the novelty of Machiavelli's republic and that bear some marked resemblances to our own.

The *Discourses* begins with a reflection on whether it is preferable for a regime to be established by a single lawgiver or to grow haphazardly over time. The model for the former is Sparta, whose laws and constitution were given by a single man, Lycurgus, and remained intact for eight centuries. The latter model, the regime that is the product of chance—or fortuna, in Machiavelli's language—is Rome, which lacked a single founder and was forced to refound and adapt itself to circumstances as they arose. Machiavelli presents this as something of a debate, considering the pros and cons of each side. Yet contrary to expectation, he draws a surprising conclusion: "In spite of the fact that Rome had no Lycurgus to give it at the outset such a constitution as would ensure to it a long life of freedom, yet owing to friction between the plebs and the senate, so many things happened that chance effected what had not been provided by a law-giver. So that, if Rome did not get fortune's first gift, it got its second. For her early institutions, though defective, were not on wrong lines and so might pave the way to perfection" (I.2/215).

The claim that Rome achieved its longevity and freedom not thanks to conscious design but as a consequence of chance and luck merely paves the way for Machiavelli's most daring and arresting thesis. It is the claim that conflict, not consensus, was what contributed most to the greatness of Rome. Not unity but disunity gave Rome its strength. Machiavelli is above all a theorist of social conflict—of class conflict—which he treats, when it is kept within bounds, as a positive good.

Machiavelli remained deeply controversial for his rejection of the model of class consensus or harmony so beloved by the humanists of his time. He returns to this theme again in book 1, chapter 4: "To me those who condemn the quarrels between the nobles and the plebs, seem to be cavilling about the very things that were the primary cause of Rome's retaining her freedom, and that they pay more attention to the noise and clamor resulting from such commotions than to what resulted from them. . . . Nor do they realize that in every republic there are two different dispositions, that of the plebs and that of the nobles and that all legislation favorable to liberty is brought about by the clash between them" (I.4/218; translation modified).

This passage makes two important points. The first goes back to Machiavelli's statement in *The Prince* always to look at "the effectual truth of things." It is consequences that count, and one should not be misled by other considerations. And second, conflict is rooted deeply in human psychology, in the two "humors" or dispositions, the desire of the nobles to rule and dominate and the desire of the plebs to be free. National strength and greatness are the outcome of a clash of these opposing dispositions, not of some specious appeal to consensus. *All* politics is for Machiavelli *partisan* politics. Consensus is a fraud. Appeals to consensus are just a smokescreen for the dominance of one class. Human life is essentially an inescapable conflict. To claim that people can rise above partisanship and all embrace some idea of the common good is one of those pleasing illusions that belong to "principalities in the air." The aim of politics should not be to eliminate conflict but to organize it and make it serve the cause of national greatness.

The second major claim of the *Discourses* is introduced in book 1, chapter 5, in a debate over what Machiavelli calls the "guardianship" of liberty. He asks, is power better entrusted to the people or to the nobles? Once again, he sets up the question as a debate and presents arguments from both sides. Sparta and Venice are republics that have followed the aristocratic model, lodging power within the hands of the nobility. There are good reasons for them to do this. The nobles are the class that most desire to rule, so giving them political power satisfies this desire. Also, giving power to the nobles offsets the restlessness of the plebs, who are notoriously agitated and fickle. Rome, on the other hand, is the example of a republic where power was concentrated in the plebs. It was above all the power of the people that contributed to the greatness of Rome. Although Sparta may have lasted longer, it was Rome that demonstrated greater virtue. Machiavelli sets himself firmly on the side of Rome.

Machiavelli's preference for the plebs—the common people—is perhaps a first in political theory.[15] Unlike the Aristotelian model of the *politeia*, or constitutional government that sought a balance of the different factions or classes, Machiavelli clearly favors the dominance of what Aristotle calls the *demos*. The people, Machiavelli believes, are the most reliable support of liberty. The Aristotlelian balanced constitution has become with Machiavelli a democratic republic. Machiavelli returns to this theme near the end of book 1 of the *Discourses*. In chapter 55 he defends republics that have established a wide degree of social equality. He goes on a tear against the nobles, who "live in idleness on their abundant revenue derived from their estates" and perform no essential labor for the republic (I.55/335). Such a class is a drain on the republic and should be eliminated. In other words, occasional purges are necessary to keep the republic pure—a lesson later adopted by the French and Russian revolutionaries who instituted bloody purges of those deemed to be "enemies of the people." This is surely one of Machiavelli's most bloodthirsty moments.

This argument is further developed in book 1, chapter 58, entitled "The Multitude Is Wiser and More Constant Than the Prince." Here Machiavelli sets out his differences with Livy. Where Livy had said that the people are the most inconstant faction, Machiavelli stands this on its head. "I propose to defend a position that all writers attack," he declares (I.58/341). Having just declared himself in favor of a bloody purge of the nobles in chapter 55, he now proclaims: "There can be no harm in defending an opinion by arguments so long as one has no intention of appealing either to authority or force" (I.58/341). It is odd that in a book designed to help us become better readers, Machiavelli seems to assume here that we have forgotten what he said just a few pages before!

Machiavelli's arguments in defense of a democratic republic develop what he says in chapter 9 of *The Prince,* where he calls the people more "decent" than the prince. The people as a whole—not as any particular individual or group—reveal better judgment, more prudence, than a prince. Machiavelli develops arguments that attribute great foresight and intelligence to the people. When two speakers with equal rhetorical gifts are advocating for different positions, he asserts, the people never fail to make the right choice. I am not sure what evidence there is to support this claim. Machiavelli remarks that in the entire history of Rome, only four times—he does not say which four—did the people have cause to repent their decisions (I.58/344). Further, it is far easier to corrupt a single individual ruler than the great body of the people. In short, the people are more reliable and better judges of character than a prince. And finally, Machiavelli is prepared to excuse the brutalities of the people because, he says, they are more likely to be directed against the enemies of the republic, while the brutalities of a prince are directed against his private enemies (I.58/345).

There is one further feature of Machiavelli's democratic republic that is worth noting. This is the Roman institution of public indictments (I.7/227–30). These were similar to people's courts, where those accused of conspiring against the public good would have to defend themselves. Machiavelli approves the Roman practice of bringing public accusations against citizens deemed to be enemies of the people. This sounds more than a little like the practice of public denunciations during Mao's Cultural Revolution or the infamous "show trials" under Stalin. Machiavelli approves this as an outlet for venting public hostility and also as a tool for keeping the aristocracy in check. He criticizes modern Florence for lacking such an institution, which leaves no means of chastising ambitious citizens. Note that Machiavelli says nothing about the possible injustice of such indictments. He will gladly sacrifice one person—recall Remirro d'Orco from *The Prince*—if it brings satisfaction to the many. In Rome public indictments were a weapon of the plebs against the rich and powerful and a chief outlet for what Machiavelli calls the "malignant humors"—jealousy, resentment, envy—to which all of us are prone.

This brings us to the fourth feature of Machiavelli's republic. In book 1, chapter 6, Machiavelli sets out another point for the reader to consider: "Should anyone be about to set up a republic, he should first inquire whether it is to expand, as Rome did, both in dominion and in power, or is to be confined to narrow limits" (I.6/225). Traditionally, republics were understood to be small, self-contained city-states. Aristotle, recall, had praised the city that could be "taken in at a glance." A large state undercuts the ethos necessary for political participation and civic engagement; it also encourages luxury that tends toward corruption. Machiavelli even admits that if your concern is longevity, you should follow the Spartan and Venetian models.

But after appearing to endorse the city-state model that he associated with aristocratic predominance, Machiavelli immediately goes on to undercut it. The goal of Rome was not simply longevity but greatness, and greatness is only possible with a policy of imperial expansion and conquest. Machiavelli's republic is a republic on the march. His point is connected with the republic's ability to control its own environment. All cities have enemies and live in the domain of fortuna; to adopt a purely defensive posture is to render oneself vulnerable to attack from others. One should therefore follow the policy of the Romans, who resolved upon empire as a means of conquering their environment and thus rendering themselves immune to the winds of fortune. They achieved this first of all by arming the plebs, which contributed to Rome's military greatness. Arming the plebs was the source of continual tumult and dissension, but it was also the source of glory and power.

Machiavelli defends this claim with a kind of ontological argument about the nature of political reality. We live in a world of flux. States of affairs are in constant change, and the fortunes of nations constantly go up and down. A state that seeks merely to preserve itself thus risks disaster. There is no perfect balance or stable point of equilibrium to be found; therefore one has to grow and expand in order to survive. States must expand their power or face ruin—it's that simple.

Machiavelli concludes this part of his discussion as follows: "Since it is impossible, so I hold, to adjust the balance so nicely as to keep things exactly to this middle course, one ought, in constituting a republic, to consider the possibility of its playing a more honorable role, and so to constitute it that, should necessity actually force it to expand, it may be able to retain possession of what it has acquired. . . . I am convinced the Roman type of constitution should be adopted and not that of any other republic, for to find a middle way between the extremes, I do not think possible" (I.6/226–27).

Machiavelli's dismissive reference here to the "middle course" is a clear reference to Aristotle and his policy of seeking the mean or the moderate course of action. As Machiavelli suggests here, moderation is not possible in a world characterized by constant flux, because there is no stable point of equilibrium from which to measure the mean. His advice: a republic must either expand or die. Does Machiavelli's contentious, large-scale, imperialistic republic sound familiar? It should, because Machiavelli is describing us.

The New Christianity

We cannot leave the *Discourses* without a word about religion—a theme that Machiavelli alludes to several times throughout the book. In the Preface he blames Christianity—he calls it "the religion of today" (what about tomorrow?)—for abetting the weakness and disunity of present-day Italy. He also refers to the evils brought about by ambition mixed with idleness, a standard form of reference to priests and their influence (Preface/206). Much of his language is that of a religious reformer—sometimes a radical reformer—much like his German contemporary Martin Luther. Yet there is a difference—a big difference.

Machiavelli is a great admirer of Numa Pompilius, the founder of the pagan religion of ancient Rome.[16] "The religion established by Numa," he writes at I.11, "was among the primary causes of Rome's success." What was it that Machiavelli admired? He freely acknowledges that the religion founded by Numa was a kind of fraud created to establish political virtue. Numa "pretended to have private conferences with a nymph who advised him about the advice he should give the people. This was because he wanted to introduce new institutions to which the city was unaccustomed and doubted whether his own authority would suffice" (I.11/241). In short, political innovation requires that it be shrouded in the mystique of divine authority.

The religion created by Numa is contrasted with what Machiavelli calls in the next chapter "our religion" (I.12/244). He begins this chapter by acknowledging—or pretending to acknowledge—the authority of existing religion. It is important that the prince or rulers of a republic or a monarchy uphold the principles of the religion of their state. Machiavelli takes a position of apparent neutrality toward the content of any particular religion; it is important that those in positions of political authority practice the established religion. He goes on to contrast this with the way that Christianity has historically evolved from its original teachings. "If such a religious spirit had been kept up by the rulers of the Christian commonwealth or as was ordained for us by its founder, Christian states and republics would have been much more united and much more happy than they are" (I.12/244). The cause of political decline, he says in the next sentence, can be laid at the doorstep of the Church of Rome. It is the church, more than any other institution, that has kept Italy weak and divided. "The reason why Italy is not in the same position," he continues, "why there is not one republic or one prince ruling there is due entirely to the Church" (I.12/245). So far Machiavelli sounds like a critic of papal abuses of power, a complaint quite common and even conventional in his day.

It is not until considerably later that Machiavelli lets the cat out of the bag. In book 2, chapter 2, he asks the question, why it is that the ancients seemed more fond of liberty than the moderns? The difference, he answers, is due to the difference between our religion and theirs. It is not the corruption of Christianity that is responsible for the loss of liberty and the disunity of Italy; the problem goes back to the founding principles themselves. Machiavelli then goes on to provide a sharp and devastating series of contrasts: "Our religion has glorified humble and contemplative men, rather than men of action. It has assigned as man's highest good humility, abnegation, and contempt for mundane things, whereas the other identified it with magnanimity, bodily strength, and everything else that conduces to make men very bold. And if our religion demands that in you there be strength, what it asks for is strength to suffer rather than strength to do bold things" (II.2/364). Here is where Machiavelli drops his bombshell:

> This pattern of life, therefore, appears to have made the world weak, and to have handed it over as a prey to the wicked, who run it successfully and securely since they are well aware that the generality of men, with paradise for their goal, consider how best to bear, rather than how best to avenge, their injuries. But, though it looks as if the world were become effeminate and as if heaven were powerless, this undoubtedly is due to the pusillanimity of those who have interpreted our religion according to idleness [*l'ozio*] and not in terms of virtue. For, had they borne in mind that religion permits us to exalt and defend the fatherland, they would have seen that it also wishes us to love and honor it, and to train ourselves to be such that we may defend it. (II.2/364; translation modified)

What is Machiavelli saying here, and why does he wait until almost the midpoint in the book to announce it? What does he want us to do? Rather than simply advocating the reform of Christianity, he seems to be advocating the creation of a wholly new religion to replace it, in the way that Christianity once replaced the pagan Roman religion. The founder of a new republic needs to be the founder of a new religion; he should follow the example of Numa and create new rites and ceremonies from scratch. He will be a transformative, even a redemptive, leader such as Machiavelli speaks about in the final chapter of *The Prince*. But what would such a Machiavellian civil religion look like? Here Machiavelli is tantalizingly and, I suspect, deliberately obscure. One cannot legislate these matters in advance. This is why the founder needs constantly to read history: to see what others have done in the past so as to discover what to do and what to avoid and how to make not only a new Rome but a new Jerusalem.

Machiavellianism Comes of Age

Machiavelli's call for the replacement of Christianity by some kind of fortified paganism did not fall on deaf ears. His most obvious disciples were those who followed the "Erastian" creed of submitting religion to political control. The most famous—or infamous—of these Erastians was Thomas Hobbes, who in both his *De Cive* and his *Leviathan* defended the proposition that religion is simply too important to be left to the priests. It must be put under secular authority. Hobbes's goal, as we will see in the next chapter, was to establish religion on such a footing that it could not interfere with the requirements of political order.

Yet the most ferocious Machiavellian of all was Rousseau. We have already seen how Rousseau, like Spinoza, interpreted Machiavelli as providing a satire on monarchy and an esoteric defense of democracy. In the final chapter of *The Social Contract,* he takes up Machiavelli's unanswered question, "What kind of religion can best serve republican government?" Like Machiavelli, and almost all who went before him, Rousseau accepted the sociological fact that "no state has ever been founded without religion serving as its base" (IV.8/146). He takes for granted the power or muscle of religion to serve as the foundation of political morality. But what kind of religion will this be? Rousseau contrasted the various polytheisms of the Greek and Roman world with the universalist monotheisms that emerged first with Judaism and later with Christianity and Islam. The pagan religions of the ancients drew no distinction between their gods and their laws. Religion could serve as a force of national strength and unity. It was also relatively tolerant, since the power of the gods extended only as far as the city walls. Even the Romans were inclined to leave peoples' gods intact, a point with which the Jerusalemites might have taken issue. All of this changed, so Rousseau argues, with the introduction of Christianity.

Christianity was the first religion to offer itself as a purely "spiritual" kingdom apart from politics. Rousseau even has some kind words for Islam: "Muhammad had very sound views" in tying his system of law (*Sharia*) to his form of government. But Christianity introduced a conflict of jurisdictions between church and state, which will forever be at odds with each other. Rather than a source of unity, Christianity became a source of conflict, and religion became dominated by priests who would use it to advance their own interests. Although he recognizes that the pure religion of the Gospels contains teachings that are "saintly" and "sublime," these are not fit for men in society. "We are told," he writes, "that a people of true Christians would form the most perfect society imaginable. I see only one major difficulty with this supposition; which is that a society of true Christians would no longer be a society of men" (IV.8/148). He goes on to explain this point: "Christianity is a wholly spiritual religion, exclusively concerned with the things of Heaven: the Christian's fatherland is not of this world. He does his duty, it is true, but he does it with profound indifference to the success or failure of his efforts. . . . True Christians are made to be slaves; they know it and are hardly moved by it; this brief life has too little value in their eyes" (IV.8/148–49).

Rousseau's attack on "the religion of the priest" was the reason why *The Social Contract* was burned in his home city of Geneva. Nonetheless, the attack on "the domineering spirit of Christianity" as a cause of political conflict was widely heralded by the French revolutionaries as a basis for their new cults and rituals. These experiments with a religion of reason were short-lived, but in fact these often became in a modified form the foundation of the nationalisms of the nineteenth century, with their worship of the nation, *la patrie*, and the fatherland. The nation and the sovereignty of the people, as Tocqueville later saw, became substitutes for religion, or the place where religion managed to live on in a kind of ghostly half-life. Rousseau's civil religion, which is nothing more than Machiavellianism come of age, survives today in many of the debates over the secular identity of France and its resistance to efforts—think of the debate over Muslim women wearing head scarves—by religion to intrude into public life.

Machiavelli's dream of a new political religion that would surpass or supplant the revealed religions of the past was not confined to France. In 1967 the American sociologist Robert Bellah revived this debate in a groundbreaking article called "Civil Religion in America."[17] "What we have from the earliest years of the republic," Bellah wrote, "is a collection of beliefs, symbols, and rituals with respect to sacred things and institutionalized in a collectivity. This religion—there seems no other word for it—while not antithetical to and indeed sharing much in common with Christianity, was neither sectarian nor in any specific sense Christian."[18] This might be called the domestication of Rousseau's ferocious Machiavellianism. Americans, Bellah claimed, maintained a civil religion that retained key elements of the prophetic tradition but combined these with worship of the Constitution and reverence for the American Framers. "The American civil religion," he continued, "was never anticlerical or militantly secular. On the contrary, it borrowed selectively from the religious tradition in such a way that the average American saw no conflict between the two."[19]

There has been no greater avatar of this American civil religion than Abraham Lincoln. For him the Declaration of Independence and the Constitution were sacred texts, and Washington and Jefferson like the prophets who led their people out of tyranny. Nowhere does Lincoln give more passionate expression to this civil creed than in his 1838 address to the Young Men's Lyceum in Springfield, "The Perpetuation of Our Political Institutions." Shocked at the recent rise of lawlessness and the outbreaks of mob violence, Lincoln exhorted his listeners to reattach themselves to their form of government. But how to do this, he asked, at a time when the living connection to the revolution was fading, and the Founding was little more than a distant memory? His answer is as follows:

> Let every American, every lover of liberty, every well wisher to his posterity, swear by the blood of the Revolution, never to violate in the least particular, the laws of the country; and never to tolerate their violation by others. As the patriots of seventy-six did to the support of the Declaration of Independence, so to the support of the Constitution and Laws, let every American pledge his life, his property and his sacred honor;—let every man remember that to violate the law, is to trample on the blood of his father, and to tear the character of his own, and his children's liberty. Let reverence for the laws, be breathed by every American mother, to the lisping babe, that prattles on her lap—let it be taught in schools, in seminaries, and in colleges;—let it be written in Primmers, spelling books, and in Almanacs;—let it be preached from the pulpit, proclaimed in legislative halls, and enforced in courts of justice. And, in short, let it become the *political religion* of the nation; and let the old and the young, the rich and the poor, the grave and the gay, of all sexes and tongues, and colors and conditions, sacrifice unceasingly upon its altars.[20]

Lincoln's effort to enlist the power of religion in support of the Constitution and its laws has a distinctively Machiavellian ring to it. Religion is to be made instrumental to the cause of liberty and republican government. There is nothing here with which the great Florentine would have disagreed. Are we to conclude, then, that America is a Machiavellian nation? Yes and no. The idea of an American civil religion has always remained somewhat disreputable. America may be overwhelmingly a nation of Christians, but it is not and was not intended to be a Christian nation. The attempt to enlist religion for the cause of the nation has always struck thoughtful observers as a misuse both of religion and of the patriotic ideal. The American experience is no exception. A civil religion, however ennobling its goals, is less an expression of religion than a substitute for it.

CHAPTER 8

Hobbes's New Science of Politics

Thomas Hobbes, 1588–1679. 1669. Oil on canvas. Portrait by
John Michael Wright (1617–1700). Photo credit: bpk, Berlin/
Christ's College, Oxford / Lutz Braun / Art Resource, NY

Thomas Hobbes was the author of the first and still the greatest work of political philosophy in the English language. His work virtually created the idiom of Anglophone, political theory. One could compare *Leviathan* with other English-language works like Locke's *Second Treatise of Government* and the *Federalist Papers,* but only Hobbes, as a writer, can be compared with writers such as Milton and Spenser without seeming manifestly foolish. He was a master of English prose, and his work ranks among the greatest achievements in this or any other language. *Leviathan* is an almost perfect book, and as Dr. Johnson said of Milton's *Paradise Lost*, no one ever wished it longer.[1]

Hobbes is the perfect foil for Machiavelli. He played the role of Mr. Hyde to Machiavelli's Dr. Jekyll. He carried out and recorded what Machiavelli made possible. Machiavelli had discovered a new continent; Hobbes helped to make it habitable. Machiavelli cleared the brush; Hobbes built the houses and institutions. Hobbes provided the definitive language in which we even today have come to think about the modern state.

Hobbes has always been something of a paradox to his readers. On the one hand, he is the most articulate defender of political absolutism. The Hobbesian sovereign is to have a complete monopoly of power within his given territory. The frontispiece of *Leviathan* depicts the majesty of the sovereign with a sword in one hand and a scepter in the other holding sway over a peaceable kingdom. Add to the doctrine of indivisible power Hobbes's insistence that the sovereign exercise control over the churches, the university curriculum, and what books and opinions can be read and taught. Hobbes seems the perfect model of absolute government. Yet on the other hand, Hobbes insists on the fundamental equality of all human beings, who are endowed with certain natural rights (at least the right to self-preservation); he maintains that the state is the product of a covenant or social contract between individuals; that the sovereign owes his authority to the will or consent of those he governs; and that the sovereign is authorized only to protect the interests of the governed by maintaining civil peace and security. From this point of view Hobbes helps to establish the language of the liberal opposition to absolutism. This paradox was noted in Hobbes's own time. Was he a royalist or an opponent of royalism?

To be sure, Hobbes was a product of his time. What else could he be? Hobbes lived in an age when the modern system of European states as we still have them today was just beginning to emerge. Three years before the publication of *Leviathan,* the signing of the Treaty of Westphalia in 1648 brought to an end more than a century of religious wars that had been ignited by the

Protestant Reformation. The treaty of Westphalia officially ended the Thirty Years' War, and it ratified two decisive agreements that would be given expression by Hobbes: first, the treaty declared that the individual sovereign state would henceforth become the highest level of government, thus putting an end to the claim of the Holy Roman Empire to exercise a universal monarchy; and second, the treaty declared that all parties would recognize the principle of *cuius regio, eius religio,* that the head of each state would have the right to determine the religion of the state, thus putting an end to the claims of a single universal church.

Hobbes was born in 1588, the year that the English naval forces drove back the Spanish Armada. He grew up in the waning years of the Elizabethan era and was a boy when Shakespeare's plays were first performed. He was a gifted student of classical languages and attended Oxford. After graduation he entered the service of the aristocratic Cavendish family and became a private tutor to their son. His first published work was a translation of the Greek historian Thucydides that he completed in 1629. Hobbes spent considerable time with the young Cavendish on the European continent, where he met Galileo and Descartes. It was during the 1640s that civil war broke out in England. Hobbes left England to live in France while the fighting went on. There he was a member of an important circle of English émigrés during the war and served as tutor to the future King Charles II. He was deeply distressed by the outbreak of war and spent time reflecting on the causes of war and disorder. His book *De Cive—On the Citizen*—was published in 1642 and was a kind of draft version of *Leviathan.* Hobbes returned to England in 1651, the same year *Leviathan* was published, and spent most of the rest of his life working on scientific and political problems. He wrote a history of the English Civil War called *Behemoth,* which remains a classic analysis of the causes of social conflict. Near the end of his life he published translations of Homer's *Iliad* and *Odyssey.* He died in 1679 at the age of ninety-one.

Despite the fierce reputation of his work, portraits and descriptions of Hobbes show he was a man of considerable charm and wit. John Aubrey, Hobbes's earliest biographer, tells several stories he must have heard from Hobbes himself or his acquaintances that depict him as a man who enjoyed life, the company of men (and women), and good wines (in moderation) and had a sly sense of humor. Hobbes was a man of paradoxes. He held a notoriously low view of human nature yet seems to have gone through life with great wit and humor. He emphasized the salutary uses of fear yet seems to have exhibited little himself. He could deny that we have access to the ultimate foundations of knowledge yet steadily affirmed his own views on the human world to be true. He routinely debunked the language of virtue but dedicated his book to a man named Sidney Godolphin, of whom he wrote: "There is not any virtue that disposeth a man to civil society or private friendship that did not manifestly appear in [the] generous constitution of his nature" (Letter Dedicatory). How to square this particular circle?

Hobbes was deeply controversial in his own time. *Leviathan* was immediately excoriated by all. To the churchmen he seemed a godless atheist; to the republicans he was tainted by monarchy; and to the monarchists he was a dangerous skeptic and freethinker. Hobbes was, along with Machiavelli, the chief architect of the modern state. In some respects he seems even more characteristically modern than Machiavelli. Machiavelli speaks of the "prince," while Hobbes speaks of the "sovereign," an impersonal or, in Hobbes's language, "artificial" power created out of a contract. Hobbes's method seems scientific, formal, and analytical in contrast to Machiavelli's combination of historical commentary and reflection drawn from experience. While Machiavelli had spoken of the sublime cruelty of men like Borgia and Hannibal, Hobbes speaks the more pedestrian, and more modern, language of power politics, where the goal is not glory but self-preservation. Further, Machiavelli's emphasis on arms is significantly amended by Hobbes's emphasis on laws. Hobbes tried to render Machiavelli acceptable by providing a more precise legal and institutional framework for the state.

Hobbes's New Political Science

Hobbes was intensely aware of himself as an innovator. Like Machiavelli, who claimed that he was the first to examine the "effectual truth" of things, Hobbes once boasted that "civil science is no older than my *De Cive*."[2] What, precisely, did Hobbes regard as so novel about his approach?

Hobbes saw himself as the founder of a new political science modeled along the lines of other early founders of the scientific revolution—Galileo, Harvey, and Descartes. Like these other revolutionaries, who overthrew the older Aristotelian paradigm in natural science, Hobbes set out to undermine Aristotle's authority in political science. He set himself up as the great anti-Aristotle. Consider the following passage from a chapter entitled "Of Darkness from Vain Philosophy and Fabulous Traditions": "There is nothing so absurd that the old philosophers . . . have not some of them maintained. And I believe that scarce anything can be more absurdly said in natural philosophy than that which now is called Aristotle's *Metaphysics*;

nor more repugnant to government than much of that he hath said in his *Politics;* nor more ignorantly than a great part of his *Ethics*" (XLVI, 11). What was it, exactly, that Hobbes claimed to find so absurd, repugnant, and ignorant?

Hobbes is especially concerned with the foundations or building blocks of his new science. He was very self-conscious about what today would be called "methodology." Aristotle started by stressing the limits of political knowledge. The subject matter of politics—human actions— allows of such variety and irregularity that we cannot expect the kind of strict knowledge that one might find in the natural or the mathematical sciences. In politics and ethics, Aristotle wrote, we must not ask for more certainty than the subject allows. It would be just as foolish to accept arguments of probability from a mathematician as to demand strict demonstrations from a rhetorician. He even suggests it is a sign of immaturity to demand great precision in matters political and ethical. Whatever general rules can be derived from politics will only be true provisionally or for the most part. Hobbes's approach begins almost literally with taking Aristotle to task. The failure of Aristotle's *Politics* and *Ethics* was a failure of methodology. Rather than remaining wedded to ordinary opinions—the *endoxa*—as did Aristotle, Hobbes will dissolve opinion—deconstruct it, in our terms—to derive a method that will guarantee strict theoretical knowledge.

The opening chapters of *Leviathan* present a kind of political physics where human beings are reduced to the body and the body is further reduced to so much matter in motion. Human beings can be reduced to their moveable parts, much like a machine. What is life, he asks rhetorically in the Introduction, but a motion of the limbs? What is the heart but a spring, and what is reason but a means of calculating pleasures and pains? Hobbes sets out to give a deliberately and thoroughly materialistic and nonteleological physics of human nature. A French disciple of Hobbes in the next century, a man named La Mettrie, wrote a book entitled *L'homme machine:* man, a machine.

Hobbes's beginning in *Leviathan* seems designed to offer an alternative to Aristotle's in the *Politics.* Aristotle argues that all human action is goal directed. All actions aim at preservation or change, at making something better or preventing it from becoming worse. Hobbes believed that the overriding human impulse is largely negative, not the desire to do some good but the desire to avoid some evil. Aristotle had simply seen the matter through the wrong end of the telescope. For Aristotle, human beings have a goal or telos, that is, to live in a community with others for the sake of human flourishing; for Hobbes we enter society not to fulfill or perfect our rational nature but to avoid the greatest evil, namely, death at the hands of others. Politics is for him less a matter of prudential decisions of better and worse than of the existential decision of life or death. For Hobbes, as for Machiavelli, it is the extreme situation of life and death, chaos and war, that serves as the norm for politics.

Furthermore, Hobbes blamed Aristotle—or his influence in the universities—as responsible for much of the civil conflict of his age. Aristotle had taught that man is by nature a political animal. This was the thesis of what could be called classical republicanism, according to which we only become fully human when we are engaged in political life, ruling ourselves by laws of our own making. It is precisely this desire to be self-governing, to rule ourselves directly, that Hobbes saw as one of the great root causes of civil war. It was the desire to be a free, self-legislating people, he believed, that led to the execution of one king and the exile of another.

Hobbes's answer to Aristotle and classical republicanism was the doctrine of indirect rule or, as we would call it today, representative government. The sovereign is not the people, or some faction of the people, ruling directly in their collective capacity; it is rather the artificially reconstructed will of the people in the person of their representative. The sovereign representative acts like a filter for the wills and passions of the people. The sovereign is not the direct expression of my will but an abstraction from my natural desire to rule myself. Instead of seeking to participate directly in political rule, Hobbes wants us to abstain from politics by agreeing with others to be ruled by an "artificial man" or representative called the sovereign: "For by art," Hobbes writes, "is created that great Leviathan called a Commonwealth, or State, which is but an artificial man, though of greater stature and strength, than the natural for whose protection and defense it was intended" (Introduction, 1).

Hobbes's use of the term "art" in this passage is deeply revealing of his purpose. By art he means something like *technique* or political making. For Aristotle, art presupposes nature; nature supplies not only the materials but also the models for all of the arts. For Hobbes, however, art does not so much imitate nature as create a new kind of nature, an artificial person, as it were. Through art properly understood we can begin to transform nature. We can have a science of politics because we are the makers of political life. The function of art is not mimetic or imitative but transformative; its aim is the creation of a new nature. Art is not understood here as the opposite of science. To the contrary: science is the highest form of art. By art Hobbes here understands what he calls reason or science. These are the fullest expression of human art or making,

Hobbes draws a sharp distinction between Aristotelian prudence and his own understanding of a science of politics: "Reason," he writes, "is not as sense and memory born with us, nor gotten by experience only, but attained by industry, first in apt imposing of names and secondly by getting a good and orderly method in proceeding from the elements, which are names, to assertions made by connexion of one of them to another, and so to syllogisms, which are the connexions of one assertion to another, till we come to a knowledge of all the consequences of names appertaining to the subject in hand; and that is it men call Science" (V, 17). Science consists in the imposition of a method for the conquest of nature. By science, he tells us, he means "the knowledge of consequences," especially "when we see how anything comes about, upon what causes and by what manner, when the like causes come into our power, we see how to make it produce the like effects" (V, 17).

This is why it is misleading to call Hobbes a "materialist." He believes that reason (or science) can play a causal role in the transformation of the human condition. Reason is not just about observation but about making or, as he says, how to make like consequences produce the desired effects. We can have a science of politics, Hobbes believes, because politics is a matter of human doings, of human goings-on, and we can know only what we make. His goal here is to liberate knowledge from subservience to or dependence on nature by turning science into a tool for remaking nature to fit our needs. Art—especially the political art—is a matter of reordering nature, including human nature, first by resolving it into its most elementary units, then reconstructing it in a way that will produce the desired results. This is Hobbes's answer to Machiavelli's call to master *fortuna*. But Hobbes goes further than Machiavelli. Machiavelli believed that even under optimal conditions the prince could only expect to conquer fortune about half of the time. Hobbes believes that armed with the proper method or art, we might ultimately become the masters and possessors of nature (XXIX, 1).

The State of Nature and the Problem of Authority

The central question of *Leviathan* is what makes authority possible. How can individuals who are biologically autonomous, who judge matters very differently from one another, who can never be sure whether they can trust one another—how can such individuals accept a common authority? Not just what constitutes authority but what makes this authority legitimate remains *the* question not only for Hobbes but for the entire social contract tradition that he began. Of course, the question of what makes authority possible only occurs at moments when authority is in question, when the rules governing authority have broken down.

Hobbes proposes to answer his question about authority by telling a story about what he calls the *state of nature,* a term he did not invent but will be forever associated with his name. The state of nature is not a state of grace from which we have fallen, nor is it a political condition as maintained by Aristotle. The state of nature is a condition of war or conflict. By a state of war Hobbes means a condition where there is no recognized authority to keep "all in awe." Such a condition may signify not only "battle" but, as he puts it, "the will to contend." A state of war can include what we might call a cold war, that is, a condition of constant preparedness for hostility. The state of nature is not necessarily a condition of actual fighting but consists in the "known disposition" to fight. Hobbes's description of this condition is stated in perhaps the most famous single sentence in the entire tradition of political philosophy: "In such a condition [the state of nature] there is no place for industry, because the fruit thereof is uncertain, and consequently, no culture of the earth, no navigation, nor use of the commodities that may be imported by sea, no commodious building, no instruments of moving and removing such things as require much force, no knowledge of the face of the earth, no account of time, no arts, no letters, no society, and which is worst of all, continual fear and danger of violent death and the life of man, solitary, poor, nasty, brutish, and short" (XIII, 9). All things being equal, Hobbes should perhaps have said "fortunately short."

Hobbes claims that the state of nature is the condition that we are all naturally in, that is to say, nature does not unite us in peace, harmony, and friendship. Only art or human contrivance can bring about peace. Conflict and war are primary; peace is derivative. In other words, authority and relations of authority do not arise naturally but are the products of human contrivance or will. We might ask ourselves, what makes Hobbes's story about the state of nature plausible?

From one point of view, Hobbes derives his theory of the state of nature from his physics of motion and rest, described in the opening chapters of *Leviathan.* He begins the work with an account of human nature as a product of sense and experience. We are bodies in motion that cannot help but obey the laws of attraction and repulsion. He seems to operate with a

kind of materialist physics in which human behavior exhibits the same me-
chanical tendencies as billiard balls and can be understood as obeying the
same processes of cause and effect. The state of nature is regarded not as an
actual historical condition but as a sort of thought experiment after the
manner of theoretical physics. It consists of taking human beings who are
members of families, estates, and kingdoms, dissolving these into their
fundamental units, namely, abstract individuals, and then imagining how
they would hypothetically interact with one another, like the properties of
chemical substances. Hobbes here seems to anticipate the modern experimental science of politics.

Skepticism and Individualism

The view of Hobbes as the founder of theoretical political science is not
necessarily wrong, but it is incomplete. Hobbes's view of human nature, I
would suggest, is characterized not so much by the term "mechanism" as by
the concept of individuality. He shows us what it is to exercise the qualities of
moral agency, to do for yourself rather than having things done for you. He
helped to introduce a new idiom of individuality into our moral vocabulary.
The concept of individuality seems quite natural to us, but it is in fact not
much older than the seventeenth century. Until the Renaissance—or not
much later—people considered themselves primarily not as individuals but
as members, members of a particular family, caste, guild, religious order, or
city. The idea that one is first of all an "I," an ego, or a self would have been
regarded as absurd. This new idea can be traced at least in part back to
Hobbes and a handful of other writers of his time. As late as the nineteenth
century Tocqueville could write: "Individualism is a recent expression
arising from a new idea."[3]

Hobbes's new conception of individuality stems from a process of
abstraction from the great complex web of attachments in which we find
ourselves. We are beings, he argues, whose fundamental characteristics are
willing and choosing. We are beings for whom the exercise of the will is preeminent, and a good deal of our happiness is connected with its exercise. Life
is an exercise in continual willing that may be temporarily interrupted but
can never come to an end except with the end of life itself. Hobbes's individualism is closely connected to his conception of human well-being as success
in the competition for the goods of life: "Continual success," he writes, "in
obtaining those things which a man from time to time desireth is what is
called happiness or felicity." "For there is no such thing," he continues, "as

perpetual tranquility of mind while we live here; because life itself is but motion and can never be without desire, nor without fear, no more than without
sense" (VI, 58).

Hobbes's individualism is not just a physical but also a moral condition. Because we are each individual bundles of activities and initiative, of
likes and dislikes, desires and aversions, life is a continual competition or
struggle, not just for scarce resources but also for honors and anything else
that a person might value or esteem. Hobbes is fascinated with the very diversity of human desires, that what leads one person to laughter leads another to tears, what leads one to piety leads another to ridicule, and so on.
Even moral terms like "good" and "evil," he writes, are simply expressions
of our likes and dislikes. We like something not because it is good; rather,
something is called good because we like it. These terms do not represent
some common quality or essential attribute but express the psychological
state of the person who uses them (VI, 7). It is from this general competition
for the various objects of our desires that Hobbes infers the natural condition is one of war. He posits in a famous passage "a general inclination of all
mankind, a perpetual and restless desire of power after power that ceases
only in death" (XI, 2).

What I have been calling Hobbes's individualism is supported by, is even
underwritten by, his moral skepticism. Like many of the great early modern
philosophers—Montaigne, Descartes, Spinoza—Hobbes was obsessed with
the question, "What can I know" or "What am I entitled to believe?" There
are many passages in *Leviathan* that testify to Hobbes's fundamentally skeptical view of knowledge. Hobbes is a skeptic in that he doubts that there is any
transcendent or nonhuman basis for our beliefs. This explains the importance he attributes to names and attaching the correct definition to things.
"For reason," he writes, "is nothing but reckoning, that is, adding and sub-
tracting of the consequences of general names agreed upon" (V, 2). Knowledge is in short a human construction and is always subject to what we can be
made to agree upon. If all knowledge ultimately rests on agreement about
shared terms—a philosophical stance known as nominalism—it follows that
human reason has no share in the divine, as Plato or Aristotle believed. It also
means that human knowledge does not have within it the spark of divinity;
nor does it testify to the inner voice of conscience or anything else that would
give it some indubitable foundation. Such certainty as we have is at best provisional, discovered on the basis of agreement and subject to continual revision.

This sense of skepticism has profound implications for Hobbes's views
on religion. Hobbes offers an entirely naturalistic account of religious belief.

"There are no signs or fruit of religion but in man only," Hobbes writes (XII, 1). The causes of religion can be traced back to the restlessness of the human mind, to its search for causes. It is because we are born ignorant of the causes of things that we are led to search out beginnings, and this leads us ultimately to posit the existence of a God who is the cause of all causes, so to speak. Hobbes did not deny the possibility of revelation or of the direct communication of God to any one of us. What he did deny was that this revelation gives anyone the right to impose his vision of God on anyone else because there is no way for anyone to verify the correctness of this communication. Did this make Hobbes an atheist? No, but it made him a skeptic.

It is because of this radical skepticism—a view of life as willing and choosing where there are no standards to adjudicate conflicts—that the central political question of *Leviathan* arises: What makes authority possible? How are people who are so separately and individually constituted capable of obeying common rules or having moral obligations to one another? Before answering this question, let us consider a little further Hobbes's account of the state of nature. The fact that the state of nature consists primarily of individuals is not to say that it is a state of isolation. People may have regular contact with one another in the state of nature, but their relations are unregulated; it is a condition of maximum insecurity. The emphasis on the individual is only a way of saying that no one has any natural authority over anyone else. Relations of authority exist only by consent or agreement.

The fact that relations in the state of nature are unregulated makes it a state of war of all against all. You might say that a state of war is the exception, not the rule, and that Hobbes bases his account of human nature on the state of the exception. But he is not saying that the state of war is one of permanent fighting; it is one of permanent fear and distrust. He asks the reader to consult his own "experience." Let me cite one of my favorite passages from the entire work:

> Let him therefore consider with himself—when taking a journey, he arms himself, and seeks to go well accompanied; when going to sleep, he locks his doors; when even in his house, he locks his chests; and this when he knows there be laws, and public officers, armed to revenge all injuries shall be done him—what opinion he has of his fellow subjects, when he rides armed; of his fellow citizens, when he locks his doors; and of his children and

servants, when he locks his chests. Does he not there as much accuse mankind by his actions, as I do by my words? (XIII, 10)

Finally, as this passage makes clear, it is wrong to think of the state of nature as some kind of primitive condition that existed in the ancient past. The state of nature exists even in civil society, whenever authority is not enforced or whenever we have reason to fear for the security of our lives or property. It is fear—fear of death, fear of disgrace, fear of failure—that is the most ubiquitous natural passion. Hobbes's political science plays to our fears because only fear can lead us from the state of nature to the civil condition. It is only the creation of a sovereign endowed with absolute authority that enables us to mitigate the fear and anxiety that are always present in the state of nature.

The Dialectic of Pride and Fear

Hobbes presents the state of nature as a condition of maximum insecurity and anxiety. How is it possible to escape this condition when there are no grounds for mutual trust or good will? Why should I lay down or give up my right to do whatever is in my power to protect myself when I have absolutely no expectation that others around me will do the same? This is a classic example of what today is called the prisoner's dilemma.

Maybe we could say that we lay down our right to all things and join with others in seeking peace because that is the rational thing to do. We are rational actors, and it is rational for us to desire peace rather than war. But note that this is exactly what Hobbes does *not* say. Far from having a rational actor model of politics, he operates with an irrational actor model. There is absolutely no reason to believe that people will act rationally or keep their word. It is not our reason but our passions that are the dominant feature of human psychology. And although Hobbes emphasizes the diversity of the passions, there are two main passions that he believes universally dominate human nature. These are pride and fear.

Pride and fear are Hobbes's equivalents of Machiavelli's two "humors," the desire to rule and the desire to be left alone. What Hobbes calls pride is the passion for preeminence, the desire to be first—and also to be seen to be first—in the race of life. Prideful people are those overflowing with confidence in their own abilities. We all know people like this: the alpha male, the manly man, the person capable of lurching from failure to failure with no loss of confidence in his own powers. Yet Hobbes is a great debunker of "vainglory," a kind of exaggerated confidence in one's own powers. For Hobbes, pride is the desire to lord it over others, to have your superiority acknowledged by those you have bested. As Gore Vidal once said, "It is not enough to succeed; others must fail."[4] But it is a major part of Hobbes's enlightened psychology to encourage us to forgo pride as no more than a form of glory seeking. His critique of pride is not religious—"pride goeth before a fall"—but political. Pride is dangerous because it causes conflict and war. How to control pride is the single most important teaching of *Leviathan*. Hobbes calls the Leviathan "King of the Proud," and its basic law is one that affirms equality of treatment. A humane code of equal respect is to replace the older civic ethos based on the celebration of a kind of noble pride.

But if pride is one of Hobbes's universal passions, so is its opposite, fear. Hobbes makes much of the fear of death that may come at any time in the state of nature, but there is more to fear than this. Fear is not just the desire to avoid death but the desire to avoid losing in the race of life; moreover, it is the desire to avoid the shame of being seen as a loser by others. There is a social quality to both of these passions; how we are seen by others is crucial to Hobbes's moral psychology. Each of us contains elements of these two passions, elements of both self-assertion and fear of the consequences of self-assertion. How does Hobbes balance these two universal desires?

Hobbes's answer is that he wants us to substitute fear for pride as the dominant passion. Fear is the passion to be reckoned with. It is fear, not reason, that leads us to abandon the state of nature and sue for peace. "The passions that incline men to peace are fear of death," Hobbes writes (XIII, 14). This is not to say that he believes that fear is naturally a stronger motive than pride. Far from it. There are many people of all types who act as if they have no fear of death: the proud aristocrat who prefers death before dishonor, the religious zealot prepared to sacrifice his life, and the lives of others, for the reward of heaven, even the risk-taking adventurer seeking to climb Mount Everest for the honor involved. If fear actually *were* the dominant passion, presumably Hobbes would not have to tell us so repeatedly that the fear of death is the basis of society. He repeats this as often and in as many different ways as he does because he correctly believes that people have to be *taught* to fear the right things.

It is a part of the educational or pedagogic intention of *Leviathan* to help us see the dangers of pride and the advantages of peace. Fear properly directed can lead to peace. In fact fear is the basis or cause of what Hobbes calls the various laws of nature that lead us from the state of nature to civil society. These laws of nature can be reduced to a single "precept or general rule of reason that every man ought to endeavor peace." "The first and most fundamental law of nature," Hobbes writes, "is to seek peace and follow it" (XIV, 4). It is out of fear that we begin to reason and to see the advantages of society. Not only should we seek peace, we have an obligation to lay down our right to all things on the condition that others around us do so as well. Hobbes then goes on to enumerate a total of nineteen laws of nature that constitute a kind of framework for establishing civil society. These laws can be regarded as the Hobbesian equivalent of the Golden Rule—he even compares them to the law of the Gospels—which he states in the negative: do not do unto others what you would not have them do unto you (XIV, 5). (45)

The Laws of Nature and the Ralph Esposito Problem

The laws of nature occupy a paradoxical position within *Leviathan*. Hobbes, as we have seen, sometimes writes as a scientist for whom nature and the laws of nature operate with the same kind of necessity as the laws of physical attraction. They describe how bodies in motion always and necessarily behave. Yet Hobbes also writes as a moralist for whom the laws of nature are, as he puts it, "precepts of reason" or general rules according to which we are forbidden to do anything destructive of life. We do not describe a stone rolling down a hill or a wave crashing on the shore as following a "precept of reason." These are simply the ways stones and waves react to their condition. But human beings do not merely react, they behave. If the laws of nature are moral precepts, then that suggests that we are free to obey or disobey them. A moral law is necessarily one where we have choice to obey or not obey; without the element of choice or will it would not be moral. Such laws do not describe how people actually do behave, they prescribe how people ought to behave. Hobbes seems to answer this question at the end of chapter 15 when he writes of the laws of nature: "These dictates of reason men used to call by the name of laws, but improperly; for they are but conclusions or theorems concerning what conduces to the conversation and defense of themselves" (XV, 41).

But if the laws of nature are only "improperly" called laws, why does Hobbes continue to use this terminology? In part this may be his way of paying homage to the ancient tradition of natural law while at the same time indicating his departure from it. The natural laws are not divine commands or ordinances but rules of practical reason determined by us as the optimal means of securing our well-being. They do not issue categorical laws so much as hypothetical rules of the sort "If you want X, then do Y." If you desire peace, then here are the means to it. Hobbes calls his doctrine of natural law "the true and only moral philosophy" (XV, 40).

What are we to make of Hobbes's laws of nature? On the one hand, they have a genuine moral content that can be reduced to a single formula: seek peace above all other goods. Peace is a moral good for Hobbes; the virtues are those qualities of behavior that tend toward peace, and the vices those qualities that tend toward war. Hobbes wants above all to induce the values or virtue of civility. Civility is the virtue of peace, equity, fairness, playing by the rules.

But it is at this point that the thoughtful reader might ask whether we have gone too far in presenting Hobbes as a moral philosopher whose slogan might well be "give peace a chance." And why is peace the highest good anyway? Why not justice or honor or piety or the examined life? One suggestion is that it is not so much peace that Hobbes cherishes as life. Peace is a means to life. Every creature has a built-in desire to preserve itself or persevere in its own existence, to continue in its own steady state, so to speak, and to resist invasion or encroachment by others. We are all endowed with a natural right to life. The desire to preserve oneself is not simply a biological fact—although it is that, too—it is a genuine moral right. From the biological fact that beings seek to preserve their lives, Hobbes draws a moral lesson that every being has a right to life. Every being has a fundamental right to its own life. (Later philosophers like Hume and Kant would treat this as an example of the "naturalistic fallacy," the attempt to derive an ought-statement from an is-statement, but this would take us too far afield.) We have a right not only to our own lives but also to do whatever we regard as needful to protect our lives. This right is, again, not just a brute fact of nature but a moral entitlement, the source of human worth and dignity.

But now have we really not gone too far in attributing a doctrine of moral dignity to Hobbes? Did he not cynically write: "The value or worth of a man is, as of all other things, his price" (X, 16)? Do his mechanism and materialism not seem to detract from any conception of inherent human worth? There is surely something to this, and yet Hobbes sees that life is a precious good, perhaps the most precious good, and also how fragile and endangered it is. His work as a whole is an effort to dispel what he thinks are the false beliefs that disguise this truth from us—for example, beliefs about the afterlife and all beliefs that detract from our appreciation of the value of life as it is. Hobbes repudiates the idea of a *summum bonum*, a highest good, because he wants us to focus on life as the precondition for all other goods. This is the moral basis of his humanitarianism.

Yet this raises further problems. Does Hobbes's attempt to instill in us, the readers, an appreciation for life simultaneously create an aversion to risk, an extreme fear of conflict and challenge? Does Hobbes's emphasis on the preservation of life, on the supreme moral value of life, make his mighty Leviathan a commonwealth of cowards? Whereas Aristotle had made the courage of men in combat a central virtue in his *Ethics,* Hobbes pointedly omits courage from his list of the virtues. He compares courage to a species of rashness: his example is dueling, which he says will always be honorable but unlawful. "For duels," he writes, "are many times effects of courage; and the ground of courage is always strength or skill, though for the most part they be the effects of rash speaking and of the fear of dishonor in one or both of the combatants" (X, 49). In other words, courage is a form of vanity or pride, the desire not to appear less than another.

Hobbes confirms this suspicion in his treatment of military conscription. How, he asks, can a sovereign conscript men into military service when the entire point of civil association is to avoid the risk of violent death? To make his case, Hobbes has to devalue the moral case for war. He describes battle as a mutual "running away." Furthermore, he says that allowance should be made for men of "natural timorousness." "A man that is commanded as a soldier to fight against the enemy, though his sovereign have right enough to punish his refusal with death, may nevertheless in many cases refuse without injustice, as when he substituteth a sufficient soldier in his place" (XXI, 16). In other words, why do the fighting yourself if you can find someone else to do it for you? Is this not a perfect description of our own all-volunteer army?

But the question is: Can even a Hobbesian society do without the manly virtues or qualities that involve pride, love, and honor—qualities that the Greeks called *thymos* and the Jews *ruach*—that Hobbes seems to condemn? Consider the case of Ralph Esposito. Who is Ralph Esposito, you ask. His name is not in the index of the book. Mr. Esposito is a New York City fireman who was one of the first responders on 9/11. Not long after, I invited him to Yale, where he discussed at length how people like himself daily risk their lives running into burning buildings to rescue total strangers. Why do people do this? Is it because some people have a built-in sense of thymos, pride, courage, love of risk that no society can do without? No society, not even a Hobbesian one, can do without a fire department, but if one were to follow Hobbes's risk-averse psychology, why would anyone ever become a firefighter or a soldier, risking life and limb for his or her country or a cause or even just to help other people? Even in the passage from Hobbes cited earlier, activities like navigation, exploration, and industry require people to engage in risk-taking behavior that cannot be explained by his laws of nature alone. In the end, societies require more Ralph Espositos than men of "natural timorousness."

Sovereign Power and Representation

The most characteristic doctrine of Hobbes is his theory of sovereignty. The creation of the sovereign—to which he refers by the term "mortal God"—is his answer to the state of nature. Only the creation of a sovereign possessed of absolute power is sufficient to put an end to the perpetual uncertainty of the state of war. What are some of the features of this sovereign?

In the first place it is important to bear in mind that the sovereign is less a person than an office. The sovereign is an "artificial person," by which Hobbes means the creation of a contract or covenant that brought him into being. The sovereign does not exist by nature. He—or it—is a product of art or science. The sovereign is the creation of the people or a product of the consent of the governed. The sovereign—and this is crucial—is understood as the *representative* of the people (XVI, 13). It is the people who endow the sovereign with the authority to represent them and act on their behalf. Hobbes's sovereign, then, has many of the characteristics of what we think of as modern executive power. When Louis XIV of France famously declared, "L'état, c'est moi" (I am the state), he was expressing an essentially premodern view, that the state is the personal property of the sovereign or ruler. But the Hobbesian sovereign does not own the state; he is appointed or "authorized" by the people to secure the limited end of peace and security. The Hobbesian sovereign has much the same function and impersonality as a modern-day CEO, responsible only to his or her shareholders.

Hobbes's theory of the sovereign contains elements of both secular absolutism and modern liberalism. The power of the sovereign must be unlimited, yet he is still the creation of the people whose will he represents. Although Hobbes is widely taken to be a defender of monarchical absolutism, in point of fact he displays surprising neutrality over what form the sovereign takes, so long as power is absolute and undivided. Among the powers that the sovereign has the right to determine are: laws concerning property, the right of declaring war and peace (foreign policy), the rules of justice affecting life and death (criminal law), and determining what books and ideas are permissible (censorship).

The core of Hobbes's theory of the sovereign can be boiled down to the statement that the sovereign—and only the sovereign—is the source of law. The law is what the sovereign says it is. This is the essence of what has since become known as the doctrine of *legal positivism,* that law is the command of the sovereign. This seems in one sense to recall the teaching of Thrasymachus in the *Republic,* who argued that justice is what the stronger say it is. There is, in other words, no higher or other court of appeal beyond the word of the sovereign. The sovereign is appointed—much like an umpire in baseball or football—to enforce the rules of the game, but in Hobbes's case the sovereign is not only the interpreter of the rules but the creator of them as well. Hobbes draws from this the conclusion that the sovereign can never act unjustly, because the sovereign is the source of the rules of justice (XVIII, 6).

Hobbes supports his argument about the sovereign by a creative reading of the story of David and Uriah, which we have already studied. We recall that David was king at the time he coveted Uriah's wife, Bathsheba, and in order to sleep with her, he had Uriah killed. Hobbes reasons from this that while David may have sinned against God in doing this, as the lawful sovereign he did no injustice to Uriah. Here are Hobbes's own words: "And the same holdeth also in a sovereign prince that putteth to death an innocent subject. For though the action be against the law of nature, as being contrary to equity (as was the killing of Uriah by David), yet it was not an injury to Uriah, but to God. Not to Uriah, because the right to do what he pleased was given him by Uriah himself; and yet to God, because David was God's subject, and prohibited all iniquity by the law of nature. Which distinction David himself, when he repented the fact evidently confirmed, saying, "To thee only have I sinned" (XXI, 7). Uriah might have thought differently, to say the least!

Hobbes's teaching about law is perhaps less draconian than it first appears. Hobbes makes clear that law is what the sovereign says it is. There can be no such thing as an unjust law, because it is the sovereign alone who can determine the rules of justice. He would seem to agree with President Richard Nixon's statement in his famous interview with David Frost: "When the President does it, that means it is not illegal." However—and this is a point worth noting—Hobbes distinguishes between a just law and a good law. All laws are by definition just, but it does not follow that all laws are good. "A good law," he writes, "is that which is needful for the good of the people" (XXX, 20). But what are the criteria by which the good of the people is determined?

Hobbes makes clear that the sovereign may be invested with absolute but not arbitrary power over the people. The sovereign must rule through law, and the purpose of law is not so much to control as to facilitate. Consider the following passage: "For the use of laws (which are but rules authorized) is not to bind the people from all voluntary actions, but to direct and keep them in such a motion as not to hurt themselves by their own impetuous desires, rashness, or indiscretion, as hedges are set, not to stop travelers, but to keep them in their way" (XXX, 21). Here Hobbes presents the laws as something like traffic regulations. His point, if I understand him, is that good laws exist to facilitate such things as travel, trade, and communication, to keep people "in their way." A bad law is one that aims merely to constrain and control at the sovereign's whim, while good laws exist to facilitate human agency. This is central to Hobbes's theory of law.

The power to control matters of opinion—what today we would call First Amendment issues—is especially important for the sovereign. "For the actions of men," he writes, "proceed from their opinions, and in the well-governing of opinions consisteth the well-governing of men's actions" (XVIII, 9). It follows that the sovereign has the right to decide which opinions are conducive to peace and which are aimed to stir up discontent and war. These comments by Hobbes are directed at two principal institutions: the churches and the universities. Both of these have been for Hobbes centers of seditious opinion that must be placed under the sovereign's control.

By the churches Hobbes is speaking of the reformed church, but in particular the radical Puritan sects who elevate matters of conscience and private belief over and above the law, arrogating to themselves the power to judge the sovereign. It was these dissenting Protestants who formed the rank and file of Cromwell's New Model Army during the English Civil War. Hobbes would banish all doctrines that profess to make the individual or the sect the judge of the sovereign (XXIX, 6–7). It is only in the state of nature, recall, that individuals have the right to determine for themselves the definitions of right and wrong; once we enter society, we pass to the sovereign the right to determine these matters for us.

Just as important to control is the power of the university and its curriculum. In particular Hobbes faults the universities for teaching Aristotle—or at least the seventeenth-century version of Aristotle—the source of republican ideas. It is above all the influence of the classics, Aristotle and Cicero especially, that Hobbes regards as an important cause of the recent Civil War and the regicide of Charles I: "As to rebellion against monarchy, one of the most frequent causes of it is the reading of the books of policy and history of the ancient Greeks and Romans, from which young men (and all others that are unprovided of the antidote of solid reason), receive a strong and delightful impression of the great exploits of war. . . . From the reading of such books, men have undertaken to kill their kings, because the Greek and Latin writers, in their books and discourses of policy, make it lawful and laudable for any man so to do, provided, before he do it, he call him a tyrant" (XXIX, 14).

This passage is interesting not only for its humor and characteristic exaggeration but also because it shows just how much emphasis Hobbes puts on the reform of opinion. Like Machiavelli, Hobbes saw himself as an educator of princes. There is a kind of internal irony here because he sometimes writes as if human beings are nothing more than complex machines that mechanically obey the laws of attraction and repulsion. But he also writes as if we are beings with will and purpose who are uniquely guided by opinions, ideas, and doctrines. Just as Plato's first order of business was the control of poetry and the arts, so must Hobbes's sovereign serve as a reformer of theological and philosophical ideas.

Hobbes even compares his *Leviathan* to Plato's *Republic*. In a rare moment of self-reflection that will make the careful reader sit up and take notice, he notes that the novelty of his ideas will make it difficult for them to receive an audience. "I am at the point of believing this my labor as useless as the commonwealth of Plato," he says in a moment of uncharacteristic despair. "For he [Plato] also is of the opinion that it is impossible for the disorders of state ever to be taken away, till sovereigns be philosophers" (XXX, 41). Although initially despairing of the possibility of a friendly reception for his work, Hobbes goes on to note more optimistically that his own work is considerably simpler and easier to learn than Plato's and may still catch the ear of a sympathetic prince. "I recover some hope," he says, "that one time or other, this writing of mine may fall into the hands of a sovereign who will consider it himself (for it is short and I think clear) without the help of any interested or envious interpreter and by the exercise of entire sovereignty in protecting the public teaching of it, convert this truth of speculation into the utility of practice" (XXXI, 41).

Hobbes may have underestimated the length and overestimated the accessibility of his book, but his desire that it should serve as wide an audience as possible is something he returns to again at the very end of *Leviathan*. The universities, he writes there, are "the fountains of civil and moral doctrine" and have an obligation to teach the correct doctrine of rights and duties. This means, first of all, adopting Hobbes's own book as the authoritative teaching on moral and political doctrine in the universities. "Therefore I think it may be profitably printed and more profitably taught in the universities," he confidently concludes. The ideal audience for it should be the preachers, the gentry, the lawyers, all men of affairs who "drawing such water as they find" from the book can use it "to sprinkle the same (both from the pulpit and in their conversation) upon the people" (Review and Conclusion, 16). Hobbes's hope was shared by all the great political philosophers: to someday be a legislator for humankind.

Hobbesian Liberalism

Hobbes enjoys describing the powers of the sovereign in the most absolute and extreme of terms. The sovereign is to have supreme command over matters of life and death, war and peace; his word in all matters is to be regarded as final. Yet Hobbes also allows ample room for individual liberty and even sets some limits to the legitimate use of sovereign power. For all his tough talk, Hobbes takes justice and the rule of law very seriously. Thus at one point he maintains that a person cannot be made to accuse himself without the assurance of a pardon; similarly a wife or parent cannot be coerced to accuse a loved one (XIV, 30). On a related point he maintains that punishment can never be used as an instrument of revenge, only for what he calls "the correction [that is, the rehabilitation] of the offender" (XV, 19).

Hobbes also repeatedly insists that law must serve as an instrument for achieving social equality. In a chapter entitled "Of the Office of the Sovereign Representative," he argues that justice be equally administered to all classes of people, rich as well as poor. He maintains that titles of nobility are of value only for the benefits that they confer on those of lesser rank "or not at all" (XXX, 15). Equal justice requires equal taxation policy. Hobbes seems to be proposing a consumption tax so that the rich, who consume more than the poor, will have to pay their fair share. And he argues that those indigent citizens who are unable to provide for themselves should not be forced to rely upon the private charity of individuals but should be maintained at public expense (XXX, 18). Here he seems almost to anticipate the modern welfare state.

Maybe most important is the centrality given to the individual in Hobbes's philosophy. Hobbes derives the power of the sovereign from the natural right of each individual to do as he likes in the state of nature; in the

Hobbesian scheme rights are primary, duties are derivative. One of the interesting paradoxes about Hobbes is that he is so absolutist not despite his individualism but because of it. It follows, then, that the purpose of the sovereign is to safeguard the natural rights of each individual by making them consistent with the rights of others. It is this priority of rights over duties that, arguably, makes Hobbes the founding father of liberalism.[5]

Hobbes's defense of the natural right of the individual is expressed in his novel teaching about liberty. He distinguishes his teaching about liberty from that of the ancients. The ancients, he believes, operated with a defective understanding of human freedom. For them, liberty meant being a member of a self-governing republic. Liberty was a property not of the individual but of the regime of which one was a member. "The Athenians and Romans," he writes, "were free, that is, free commonwealths, not that any particular men had the liberty to resist their own representative, but that their representative had the liberty to resist or invade other people" (XXI, 8).

But this sense of collective liberty—the freedom to resist or invade other people—is not the same, indeed, is opposed to, the modern idea of liberty that Hobbes proposes. By liberty he means the absence of constraints or impediments to action. We are free to the extent that we can act in an unimpeded manner. It follows, then, that political liberty means the freedom to act where the law is silent (XXI, 6). Hobbes's sovereign is more likely to allow citizens a zone of private liberty where they are free to act as they choose than is the ruler in the classical republic based on coerced participation in political deliberation. Hobbes makes a dig at defenders of the view that only citizens of a republic can be accounted free. "There is written on the turrets of the city of Lucca in great characters at this day the word 'LIBERTAS'; yet no man can thence infer that a particular man has more liberty or immunity from the service of the commonwealth there than in Constantinople" (XXI, 8). Freedom, as he puts it here, requires "immunity" from service. A regime is to be judged by how much private liberty it allows to its citizens—this idea of individual liberty was unknown to the ancients and unprecedented in the modern world.

Hobbes's Children

Hobbes provides us with the definitive language of the modern state. Yet he remains as contested a figure for us as he was in his own time because the state itself is a contested legacy. For many today his conception of the Leviathan state is synonymous with antiliberal absolutism. For others, he opened the door to John Locke and the liberal theory of government. He taught the priority of rights over duties, and argued that the sovereign should serve the lowly end of providing peace and security, leaving it to individuals to decide for themselves how best to live their lives. Nevertheless, the liberty that subjects enjoy in Hobbes's system falls in the area that the sovereign omits to regulate; Hobbes does not praise vigilance in defense of liberty, and he denounces all efforts to resist government. At best one could say that he is a part-time liberal.

Hobbes is at his best when providing the moral and psychological language in which we think about the state. The state is a product of a psychological struggle between the contending passions of pride and fear. Fear is associated with the desire for security, order, and rationality; pride with the love of glory, honor, and recognition. All the goods of civilization stem from our ability to control pride. The very title of the book comes from a biblical passage in Job where Leviathan is described as "king of the children of pride" (XXVIII, 27). The nineteen laws of nature that Hobbes enumerates are intended to instruct us in the virtues of sociability and are especially directed against pride or hubris.

The modern state as we know it grew out of the Hobbesian desire for security that could only be achieved at the expense of the desire for glory. The Hobbesian state was intended to secure the condition of life, even a highly civilized and cultivated life, but one calculated in terms of self-interest and risk avoidance. The Hobbesian fearful man is not likely to be someone who risks life for liberty, honor, or a cause. He is more likely to be someone who plays by the rules, avoids danger, and bets on the sure thing. The Hobbesian citizen is not likely to be a risk taker like George Washington, Andrew Carnegie, or Steve Jobs. He is more likely to think like an actuary or an insurance agent, always calculating the odds and finding ways to cover the damages. Later political theorists like Rousseau would develop a name for this Hobbesian man: the bourgeois, or what Nietzsche would later call the "last man."[6]

Hobbes was remarkably successful. The type of individual that he tried to create—careful, self-interested, risk averse—is the dominant ethos of our civilization. We have all become Hobbesians whether we choose to admit it or not. At the same time, even a Hobbesian society cannot entirely exist without some individuals who are willing to risk life for the sake of honor, self-respect, or even the sheer joy that comes from risk itself. Why do people become policemen, firemen, soldiers, freedom fighters—all activities that cannot be explained in terms of self-interest alone? But will not even a Hobbesian society require policemen, firemen, soldiers, and armies? Where will these recruits come from?

Hobbes regards these risk-loving passions—for which Plato used the term thymos—as barbaric, uncivilized, and warlike. To some degree he was right. But even the Hobbesian state lives in the midst of a Hobbesian world— that is to say, the world of international relations is the Hobbesian state of nature writ large. States stand to one another on the world stage as individuals stand to one another in the state of nature, as potential enemies with no higher law or authority to adjudicate their conflicts. In such a world even the sovereign state will be endangered, either by other sovereign states or by groups and individuals devoted to terror and destruction, as the example of 9/11 surely brought home. Political scientist Pierre Hassner has described this as "the dialectic of the bourgeois and the barbarian," a struggle between the modern state, with its largely pacified and satisfied citizen bodies, and those premodern states prepared to use the instruments of violence, terror, and suicide bombings to achieve their ends.[7] A Hobbesian state, paradoxically, still requires men and women who are prepared to fight, to risk all, in defense of their state. The Hobbesian bourgeois cannot entirely do without the barbarian. Can Hobbes explain this paradox?

This point has been further reinforced in James Bowman's book *Honor: A History*.[8] Bowman points out that while affairs of honor, as they are quaintly called, have largely disappeared from advanced modern societies, honor still remains a consuming passion in many parts of the world today, including most importantly the Middle East. Honor in most societies throughout history is not merely a personal quality, like medieval chivalry, but is above all group honor, the honor that surrounds the family, the extended clan, or the religious sect. An assault on any one member of the group is an assault on the dignity of all. This helps to explain, for instance, why in many cultures the concept of saving face is so important, even if to modern Americans it seems relatively trivial. One reason, Bowman believes, that Westerners have such a difficult time understanding other peoples and cultures is that the very idea of defending one's honor has largely been devalued in the West. We tend to look at human behavior as a matter of providing rational incentives, while most people are driven by a need for esteem and a desire to avoid humiliation. When during the Vietnam War Nixon spoke of achieving "peace with honor," this was largely mocked as ludicrous. Honor, to so many of us, sounds like some kind of primitive group ethic, and therefore we don't understand people for whom loyalty to the group or sect remains inviolable. What we don't often see is that in large part it is Hobbes's effort to discredit this ancient warrior ethic that is responsible for our current blindness.

Our Hobbesian civilization conceals from us an uncomfortable truth. Hobbes teaches us the virtues of civility. His nineteen laws of nature constitute what he calls "the true and only moral philosophy," which contains the virtues of modesty, peace, justice, equity, and gratitude, all necessary to sustain a civil society. But are these virtues enough to guarantee the survival of civilization, especially when it is confronted with enemies, often unscrupulous and savage enemies, that will use any means necessary to achieve their ends? Our peace, security, and safety—our bourgeois freedoms, as it were—still require people who are willing to put their lives at risk for the values of civilization. Where will such people be found if the very values of civility have rendered us too civilized to be able to defend ourselves? Society requires the twin dispositions of pride and fear, spiritedness and caution, if it is to survive. Hobbes diminishes pride and spiritedness as dangerous antisocial passions, but today we may do well to rethink the qualities of great ambition, love of fame, and the desire for honor—qualities that the ancients took for granted and too often we moderns fail to remember. The bourgeois is still in need of the barbarian.

CHAPTER 9

Locke and the Art of Constitutional Government

John Locke, 1632–1704. 1697. Oil on canvas. Portrait by Godfrey
Kneller (1646–1723). Photo credit: bpk, Berlin / State Hermitage Museum,
St. Petersburg / Roman Beniaminson / Art Resource, NY

John Locke gives the modern state the expression that is most familiar to us. His writings seem to have been so completely adopted by Thomas Jefferson in the Declaration of Independence that Locke is often thought of as almost an honorary member of the American founding generation. Among other things, he advocates the natural liberty and equality of human beings; the individual's right to such things as life, liberty, and property; government by consent; limited government with a separation of powers; and a right to revolution. In addition, Locke was an advocate of religious toleration. His name is forever linked to the idea of liberal or constitutional democracy.[1]

Yet Locke's teachings did not arise *ex nihilo*. They were prepared in part by Machiavelli, who died approximately a century before Locke's birth, but more importantly by Locke's immediate predecessor, Hobbes. Hobbes had taken Machiavelli's idea of the prince and in effect turned it into the doctrine of sovereignty. The Hobbesian sovereign is at the basis of our idea of impersonal government; Hobbes transforms princely rule into an office which is at once a creation of a social contract or "covenant" and responsible to the agents or persons who have created the contract. Hobbes had taught that the sovereign is representative of the people who create this office in order to ensure peace, justice, and order. Without the power of the sovereign, we would find ourselves in a state of nature—a term coined by Hobbes to indicate a world without civil authority. Hobbes gives voice to the doctrine of secular absolutism, one that invests the sovereign with virtually unlimited power to do whatever is necessary to ensure peace and stability.

Out of such harsh and formidable premises grew Locke's new, more liberal constitutional theory of the state. Locke set out to tame or domesticate Hobbes, whose theory of absolute government found few immediate defenders. Locke's most important work of political theory is the *Two Treatises of Civil Government*. The *First Treatise* was an elaborate and painstaking refutation of the theory of the divine right of kings advocated by Sir Robert Filmer in a book called *Patriarcha*. Here Locke demolishes the claim that kingship derives from God's grant of dominion to Adam and hence that all authority is acquired by divine right. The *First Treatise* is an important but long and tedious work that even Locke must have found tiresome. It is in the *Second Treatise,* written we now believe shortly before the Glorious Revolution of 1688, that Locke advanced his bold and innovative ideas on the role of government.

Locke's *Second Treatise* was intended as a practical work, addressed not so much to philosophers as to Englishmen, in the everyday language of his time. Locke wrote to capture the common sense of his age, although this is not to say that he was not extremely controversial. He was a deeply political man, although a cautious and reticent one, who lived in a period of intense religious and political conflict. He was a boy when Charles I was executed and an adult when James II was overthrown and forced into exile. He spent many years at Oxford, where he was suspected of harboring radical sympathies but was so cautious and careful in expressing them that even after many years the head of his college could call him "a master of taciturnity." Locke was private secretary and physician to a man named Anthony Ashley Cooper—later Lord Shaftsbury—who formed a circle of radical opponents to the monarchy. Locke was forced into exile in 1683 and lived in Holland for several years before returning to England, where he remained until his death in 1704. At the time of his death he was the most famous philosopher in Europe.

Locke's Bestiary

More than any other modern thinker, Locke makes the natural law the centerpiece of his political theory. To understand the natural law, it is necessary to see it in the natural condition, the state of nature. For Locke the state of nature is not a condition of ruling and being ruled as it was for Aristotle but one of "perfect freedom" (II/4). While Aristotle understood that by nature we are members of a family, a polis, a moral community of some sort bound by ties of obligation, Locke means this as a condition without civil authority or civil obligation. The state of nature is not an actual historical state—although Locke sometimes compares the state of nature to the vast tracts of North America—but a kind of thought experiment. What is human nature, Locke asks, in the absence of all authority?

On the surface Locke's state of nature seems the virtual antithesis of Hobbes's. The state of nature is not an amoral condition of violence and murder, as Hobbes had opined. The state of nature is a moral condition governed by a moral law that dictates peace and sociability. This law "willeth the peace and preservation of all mankind" (II/7).

Locke's natural law seems like a traditional form of moral law that would have been familiar to readers of Cicero, Thomas Aquinas, and Richard Hooker ("the judicious Hooker"). It sounds very comforting and traditional. All civil authority has its foundation in a law of nature that is knowable to all human beings by virtue of their reason alone. The law of nature declares that as we are all the "Workmanship" of "one Omnipotent and infinitely wise

Maker," we ought never to harm any others in their lives, liberties, or possessions (II/6). Locke seems to weave together effortlessly the Stoic tradition of natural law and the Christian conception of divine workmanship into one seamless whole.

But even within the opening paragraphs, Locke's law of nature turns into a right of individual self-preservation. From the beginning it is not altogether clear whether the natural law is a theory of moral duties and obligations toward others or a Hobbesian doctrine of natural right that mandates that priority be given to individual self-preservation and what is necessary to achieve it. The state of nature is a condition without civil authority. The law of nature has no person or office to oversee its application. The state of nature, at first described as a condition of peace and mutual trust, quickly degenerates into a state of war, with every individual serving as the judge, jury, and executioner of the natural law. The state of nature quickly has become a Hobbesian condition of every man for himself: "The damnified Person has this Power of appropriating to himself, the Goods or Services of the Offender by *Right of Self-preservation,* as every Man has a Power to punish the Crime, to prevent its being committed again, *by the Right he has of Preserving all Mankind,* and doing all reasonable things he can in order to that end" (II/11).

The "Fundamental law of Nature," as Locke calls it, is the right of self-preservation, which states that each person is empowered to do whatever is in his power to do to preserve himself. "And one may destroy a Man who makes War upon him, or has discovered an Enmity to his being, for the same Reason that he may kill a *Wolf* or a *Lyon;* because such Men are not under the ties of the Common Law of Reason, have no other Rule, but that of Force and Violence and so may be treated as Beasts of Prey, those dangerous and noxious Creatures that will be sure to destroy him, whenever he falls into their Power" (III/16).

One might call this Locke's bestiary. The state of nature is a condition populated not by gentle, peace-seeking, and cooperative persons but by various "Beasts of Prey" of all descriptions—lions, tigers, and bears. The very freedom that such beings enjoy in the state of nature leads to its abuse, which in turn requires the need for government. In the meantime, however, is the state of nature—as Locke initially asserts—a moral condition overseen by a natural law of peace or is it a thinly veiled description of a Hobbesian war of all against all?

Locke seems to be speaking two different languages: one of traditional natural law that posits duties to others, and the second of a modern Hobbesian conception of natural right that maintains the priority of rights, especially the right to one's self-preservation. Is Locke a member of the Ciceronian and Thomistic natural law tradition or a modern Hobbesian? Do his politics derive from a theological conception of divine "workmanship" or from an ultimately naturalistic account of the human passions and the struggle for survival? These are the questions that have long bedeviled readers of the *Second Treatise*.

Some readers argue that Locke's idea of equality in the state of nature relies specifically upon a Christian context of argument.[2] His statement that "there being nothing more evident, than that Creatures of the same species and rank, promiscuously born to all the same advantages of Nature, and the use of the same faculties, should also be equal one amongst another" (II/4) is said to rely on an idea of God's workmanship. What it means to belong to a species and why belonging to the same species confers a special rank and dignity on its members only makes sense if one believes that the species in question has a specifically moral relation to God. In the end, as I will try to show later, it is not the theological conception of divine "workmanship" but the utterly worldly and secular doctrine of "self-ownership" that best characterizes Lockean political philosophy.

The question of whether Locke's idea of natural law relies upon theological belief or whether it can be inferred from nontheological, purely naturalistic grounds is not simply a philosophical problem. If we consider that Locke's doctrine about natural law forms an important support of the Declaration of Independence, how we interpret his thought will carry major implications for how we think about a host of public policy issues. For example, the Declaration's reference to "the Laws of Nature and of Nature's God" seems to come right out of the *Second Treatise*. But if the laws of nature are underwritten by "Nature's God," this has major implications for issues such as school prayer and the display of the Ten Commandments in courthouses and other public spaces. To what extent do our rights and duties depend upon a theological conception of nature and human nature? How one thinks about this issue will often determine the place, if any, of religion in the public arena.

Let us consider this question by examining Locke's most characteristic doctrine: his theory of property.

"The Labour of his Body"

The core of Locke's theory of government is arguably lodged in his account of property in chapter 5 of the *Second Treatise*. Locke's conception of human nature is very much that of man as the property-acquiring animal.

Our claims to property derive from our own work; the fact that we have expended our labor on something gives us the title to it. Labor is the source of all value. The state of nature is a condition of communal ownership— what Marx would have called primitive communism. The fact that we add our labor to something marks it off as ours: "Every man has a *Property* in his *Person*. This no Body has any Right to but himself. The *Labour* of his Body and the *Work* of his Hands, we may say, are properly his. . . . For this *Labour* being the unquestionable Property of the Laborer, no Man but he can have a right to what that is once joyned to, at least where there is enough, as good left in common for others. . . . That *labour* put a distinction between [him] and the common. That added something to them more than Nature, the common Mother of all, had done; and so they became his private right" (V/27–28).

The natural law, according to Locke, dictates a right of private property, and it is to secure this right that government is established. In a striking passage he says that the world was created in order to be cultivated and improved. Those who work to improve and develop nature are the true benefactors of mankind. "God gave the World to Men in Common," he writes, "but since he gave it to them for their benefit, and the greatest Conveniences of Life they were capable to draw from it, it cannot be supposed he meant it should always remain common and uncultivated. He gave it to the use of the Industrious and Rational . . . and not to the Fancy or Covetousness of the Quarrelsome and Contentious" (V/34).

From this passage we can see at once that the Lockean state will be a commercial state. Ancient political theory regarded commerce and property as subordinate to the life of the citizen. Plato advocated communism among his Guards; Aristotle regarded the necessity of private property as a means for the few to engage in a life of politics while still being supported by a class of slaves. Economy was subordinate to polity. For Locke, however, the world belongs to "the Industrious and Rational," namely, those people who through their own efforts increase and enhance the plenty of all. "He who appropriates land to himself by his labour," Locke writes, "does not lessen but increase the common stock of mankind" (V/37). It is only a relatively short step from Locke's *Second Treatise* to Adam Smith's *Wealth of Nations*.[3]

For Locke there are no natural limits to property or acquisition. This is the absolutely essential point. Accumulation may be initially limited by use, but the introduction of money or coinage makes unlimited capital accumulation not only possible but even a moral duty (V/36). By enriching ourselves we unintentionally contribute to the benefit of others. "A King of a large and fruitful Territory [in America]," Locke writes, "feeds, lodges, and is clad worse than a day Labourer in *England*" (V/41). The creation of general plenty—the "common-wealth," to use a revealing term—is due entirely to the emancipation of labor from its previous moral and political restrictions. Labor becomes the title and source of all value. In a remarkable series of rhetorical shifts, Locke makes not nature but human labor and acquisition the source of different degrees of property and material possession.

He begins the chapter with the assertion that "God hath given the world to men in common," suggesting that the original state of nature is one of collective ownership. He then suggests that, since every person is the owner of his own body, we acquire a title to those things with which we have "mixed" our labor. But what starts as a very modest title to those objects that we have worked on ourselves, such as picking apples from a tree, soon turns into a full-scale explanation of the rise of property and a kind of market economy. Labor accounts for ten times the amount of value that is provided by nature alone, but Locke then goes on to add quickly: "I have here rated the improved land very low in making its product but as ten to one, when it is much nearer an hundred to one" (V/37). Later he even asserts that the value of anything is improved a thousandfold due to labor (V/43). What began as a fairly rudimentary discussion of the origins of property limited by the extent of use and spoilage has by the end of the same chapter turned into an account of large-scale ownership with considerable inequalities of possession. There appears to be an almost direct link between Locke's dynamic theory of property and Madison's claim in *Federalist* No. 10 that "the protection [of different and unequal faculties of acquiring property] is the first object of government."[4]

Locke gives to commerce, moneymaking, and acquisitiveness not only pride of place but a moral status that such activities never enjoyed in the ancient and medieval worlds. Locke is the author of the idea that the task of government is the protection of the right of property. The new politics will no longer be concerned with glory, honor, virtue, but will be sober, pedestrian, hedonistic, though without sublimity or joy. Commerce does not require us to spill blood or risk life. It is solid, reliable, and thoroughly middle class.

The Spirit of Capitalism

The first five chapters of the *Second Treatise* take the form of a speculative history or anthropology of human development that walks us through the state of nature, the state of war, and the creation of property. The fifth chapter begins with a condition of primitive communism, discusses the creation of property through work, and ends with the creation of a market economy marked by vast inequalities of wealth and property. How did this occur and, what's more important, what makes it legitimate?

Locke retells or rather rewrites the narrative of human beginnings that had previously belonged to the Bible. He tells the story of how human beings finding themselves in a state of nature without authority to adjudicate their disputes and governed only by the natural law are nevertheless able to create and enjoy the use of property acquired through "the *Labour* of their Body and the *Work* of their Hands" (V/27). Man is a property-acquiring animal even in the state of nature where there are no laws but the natural law to govern human association.

The problem, of course, with the state of nature is its instability. With no civil authority to adjudicate disputes—especially disputes over property—the peaceful enjoyment of the fruits of our labor are constantly threatened by war and conflict. How can we be secure in our person or property with no enforcement agency to resolve breaches of the peace? The need for government arises out of the real need to resolve disputes over property rights.

In many respects the very familiarity of Locke's doctrine conceals its radicalism. Locke has made the protection of property "the great and *chief end* of Men's uniting into Commonwealths" (IX/124). No one prior to Locke—I would submit—had ever believed that the purpose of politics was the protection of property rights, and by property, it should be said, Locke meant more than real estate: he meant everything that encompasses our lives, liberties, and estates. All of these are property in the literal and most revealing sense of the word: they are things that are proper to us.

Locke continually emphasizes that it is the uncertainty or "inconveniences" of the state of nature that leads us into civil association. Hobbes had emphasized the absolute fearfulness of the state of nature; for Locke it is the fact that we are beings continually beset by unease and anxiety that is the problem. It is unease—restlessness—that is both the source of our insecurities and the spur to labor and the acquisition of property.

What is it about Locke that led him constantly to emphasize the restless, uneasy, and perpetually anxious character of human nature? Certainly one never hears Plato or Aristotle refer to the fearful character of human nature. Was this an expression of Locke's own psychological disposition that was especially prone to caution, reticence, and fearfulness? Or does his emphasis on uneasiness represent the qualities of a new class—the commercial class—seeking to establish its claim to legitimacy? When Locke writes that the world is intended for the use of the "Industrious and Rational," he is speaking of a new middle class whose title to rule rests not on heredity or tradition or claims to nobility but on the exercise of the capacities of hard work, thrift, and opportunity. Locke's goal in the *Second Treatise* seems to have been to provide this new class with a title to rule. Consider the following words of a distinguished twentieth-century commentator: "The new and politically inexperienced social classes which, during the last four centuries, have risen to the exercise of political initiative and authority, have been provided for in the same sort of way as Machiavelli provided for the new prince of the sixteenth century. None of these classes had time to acquire a political education before it came to power; each needed a crib, a political doctrine, to take the place of a habit of political behavior. . . . This is pre-eminently so of Locke's *Second Treatise of Civil Government*."[5]

Locke's new commercial state is Machiavellianism with a human face. It is the rule not of the prince but of a new entrepreneurial middle class that operates outside the traditional sources of authority. It is the ethic, literally, of the self-made man, with all the insecurities that self-making represents. Locke's self-made man is virtually identical to the Protestant images of the self in books like John Bunyan's *Pilgrim's Progress,* Daniel Defoe's *Robinson Crusoe,* and the greatest single work of this genre, Benjamin Franklin's *Autobiography.* Locke's account of property and the urge toward accumulation reveals the deeply Calvinist structure of his thought. His Calvinism domesticates or tranquilizes Machiavelli by turning Machiavellian *virtù*—manliness or daring—into the virtues of labor, industry, and hard work.

Locke's account of our self-making, particularly our struggle to overcome the penury of nature through work and self-discipline, anticipates the genre of the "Robinsonade," the great romance of adventure and affective individualism created by Defoe. Young Robinson Crusoe, contrary to the wishes of his father, abandons his home in England for a life of adventure and discovery abroad. A storm shipwrecks him on a deserted island where he is forced to recapitulate the experience of mankind's struggle out of the state of nature. Severed from all social ties, he is forced back on his own resources to provide for his own self-preservation. Due to his passion for cataloguing and making use of all of the items at his disposal, Crusoe is able to re-create himself, the essence of the autonomous, self-reliant individual that would provide the model for so many of the great novels of individual self-improvement.

Defoe, like Locke, depicted the new ethic of the bourgeois class in the early stages of its vigor and optimism. They present not the warlike qualities of the martial nobility but the more homely virtues of frugality, economy, prudence, thrift, and hard work. No less an authority than Karl Marx saw in the Crusoe story the origins of the very bourgeois science of modern political economy. I cannot resist quoting at length Marx's wonderful depiction of the Robinsonade in the first volume of *Das Kapital:*

> Since Robinson Crusoe's experiences are a favorite theme with political economists, let us take a look at him on his island. Moderate though he be, yet some few wants he has to satisfy, and must therefore do a little useful work of various sorts, such as making tools and furniture, taming goats, fishing and hunting. Of his prayers and the like we take no account, since they are a source of pleasure to him, and he looks upon them as so much recreation. . . . Necessity itself compels him to apportion his time accurately between his different kinds of work. Whether one kind occupies a greater space in his general activity than another depends on the difficulties, greater or less as the case may be, to be overcome in attaining the useful effect aimed at. This our friend Robinson soon learns by experience and having rescued a watch, ledger, and pen and ink from the wreck, commences, like a true-born Briton, to keep a set of books. His stock-book contains a list of the objects of utility that belong to him, of the operations necessary for their production; and lastly, of the labor-time that definite quantities of those objects have, on the average cost him. All the relations between Robinson and the objects that form his wealth are his own creation, are here so simple and clear as to be intelligible without exertion. . . . And yet those relations contain all that is essential to the determination of value.[6]

Lockean political philosophy gives expression precisely to what the great German sociologist Max Weber called the "the spirit of capitalism." In his classic work *The Protestant Ethic and the Spirit of Capitalism,* Weber argued that the capitalist ethic that made a high moral duty of the limitless accumulation of capital was the outgrowth of Puritanism and Calvinism. For Weber, it was through the Protestant Reformation that took root in the countries of northern Europe that capitalism first developed, along with a wholly new moral attitude to such things as wealth and moneymaking. It would take us too far afield to examine Weber's famous thesis about the religious origins of capitalism and the ethic of capital accumulation, but Locke seems to be exhibit A in this changed moral view toward economic activity.

Weber regarded Benjamin Franklin most of all as epitomizing the new bourgeois attitude toward wealth and capital accumulation. But rather than depicting this attitude, as had Defoe and Locke, as one of liberation from feudal hierarchies of status and tradition, Weber saw in it little more than a crabbed and colorless ethic of utilitarianism and materialism. Weber could see nothing to admire in Franklin's ethic. It seemed to him merely a mask for hypocrisy. To view the virtues as a means to the ends of prosperity and well-being was to diminish the beauty and dignity of virtue that should be treated as an end in itself. This kind of low-minded utilitarianism was for Weber the essence of the new bourgeois creed. Franklin's ethic represented for Weber the transformation of the Calvinist idea of a "calling" into a purely worldly ethic of success and profit seeking:

> In fact, the *summum bonum* of this ethic, the earning of more and more money, combined with the strict avoidance of all spontaneous enjoyment of life, is above all completely devoid of any eudaimonistic, not to say, hedonistic, admixture. It is thought of as so purely as an end in itself, that from the point of view of the happiness of, or utility to, the single individual, it appears entirely transcendental and absolutely irrational. Man is dominated by the making of money, by acquisition as the ultimate purpose of his life. . . . At the same time it expresses a type of feeling which is closely connected to certain religious ideas. If we thus ask, *why* should "money be made out of men," Benjamin Franklin himself, although he was a colorless deist, answers in his autobiography with a quotation from the Bible . . . "Seest thou a man diligent in his business? He shall stand before kings" (Proverbs, XXII:19).[7]

Weber conceives of capitalism as torn between two competing ethical ideals: one is Puritan asceticism and self-denial, the other is a eudaimonism that seeks worldly happiness through wealth accumulation and property. This tension is something that worried not only Weber but also those who have been deeply influenced by him. Leo Strauss, for example, regarded the Lockean teaching concerning property as openly "hedonist," an "aimless" search for those things that provide satisfaction but are no longer sufficiently moored in a substantive conception of the *summum bonum.* "Life," in Strauss's famous formulation, "is the joyless quest for joy."[8] The great American sociologist Daniel Bell similarly regarded the capitalist spirit as torn between an ethic of accumulation and an ethic of consumption. These tensions constituted "the cultural contradictions of capitalism," a contradiction between the Puritan ethic of work, discipline, and deferred gratification and a hedonistic ethic of enjoyment, pleasure, and the limitless pursuit of happiness.[9] This tension still remains at the core of our capitalist system as we try to find a way to manage our contradictory impulses toward our urge to save and our urge to spend, our Calvinism and our hedonism.

It would be a mistake to think of Locke's capitalistic revolution as due to religious sources alone. Weber struggled with the question of how a doctrine originally as morally elevated and austere as Calvin's could morph into something like a worldly "spirit of capitalism" with its gospel of success. Even Weber was forced to admit that it was not so much Calvinism but a "corruption" of Calvinism that led its followers to see in economic well-being a sign of spiritual election. Locke was without doubt indebted to Calvinism and its Puritan offshoot in England, although he also follows secular philosophical sources initiated by Machiavelli and especially an Englishman named Sir Francis Bacon. The moral autonomy of the individual, so central to Locke's philosophy, depends in part on Calvinist and Puritan doctrines but also on fundamental changes in the philosophical tradition that preceded by decades the writings and influence of Calvin and his acolytes.

Advise and Consent

The origin of all government—or at least all legitimate government—is said to derive from consent. In chapter 8 of the *Second Treatise* Locke provides a hypothetical reconstruction of the origin of all societies. "The only way whereby anyone divests himself of his Natural Liberty," he writes in section 95, "and *puts on the bonds of Civil Society* is by agreeing with other Men to joyn and unite in a Community, for their comfortable, safe, and peaceable living." Locke goes on to affirm that whenever a sufficient number of people have consented to make one community, "they are thereby presently incorporated and make *one Body Politik,* wherein the *Majority* have a right to act and conclude for the rest" (VIII/95).

This short and apparently unobtrusive statement makes the first and most powerful case for democracy. On the basis of this statement a famous

Yale professor and author of an important book on Locke declared Locke to be the font of "the faith of a majority-rule democrat."[10] Locke a radical democrat? Consider the following: "For when any number of Men have, by the consent of every individual, made a *Community,* they have thereby made that *Community* one Body, with a Power to Act as one Body, which is only by the will and determination of the *majority*" (VIII/96). To be sure, it would have come as a surprise to the king of England or any other existing monarch to learn that he ruled only by the consent of the governed.

Is Locke denying the legitimacy of all governments that have not received the consent of the majority? This is certainly what David Hume, writing approximately half a century after Locke's death, believed him to be saying. For Hume the doctrine of consent constituted the essence of anarchy. There was not now nor never has there been a government based on the consent of the governed, Hume argued. Government, like all institutions, rests upon habit and custom. To argue that only consent could lend legitimacy to government was to destabilize all governments: so said the Tory Hume against the Whig Locke.[11]

Locke did not use his theory of consent to defend democracy as the only legitimate form of government. The *Second Treatise* argues that government derives its just powers from the consent of the governed, but it does not specify which particular form of government is best. The majority may agree to keep political power in its own hands in which case it remains a democracy. But it may agree to be ruled by some body or even a single individual. The point seems to be that all government is elective, all government derives its power and legitimacy as a grant from the majority. Oligarchies and monarchies only exist due to the consent of the governed. Without that consent, Locke contends, even "the mighty Leviathan"—an unequivocal reference to Hobbes—could not "outlast the day it was born" (VIII/96).

Locke's doctrine of consent could be called the cornerstone of his political theory—even more so than his doctrine of property. It is largely through Locke that the language of consent entered American political discourse. Not only did the Declaration of Independence affirm that all lawful government derives from the consent of the governed, Lincoln reaffirmed the importance of consent in the course of his struggle against slavery. Consider the following passage from his speech on the Kansas-Nebraska Act of 1854: "When the white man governs himself, that is self-government, but when he governs himself and also governs another man, that is more than self-government—that is despotism. If the negro is a *man,* why then my ancient faith teaches me that 'all men are created equal;' and that there can be no moral right in connection with one man's making a slave of another. . . . What I do say is that no man is good enough to govern another *without that other's consent.* I say this is the leading principle—the sheet anchor of American republicanism."[12] Lincoln's statement here was part of his debate with Stephen Douglas over the issues of slavery, but it cut to the core of the doctrine of consent. Douglas defended the theory of "popular sovereignty" according to which whatever the majority of a people in a state or territory desired was the legitimate source of law. From this premise he could argue that slavery to him was a matter of "indifference" since it all depended on what the popular will desired. Lincoln argued otherwise. The doctrine of consent was not a blank check for majority rule. It implied a set of moral limits on what a majority can do. Consent was inconsistent with slavery because no one person can rule another without that other's consent.

Locke was clearly aware of the radical, unsettling implications of his theory of consent. In particular, how did he believe that consent was actually conferred? We are citizens of the oldest democracy in the world, yet did anyone ever ask any of us to give our consent to our form of government? The idea of giving one's consent to something suggests an active, emphatic voice, yet has anyone after the first generation of founders who created and ratified the Constitution ever been asked or required to give his or her consent to it? What is Locke's answer to this problem?

Locke clearly struggles with the problem of how consent is conferred. His answer to this question is quite different from our views on citizenship. "A child," he writes in section 118, "is born a subject of no country or Government." In other words—and contrary to our own Fourteenth Amendment—citizenship is not conferred by birth. Every person, Locke continues, referring to his argument from the state of nature, is born free and equal and is only under the authority of his parents. Whatever government we may choose to obey is a matter not of birth but of choice.

It is only when one reaches the "Age of Discretion" that one is obligated to choose through some sign of agreement to accept the authority of government. Locke is unclear as to how this sign or act of consent is given. One suspects he is referring to some kind of oath or civil ceremony where one pledges with one's word to accept the form of state. "Nothing can make any man so"—an actual citizen of the state—"but his actually entering into it by positive engagement and express promise and compact," Locke writes at section 122. Such an expressed promise or agreement leaves one "perpetually and indispensably obliged to be and remain unalterably a Subject to it" (VIII/121).

One can see from this passage just how seriously Locke takes the idea of consent. One's word is one's bond. To give voice or consent to government is not an act to be entered into lightly but suggests a lifetime commitment. It also shows just how different Locke's views on citizenship are from ours. For Locke, the only people to be full citizens are those who have given their active consent. The only people in our regime who have given their consent in this Lockean manner are what we call "naturalized" citizens, those who have through an official ceremony pledged their support to the form of government under which we live.

For all others, Locke contends, only a "tacit" consent has been given. But how is tacit consent conferred? How can we infer consent when it is not expressly given? This is a question that Locke does not ponder. He suggests that if we have enjoyed the safety of our person and property, one can infer our consent. When, for example, in a wedding ceremony, the minister or justice of the peace asks the congregation to "speak now or forever hold your peace," he is asking for their consent to the legitimacy of the marriage. Generally—except in the movies—there is silence, and silence implies consent. But how do we really know under what conditions silence confers consent or when it is only silence? Silence can equally be the result of threat or intimidation. This is always the problem of inferring intention *ex silentio*.

"God-like Princes"

Locke's doctrine of consent does not appear to endorse any one particular form of government. The task of forming a government will fall to the decision of the majority, but what form the majority will choose must remain an open question. What gives Locke his distinctive voice is his claim that whatever kind of government a majority decides upon, it must be one that limits the power of the sovereign.

Locke's answer to the problem of what kind of government is best is, in a phrase, a system that checks power, especially the power of the monarch or executive. Although we typically think of the father of the doctrine of the checks and balances as the great Montesquieu, who wrote half a century after Locke, in the *Second Treatise* Locke spends several chapters dealing with what he calls the "subordination of powers." His doctrine of the separation or subordination of powers is somewhat different from our own constitutional separation of executive, legislative, and judicial powers.

In the first place Locke emphasizes—in fact continually affirms—the primacy of legislative authority. He states that "the first and fundamental positive Law of all Commonwealths is the establishing of the Legislative power" (XI/134). In England this meant a doctrine of parliamentary supremacy. It is the law-making authority of government that is supreme. There is nothing more important than having settled or known laws that serve as a fence against arbitrary rule. The purpose of government is less to offset the danger of lapsing back into the state of nature (as Hobbes believed) than to prevent the possibility of a tyrant or despotic sovereign with arbitrary power over our lives and property.

Here is where we see Locke's greatest difference with Hobbes. While Hobbes had been an unwavering defender of a united sovereign power, Locke warns continually against the dangers of too great an executive authority. In one of the few jokes to appear in the *Second Treatise,* Locke says the following of *Leviathan:* "As if when Men quitting the State of Nature entered into Society, they agreed that all of them but one, should be under the restraint of Laws, but that he should still retain all the Liberty of the State of Nature, increased with Power, and made licentious by Impunity. This is to think that men are so foolish that they take care to avoid what Mischiefs be done them by *Pole-Cats,* or *Foxes,* but are content, nay think it Safety, to be devoured by *Lions*" (VII/93). Here is another example of Locke's bestiary. Hobbes had identified a real problem, but his cure was worse than the disease. Locke's answer to Hobbes seems to be that if you thought you were bad off in the state of nature, think how much worse off you would be under the power of an absolute sovereign armed with the powers of taxation and conscription. It is not the state of nature but the use of arbitrary power that is the chief evil to be avoided.

Yet even Locke, the great constitutionalist and critic of absolutism, could not dispense entirely with the necessity for executive power. He often treats the executive—and it is not clear whether this refers to one person or a body of persons—as if it were simply an agent of the legislative power. The purpose of the executive often seems to be merely carrying out the will of the legislature. In Locke's language, the executive power is "ministerial and subordinate to the Legislative" in its law-making capacity (XIII/153). The executive seems to be little more than a cipher in Locke's view of legislative supremacy.

Yet there is in every community, Locke affirms, the necessity for a distinct branch of government dealing with matters of war and peace. He calls this the federative power. Every community, he affirms, is to every other community what every individual is to every other individual in the state of nature (XII/145). A distinct federative or war power is necessary in dealing with matters of international conflict between states. In a remarkable passage he notes that this power cannot be bound by "antecedent standing positive Laws" but must be left to "the Prudence and Wisdom of those whose hands it is in, to be managed for the public good" (XII/147).

In other words, matters of war and peace cannot be left to the legislature; they require the intervention of strong leadership—what Locke in an absolutely stunning turn of phrase refers to as "God-like princes" (XIV/166). It is necessary for the executive in extreme situations to call on the use of the prerogative power. "It is impossible," Locke writes, "to foresee, and so by laws to provide for, all Accidents and Necessities, that may concern the public" (XIV, 160). During contingencies or emergencies, the executive must be empowered to act on its own initiative for the good of the community. For this reason it is necessary that the executive be entrusted with a reservoir of prerogative power that Locke defines as "the power to act according to discretion for the public good without the prescription of the Law" (XIV/160).

Locke's prerogative power is the result of the inability of the law to foresee all possible contingencies. Our inability to make rules that can apply to all possible events makes it necessary to leave some discretionary power in the hands of the executive to act for the public safety. He gives as an example the necessity to tear down a person's house to prevent a fire from spreading to the entire neighborhood (XIV/159). Locke's example calls to mind certain contemporary decisions concerning the right of eminent domain. Under certain circumstances it is permissible under the laws of eminent domain for the government to seize private property for the purpose of enhancing the public welfare, for example, building a school or expanding an airport. But when do such acts become abuses of power? Is this an example of using prerogative power for the public good or an unjust usurpation of property rights? Under certain emergency circumstances, in other words, it is necessary to go beyond the letter of the law to act for the public good. The question is whether prerogative power is contained within a constitution or whether it is some kind of extraconstitutional power. And what are the limits of the executive's prerogative power? What check, if any, is there on the use and abuse of this power?

Locke does not exactly say, yet this is a point that raises questions of fundamental importance for constitutional government. Does executive authority extend to all things in times of war, for example? Can traditional limits on presidential power (e.g., the Geneva Conventions) be curtailed under emergency circumstances or are such departures destructive of constitutional government and the rule of law? It is clear that Locke's doctrine of prerogative power vastly expands the legitimate sphere of executive authority, as opposed to a more legalistic definition. Does Locke demonstrate to us the limits of legalism or does his advocacy of prerogative power dangerously skirt the boundless field of absolutism?

I will leave it to you to judge the extent of Locke's prerogative power. He praises the "wisest and best princes" of England as those who exercised the largest prerogative. Such power comes into play especially during times of national crisis or emergency when the rule of law may have to be suspended for the sake of national security and protection. At such times a sovereign may find it necessary to invoke the law of nature that gives him the power to do whatever is in his power to ensure the survival of the state. Locke's acknowledgment of a distinct power that can act on its own authority without the guidance of law is clearly in tension with his theory of legislative supremacy. His reference to "God-like princes" recalls Machiavelli's "armed prophets" and undermines his commitment to law and limited government. Does his idea of an executive prerogative put his reputation as a founder of constitutional democracy into doubt? Was Locke aware of these paradoxes? I think so.[13]

Locke's theory of prerogative power has special resonance today as we face issues of emergency (as in the wake of 9/11) and states of exception. There are some thinkers, like Carl Schmitt, the German legal theorist of the Weimar period, who believed that the state of emergency—the state of the exception—is the essence of the political and that the person or body who has the power to declare the exception is the sovereign. From Schmitt's point of view, this is an extraconstitutional power that statesmen must necessarily utilize when ordinary constitutional operations like the rule of law prove inadequate. Such extensive power, even if it exceeds the authority granted by a constitution, is necessary to confront unforeseen situations.

But is it possible that prerogative powers are granted by our Constitution? Consider Lincoln's decision to suspend habeas corpus during the Civil War. Lincoln did not take this extraordinary step by appealing to an extraconstitutional power that obtains in times of emergency only. He was deeply concerned about the dangers and temptations of dictatorship but argued effectively that the Constitution grants extraordinary powers to deal with extraordinary situations. He cites the Constitution: "The privilege of the writ of habeas corpus shall not be suspended, unless when in cases of rebellion or invasion, the public safety requires it."[14] In other words, the

Constitution contains within itself the provision for the executive to act with prerogative power in times of rebellion or invasion, as the public safety demands. Are such arguments equally applicable to current issues relating to the detention of prisoners at Guantanamo Bay or the National Security Agency's claims about domestic spying?

At the end of the same chapter Locke asks the question, Who shall judge—who shall arbitrate—in cases of conflict between the legislative and executive powers? He seems to be referring to moments of high constitutional crisis between conflicting powers of government. In cases of such conflict, he writes, "there can be no *Judge on Earth*." "The people," he says, "have no other remedy in this but to appeal to Heaven" (XIV/168). How much is contained in this phrase "appeal to Heaven"!

By an appeal to Heaven Locke refers to his doctrine of the right of a people to dissolve their government. He raises this question again at the very end of the book. When a conflict between the people—or their representatives—and the executive becomes so great that the very conditions of social trust have been dissolved, who shall judge? Locke answers emphatically, "The people shall be judge" (XIX/240). In other words, all power derives from and reverts back to the people.

Locke affirms a right of revolution. An appeal to Heaven refers to an appeal to arms, to rebellion, and the need to create a new social contract. He attempts to hold together a belief in the sanctity of law and the necessity for prerogative power that may sometimes have to circumvent the rule of law. Are these two compatible? Can the prerogative power of the executive be constitutionalized so that it does not threaten the liberty of its citizens? Locke alerts us to, even if he does not solve, this timeless problem.

In the end Locke was a revolutionary, but a moderate and cautious one—if this is not too much of a contradiction in terms. His doctrine of consent and legislative supremacy should make him a hero to radical democrats; his beliefs about limited government and the rights of property should make him a hero to constitutional conservatives and libertarians. Ultimately, Locke was neither and both. Like all great thinkers, he defies simple classification. But there is no doubt that he gave the modern constitutional state its definitive form of expression.

Locke's America

No one who reads Locke can fail to recognize the profound influence his writings had on the formation of the American republic. His conception of natural law, individual rights, government by consent, and a right to revolution were the inspiration of the Declaration of Independence and other founding U.S. documents. To some degree a judgment on Locke is a judgment on America, and vice versa. He is—to the extent that anyone is—America's philosopher-king. So what, then, should we think now just over three centuries after Locke's death?

For many years the affiliation between Locke and America was regarded in a largely positive light. For historians and political theorists, our political stability, system of limited government, and market economy have been the result of a broad consensus on Lockean principles. But for many, this relation has also been seen as problematic. The famous historian Louis Hartz complained of America's "irrational Lockeanism," by which he meant a kind of closed commitment to Lockean ideals that shut off other political alternatives and possibilities. For others, Locke legitimized a narrow ethic of "possessive individualism" that focused entirely on market relations. And for still others, his emphasis on rights suggested a legalistic conception of politics that has no language for talking about the common good, the public interest, or other collective goods.[15]

Today, however, Locke's theory of liberalism is confronted with another alternative that also has deep roots in the liberal tradition. I am referring to John Rawls's widely read and widely acclaimed book *A Theory of Justice*.[16] Rawls's book is in many ways a contemporary attempt to update the theory of the state of nature and the social contract through the insights and techniques of contemporary philosophy and game theory. It is certainly the most important work of Anglo-American political philosophy of the past generation. It is a work that situates itself within the liberal tradition of philosophy begun by Locke but developed by Immanuel Kant and John Stuart Mill, and which Rawls hopes to put in a completed or perfected form.

Rawls's *Theory of Justice* stands or falls on its theory of rights, from which all else is derived. Consider the following propositions:

Locke: "Every man has a property in his own person. This nobody has any right to but himself." (V/27)

Rawls: "Each person possesses an inviolability founded on justice that even the welfare of society as a whole cannot override. For this reason justice denies that the loss of freedom for some is made right by a greater good shared to others."[17]

So far so good. Both of these authors present theories of justice, and both justify them by recourse to liberal principles of freedom and equality.

Both regard the purpose of government as securing the conditions of justice, and both regard justice as deriving from the consent—the informed consent—of the governed. But they differ profoundly over the source of rights and therefore over the role of government in securing the conditions of justice.

For Locke, rights derive from a theory of self-ownership. According to this view, everyone has a property in his or her own person, that is, no one has any claim on our bodies or our selves. On the rock of self-ownership Locke builds his edifice of natural rights, justice, and limited government. We possess an identity—what we might call moral personality—by virtue of the fact that we alone are responsible for making ourselves. We are literally the products of our own making. We create ourselves through our own activity, and our most characteristic activity is our work ("the *Labour* of his body and the *Work* of his hands, we may say, are properly his"). Locke's doctrine is that the world is the product of our own making, of our own free activity. Not nature but the self is the source of all value. It is this self that is the unique source of rights. The task of government is to secure the conditions of our property in the broadest sense of that term, namely, everything that is proper to us.

Now contrast Locke's theory of the source of rights to Rawls's. Rawls adds to his conception of justice something he calls the "difference principle." This principle maintains that our natural endowments—our talents, abilities, our family backgrounds and history, our place on the social hierarchy—are, from a moral point of view, something completely arbitrary. They are not "ours" in any strong sense, they do not belong to us, but are the result of an arbitrary genetic lottery of which each of us is the wholly undeserving beneficiary. The result is that no longer can I be regarded as the sole proprietor of my assets or the unique recipient of the advantages or disadvantages that accrue from them. Fortune—Machiavellian *fortuna*—is utterly arbitrary, and therefore I should be regarded not as the possessor but merely the recipient of what talents, capacities, and abilities that I may possess.

The result of Rawls's principle—and its differences from Lockean self-ownership—could not be more striking. The Lockean theory of justice supports a meritocracy, sometimes referred to as an equality of opportunity; that is, what a person does with his or her natural assets belongs exclusively to that person. No one has the moral right to interfere with the products of our labor, which include not just the "labor of our body and the work of our hands" but also our intelligence and natural endowments. For Rawls, on the other hand, our endowments are never really our own to begin with. The capacities for hard work, intelligence, ambition, and just plain good luck do not properly belong to you at all. They are part of a common or collective possession to be shared by society as a whole. Consider the following: "The difference principle represents, in effect, an agreement to regard the distribution of natural talents as a common asset and to share in the benefits of this distribution whatever it turns out to be."[18]

It is this conception of common assets that underwrites Rawls's theory of distributive justice and the welfare state, just as it is Locke's theory of self-ownership that justifies his conception of private property and limited government. According to Rawls's view, justice requires that social arrangements be structured for the benefit of the "least advantaged," that is, the worst off in the genetic lottery. For Rawls, a society is just if, and only if, it is engaged in redressing social inequalities, if it serves to benefit those whom he calls the least advantaged. Redistributing our common assets does not violate the sanctity of the individual, because the fruits of our labor were never really "ours" to begin with. Unlike Locke, whose theory of self-ownership provides a moral justification for the self, for our moral individuality, Rawls's difference principle maintains that we never belong to ourselves alone but are always part of a "we," a social collective whose common assets can be redistributed to the advantage of the whole.

Locke and Rawls represent two radically different visions of the liberal state, one broadly libertarian, the other broadly egalitarian, one emphasizing liberty, the other equality. Both of these views begin from certain common premises, but they move in very different directions. Locke's theory of self-ownership regards the political community in largely negative terms as protecting our natural rights to our persons and properties; Rawls's theory of common assets regards the community in positive terms as taking an active part in redistributing the products of our individual endeavors for the common interest. The question is which of these two views is the more valid?

My own view is that Locke is far closer to American theory and practice than is Rawls. The Declaration of Independence, the charter of American liberties, states that each individual is endowed with certain "unalienable rights," among which are life, liberty, and the pursuit of happiness. The very indeterminacy of this last phrase, with its emphasis on the individual's right to determine happiness for himself or herself, suggests a form of government that allows for ample diversity of our natural talents and abilities as well as the inequalities that derive from such diversity. Although the Declaration certainly intends the establishment of justice as one of the first tasks of government, nowhere is it implied that this requires the wholesale redistribution of our individual assets. In fact Rawls's claim that a government is just to the extent—and only to the extent—that it is actively involved in the redress of inequalities would cast a pall of illegitimacy over virtually every government that has ever existed. This idea would also have come as news to thinkers as different as Plato, Aristotle, Cicero, Maimonides, and Thomas Aquinas, all of whom believed that social inequalities were necessary for societies to achieve a high degree of personal and collective excellence.

Also, although Rawls is clearly attentive to the moral ills of inequality, he seems naïve about the actual political mechanisms by which those inequalities will be rectified. He wants government to work for the benefit of the least advantaged, but this will require the extensive and often arbitrary use of judicial power to determine who has a right to what far in excess of limited constitutional government. At bottom are two very different conceptions of law. For Locke, laws are known rules used for the adjudication of conflicts; for Rawls, laws are the considerations of "fairness" in the distribution of scarce resources. For Rawls, laws are not simply procedures but designate substantive outcomes. Laws pertain not to rules but to regulations that certain rational competitors would agree is an equitable distribution of goods. It is not surprising that the warmest reception of Rawls's work today has come from those advocating the modern regulatory policies whose goal is to rearrange our collective assets for the sake of achieving a maximum degree of social equality.

A return to Locke—even if such a return were possible—would by no means be a panacea for what ails us. Some historians—Louis Hartz was the most famous—treat America as a nation uniquely built upon Lockean foundations. America, Hartz believed, remained something of a Lockean remnant in a world increasingly governed by more radical forms of modernity. Indeed, it has been our stubborn Lockeanism that has prevented the kinds of extreme ideological polarization and conflict characteristic of continental Europe throughout much of the nineteenth and twentieth centuries. Yet the image of America as something of a theoretical anomaly protected from the shocks of later modernity cannot be sustained. Those who would urge a return to the language of Locke or the American framers are blind and deaf to later developments—romanticism, progressivism, postmodernism—that have been grafted on to the character of our regime. "The United States," as Joseph Cropsey has argued, "is an arena in which modernity is working itself out. The founding documents are the premise of a gigantic argument, subsequent propositions in which are the decayed or decaying moments of modern thought."[19]

Locke's effort to build modern republican government on the "low but solid" ground of self-interest and the desire for comfortable self-preservation could not help but generate its own forms of dissatisfaction. Can a regime dedicated to the pursuit of happiness ever satisfy the deepest longings of the human soul? Can a regime devoted to the rational accumulation of property answer the needs for those higher-order virtues like honor, nobility, love of country, and sacrifice? Can a regime devoted to the avoidance of pain, discomfort, and anxiety produce anything more than contemporary forms of Epicureanism and nihilism? To understand the full scope of our dissatisfaction with the Lockean conception of modernity, it is important that we turn to modernity's greatest critic: Jean-Jacques Rousseau.

CHAPTER 10
Rousseau on Civilization and Its Discontents

Jean-Jacques Rousseau, 1712–1778. Oil on canvas. Photo credit:
The Art Gallery Collection / Alamy

189

Rousseau is commonly regarded as a critic of liberalism, of the kind of property-owning society based on rights and limited government given expression by Locke. But to see Rousseau as a critic of Lockean liberalism would be short-sighted. He was a product of the ancien régime. He was born in 1712, two years before the death of Louis XIV, and died in 1778, a decade before the outbreak of the French Revolution. His life was lived entirely in the waning years of the age of absolutism. Rousseau was aware that he lived in an age of transition, but what precisely would come after was by no means clear. He wrote with the passion and intensity of someone who expects to be instrumental in the coming of a new historical and political epoch—and he was.[1]

Do not mistake Rousseau for a Frenchman; he was a Swiss. He frequently signed his name "Citoyen de Genève," after the city where he was born. He was the son of an artisan who abandoned his family after a falling out with the local authorities. The young Rousseau was apprenticed to an engraver but left Geneva for good at the age of sixteen. For the following sixteen years, he lived a varied life, working occasionally as a music instructor and transcriber, the secretary to the French ambassador in Venice, and the lover of a wealthy woman several years his senior. After moving to Paris in 1744 Rousseau eked out a living on the margins of the Parisian literary scene until the publication of his *Discourse on the Arts and Sciences* in 1750. This work made his name. The *Discourse on the Origins and Foundations of Inequality among Men*—the so-called *Second Discourse*—was published five years later. *On the Social Contract* and *Emile,* his major work on political education, were both published in 1762. Rousseau was also the composer of a highly successful opera, *Le Devin du Village,* that was performed at the court of Louis XV, and even until the end of his life he continued to earn money as a music transcriber. During this period he fathered five children with a common-law wife and abandoned them all to an orphanage. His writings were many and various. He left volumes of autobiography, one entitled *Confessions*—after the book by Saint Augustine—and another written in dialogue form called *Rousseau Juge de Jean-Jacques.*[2]

Historians and political theorists have often been flummoxed by the nature of Rousseau's contribution. Was he a revolutionary whose work inspired the radical phases of the French Revolution? After all, *The Social Contract* begins with the incendiary lines "Man is born free and everywhere he is in chains." Rousseau's appeal to the severe political ethics of ancient Sparta and Rome, as well as his belief that the people are the sole source of sovereignty, figured into the revolutionary politics of the subsequent age. Or did Rousseau seek to release us from the bonds of society altogether, as he seems to do in the *Second Discourse*? In this work he lays the ground for the romantic individualism that would be associated later with William Wordsworth in England and Henry David Thoreau in America. His direct appeal to nature, as well as his celebration of the simplicity of peasant life, opens the door to Tolstoy and a host of social experiments in rural communal utopianism.

Rousseau's influence was manifold and various. He helped to bring the political and intellectual movement called the Enlightenment to its highest state of perfection—at least Edmund Burke thought so—and yet he was at the same time one of the Enlightenment's most profound critics. He was a close friend of Denis Diderot and the authors and contributors to the *Encyclopedia* and yet excoriated the influence of the progress of the arts and sciences on the moral life of communities. He was a writer who wore different hats. He defended what he called the savage against civilized man, he took the side of the poor and dispossessed against the elites, and he adopted the posture of loyal son and citizen of Geneva against the sophisticated intellectuals of his day. Who was Rousseau, and what did he stand for? This is what we will try to find out.

Conjectural History and Natural Science

The *Second Discourse* is in the eyes of many readers Rousseau's greatest work. It is what the eighteenth century called a conjectural history. It is a kind of philosophical history—really a philosophical reconstruction of history—though not of what actually happened in the past but of what had to have happened for history to make sense. Rousseau begins the work by comparing the effects of history to the statue of Glaucus that the winds and storms had so disfigured that it scarcely looked human at all (124). This is what history has done to us. It has so affected and transformed human nature that if we want to understand what human nature is, it is necessary to reconstruct it through a kind of thought experiment.

Rousseau compares his procedure in the *Second Discourse* to that undertaken by physicists and cosmologists who speculate about the origins of the universe. There is no empirical or physical evidence to draw on to understand exactly how the world was formed. We can only make certain inferences and conjectures based upon the evidence we have available to us. Thus Rousseau remarks in one of his most arresting sentences: "Let us therefore begin by setting aside all the facts, for they do not affect the question" (132). The investigations that he is pursuing should not be taken for historical truths, only for "hypothetical and conditional reasonings." In other words, the history he intends to unfold is an experiment much like that undertaken by geologists who try to infer the development of plant or animal life from the existence of certain fossils or skeletal remains.

Yet at the same time that Rousseau speaks of his work as tentative and experimental ("I have hazarded some guesses"), one cannot help but note that he seems extremely confident about his findings. In particular, he discusses and rejects the investigation of his predecessors, both ancient and modern: "The philosophers who have examined the foundations of society," he remarks, "have all felt the necessity of returning to the state of nature, but none of them has reached it." Rousseau believes that he alone has finally struck gold: "O man," he exclaims, "whatever land you may be from, whatever may be your opinions, listen: Here is your history such as I believed I read it, not in the books by your kind, who are liars, but in Nature which never lies" (133). Rousseau claims that for the first time human nature will be revealed and the history of civil society will be explained.

Natural Man

Rousseau follows in the footsteps of his great predecessors Hobbes and Locke by seeking human nature in a hypothetical condition that he calls the state of nature. He believes that while Hobbes and Locke were on the right track, they never really took seriously the depth of the problem. What does it mean to take nature seriously?

To understand human nature as it originally was requires us to conduct a kind of thought experiment where we peel away, onion-like, everything we have become or acquired through the influence of history, custom, and tradition. Thus when Hobbes attributes to natural man certain warlike properties, Rousseau figures that this cannot be right. War and the passions that lead us to war can only come into being once we are already in society; they cannot possibly hold true for natural man prior to all social relations. Ditto for Locke. When Locke attributes to man in the state of nature certain qualities of rationality, industry, and acquisitiveness, these, too, are qualities that can only come to light in society. Property entails social relations between persons, and man in the state of nature is a presocial animal. It is clear that for Rousseau human nature is something infinitely more remote and strange than anything his predecessors could ever have imagined.

Rousseau's natural man is in fact far more like an animal than anything we might identify as recognizably human. Rousseau deliberately animalizes human beings. When Aristotle said that man is the rational being because we possess speech, he was wrong again, Rousseau says. Language is dependent on society and could only have developed over literally thousands of generations; it cannot be a property of natural man. Human nature is little different from animal nature, and Rousseau delights in learning about orangutans and other species, several of which had only recently been discovered by Europeans. A century before Darwin, he could just as easily have called his book *On the Origin of Species*.

Yet for all our common features with other species, Rousseau specifies two qualities that set us apart. The first is the quality of freedom or what he calls free agency: "I see in any animal nothing but an ingenious machine to which nature has given senses in order to wind itself up and, to a point, protect itself against everything that tends to destroy or to disturb it. I perceive precisely the same thing in the human machine, with this difference that Nature alone does everything in the operation of the beast, whereas man contributes to his operations in his capacity as a free agent" (140).

The idea of freedom or free agency also sounds superficially similar to Hobbes and Locke. Didn't they assert that in the natural state all men are free and equal? Wasn't it precisely our natural freedom and equality that made the transition from nature to civil society possible? But Rousseau means something different. Freedom for Hobbes and Locke means the freedom to choose this or that; the freedom to exercise the will and not to be interfered with by others around us. Rousseau also believes this, but he adds something else. He connects freedom to what he calls in the same passage human *perfectibility*. What does he mean by this term?

Perfectibility suggests our openness—our virtually unlimited openness—to change. As a species we not only have the freedom to *do* this rather than that; we have the freedom to *become* this rather than that. It is our very openness to change that accounts for our mutability over time. As a species we are uniquely underdetermined, meaning that our nature is not confined in advance to what it may become. Rather, our nature is uniquely suited to alter and transform itself as circumstances change and as we adapt to new and unforeseen situations. Perfectibility is a feature not so much of individuals as of the species. Whereas Hobbes and Locke assumed that human nature itself remained more or less unchanged from the transition to civil society, Rousseau believes that human nature has undergone massive "revolutions" over the course of time. It is this "distinctive and almost unlimited faculty of perfectibility," he asserts, that is "the source of all of man's miseries" (141).

Rousseau notes that freedom alone—perfectibility—is not our sole natural characteristic, although it is responsible for almost everything that we have become. In addition to freedom there is the faculty Rousseau calls *pitié* (pity). Here is Rousseau at his most characteristic: the founder of romanticism.

Man is not the rational animal, the thinking being, the Cartesian cogito, but the sensitive creature. We are creatures not merely of sense but of sensibility. Rousseau finds all kinds of evidence for assuming that compassion was part of our original nature. There is a reluctance he finds in all species to witness the pain or suffering of others of their kind. The fact that we cry at the misfortunes of others who have nothing to do with us is evidence of our sensitivity. Do we not enjoy crying at movies? Is it rational to feel pity at the death of King Kong, a fictional creature whose fate cannot affect us? Man is the sensitive creature—so much so that Rousseau claims to find evidence here for our "natural goodness." Why does Rousseau emphasize this quality?

Long before television's Dr. Phil and a thousand other self-help gurus, Rousseau taught us "to get in touch with our feelings." But while natural man may be gentle and compassionate, this sentiment is easily overpowered by other more powerful passions once we enter society. Reason, which comes about only in society, sets us against one another. We cease to care about others and become calculating and mercenary. Selfishness and egoism are reinforced by the development of rationality: "It is reason that engenders *amour propre*," Rousseau remarks, "and reflection that reinforces it" (153). The development of rationality hastens our corruption by assisting in the development of vice. The task of the *Second Discourse* is to recover our natural selves from the artificial, corrupt, and calculating beings we have become.

Property and the Origins of Inequality

Rousseau's *Emile* begins with this sentence: "Everything is good that leaves the hands of the Author of things; everything degenerates in the hands of man."[3] This is more or less the same thought that runs throughout the *Second Discourse*. It is an attempt to show how man, who is by nature strong, independent, and free, becomes in society weak, dependent, and enslaved. How did this come about? How did savage man—and the term *sauvage* is one that Rousseau uses with great affection—become civil man? How did the natural man become a bourgeois?

The answer to these questions can be given in a single word: property. The first sentence of part 2 of the *Second Discourse* reads: "The first man who, having enclosed a piece of ground, to whom it occurred to say *this is mine,* and found people sufficiently simple to believe him, was the true founder of civil society" (161). Locke might well have agreed, but Rousseau continues as follows: "How many crimes, wars, murders, how many miseries and horrors mankind would have been spared by him who, pulling up the stakes or filling in the ditch, had cried out to his kind: Beware of listening to this impostor. You are lost if you forget that the fruits are everyone's and the earth no one's" (161).

Rousseau was not a communist. He did not feel it was either possible or desirable to do away with private property after the fashion of Plato or Marx. But there is no one who was a more acute observer of the ills of class and the effects of private property than Rousseau. He believed that there was something deeply wrong with the conception of government as the protector of private property that intervenes as little as necessary with the affairs of individuals, leaving them free to pursue life, liberty, and property as they see fit. In many respects he points back to an older conception of government, one derived from the ancients, that sees politics as supervising the pursuit of property, mitigating the harshest effects of economic inequality, and controlling the acquisitive desires of its citizens. A sentence from Rousseau's *Discourse on the Arts and Sciences,* says it all: "The ancient politicians forever spoke of morals and virtue; ours speak only of commerce and money" (18).

Amour Propre and Civil Society

If Rousseau were only interested in issues of class and economic inequality, there would be very little difference between him and Marx.[4] In fact Marx was an appreciative reader of Rousseau, and many of Marx's best lines against capitalist society are taken from Rousseau. But it is less the material aspects of inequality that bother Rousseau than the moral and psychological injuries of class. He frequently takes the side of the poor and dispossessed, but it is not poverty as such that rouses his anger so much as the attitudes and beliefs shaped by inequalities of wealth and power. It is as a moral psychologist that Rousseau truly finds his voice.

The chief villain of the *Second Discourse* is not property but something Rousseau calls *amour propre*. Amour propre is an untranslatable term, which is why it is often best left in the French. It is related to a range of psychological characteristics, such as pride, vanity, conceit, or in one translation "egocentrism." Amour propre only arises in society and is the true cause of our discontents. In a lengthy footnote Rousseau distinguishes amour propre from what he calls self-love or *amour de soi-même*: "*Amour propre* and *Amour de soi-même,* two very different passions in their nature and their effects, should not be confused. Self-love is a natural sentiment which inclines every animal to attend to its self-preservation and which, guided in many by reason and modified by pity, produces humanity and virtue. *Amour propre* is only a relative sentiment, factitious, and born in society, which inclines every individual to set greater store by himself than by anyone else, inspires men with all the evils they do one another, and is the genuine source of honor" (218). How did this sentiment arise? How did it come about? And even more important, what can be done about it?

For Hobbes, pride, the desire to be superior, is natural to us. It is part of our natural desire to dominate others. But for Rousseau, such a sentiment could only come about after the state of nature—a state that on Hobbes's own account is "solitary, poor, nasty, brutish, and short"—had begun to give way. Hobbes's account is on Rousseau's reading incoherent. If the natural state is truly solitary, as Hobbes says, then what would it mean for us to feel pride or vanity, which presupposes human sociability and the esteem of others? Rousseau uses Hobbes to prove his own point, namely, that amour propre is not a natural sentiment but a sentiment that is relative and artificial, that comes into being only once we enter society.

Rousseau speculates—and again this is a hypothetical history—that amour propre arose as soon as people began to gather around a hut or a tree and to look at one another. It is from this gaze that the fatal passion of vanity was born: "Everyone began to look at everyone else and to wish to be looked at himself, and public esteem acquired a price. The one who sang or danced best; the handsomest, the strongest, the most skillful, or the most eloquent came to be the most highly regarded, and this was the first step at once toward inequality and vice: from these first preferences arose vanity and contempt on the one hand, shame and envy on the other; and the fermentation caused by these new leavens eventually produced compounds fatal to happiness and innocence" (166).

Rousseau is on to something crucial here. Amour propre is presented in largely negative terms, but it is also inversely related to something positive, to the desire felt by all people once they enter society to be accorded recognition or respect by those around them. The desire for recognition is also at the root of justice. Underlying this is the intuition that our feelings, beliefs, opinions, and attitudes should be acknowledged and respected by others, that we matter. When we feel our opinions are slighted, when others do not recognize their worth, we feel angry and vengeful. The need for recognition is a cornerstone of justice, but at the same time this demand for recognition can easily become cruel and violent. Consider the following:

> As soon as men had begun to appreciate one another and the idea of consideration had taken shape in their mind, everyone claimed a right to it, and one could no longer deprive anyone of it with impunity. From here arose the first duties of civility even among savages, and from it any intentional wrong became an affront because, together with the harm resulting from the injury, the offended party saw in it contempt for his person, often more unbearable than the harm itself. Thus everyone punishing the contempt shown him in a manner proportionate to the stock he set by himself, vengeances became terrible, and men bloodthirsty and cruel. (166)

Does this sound familiar? It should. Amour propre, as Rousseau recognizes, is a volatile passion. It contains the desire to be respected and acknowledged that is at the root of justice, yet it is also highly malleable and can give rise to feelings of shame and indignation when we feel our basic entitlements are not respected. It makes us burn with anger at perceived slights and makes us risk our lives and endanger the lives of others to rectify perceived acts of injustice. Rousseau's question is whether amour propre is purely a negative passion or whether it can be redirected to achieve social goods like justice and equity.

In the years after Rousseau wrote the *Second Discourse,* this theme would be taken up by a famous German philosopher named Hegel. For Hegel, the struggle for esteem or recognition was not only a powerful psychological spur to action; it became nothing less than the master power of world history. In a book entitled *The Phenomenology of Mind,* Hegel described history as a life-and-death struggle for recognition in which individuals and classes battle one another for power and prestige. The struggle for recognition was at the core of the famous dialectic of world history that first Hegel—and later Marx—held could only be overcome once a society was

created that could afford every citizen an equal degree of esteem and respect. Hegel believed such a society was possible within the context of the
more-or-less constitutional monarchies of his day, but Marx radicalized
Hegel's thesis to show that only a universal classless society could satisfy
the Hegelian demand for recognition.[5]

This is obviously a long story, but it is the story of modern politics and
history at least since Rousseau and the French Revolution. Our politics
have become today the domain not only where classes contend for places of
power but where increasingly people demand to have their claims accorded
recognition or respect. (Consider the way political candidates and their
surrogates are perpetually on the lookout for what are deemed slights, and
the sense of feigned moral outrage they then express.) For Rousseau, a politics that was concerned only with the protection of person and property, to
protect people from harm, only began to scratch the surface of the problem.
For him and all who came later, politics would have to serve the higher
purpose of guaranteeing not only protection but also esteem, not only security but also recognition, not just toleration but also acceptance. Perhaps
more than any of the other philosophers in the Great Tradition, Rousseau is
our contemporary.

Civilization and Its Discontents

In *Annie Hall* Woody Allen remarks that there are two kinds of people: the
horrible and the miserable. The horrible are those who have suffered some
kind of personal tragedy, like disfigurement, or who are facing terminal ill-
ness; the miserable are everyone else. Rousseau wants us to be miserable.
He wants us to feel just how bad things have become.

The only exception to the general history of human discontent related
by Rousseau was the creation of early primitive society. The societies he describes as maintaining a "middle position" between the pure state of nature and the development of modern conditions he considers to be "the
happiest and the most lasting epoch" and "the best for man" (167). It is in
primitive society—not necessarily the pure form of the natural state—that
Rousseau finds the perfect equilibrium between human powers and human
needs that is the recipe for happiness.

The end of primitive society came with the discovery of two inven-
tions: agriculture and metallurgy. With agriculture came the division of
the land and subsequent inequalities of property; with metallurgy came the
arts of war and conquest. With these two developments humanity entered

a new stage, one where laws and political institutions became necessary to adjudicate conflicts over rights. The establishment of governments, rather than bringing peace as Hobbes and Locke had argued, had the effect of sanctioning the growing inequalities that had begun to arise. For Rousseau, there is something deeply shocking about the assertion that men who were once equal so easily consent to inequalities of property and rule by the strong. The social contract, as he presents it, is a kind of swindle that the rich and powerful use to control the poor and dispossessed. Rather than instituting justice, this compact merely legitimizes past usurpations. Political power helps to legitimize economic inequalities. Governments may operate by consent, but the consent they are granted is based on falsehoods and lies. How else can one explain why the lives of the rich are so much freer, so much easier, and so much more open to enjoyment than those of the poor?

The establishment of government is the last link in the chain of Rousseau's conjectural history. However, the emergence of this stage of civilization has led simultaneously to the creation of a new kind of human being that Rousseau was among the first to identify as the bourgeois. The bourgeois is Rousseau's invention, and he does much to define the term for the next century. Most striking about this new human type is the necessity to appear to be one thing but actually to be something else. The distinction between seeming and being is central: "To be and to appear became two entirely different things," Rousseau writes, "and from this distinction arose ostentatious display, deceitful cunning, and all the vices that follow in their wake" (170).

In the penultimate paragraph of the *Second Discourse* Rousseau describes the dilemma of the bourgeois as follows: "The savage lives within himself; sociable man, always outside himself, is capable of living only in the opinion of others, and, so to speak, derives the sentiment of his own existence solely from their judgment" (187). Natural man thought of himself, and only of himself, whereas civilized man is forced to think of others, but only as a means to his ends. The bourgeois is someone who lives in and through the opinions of others, who thinks only of others when he is alone and only of himself when he is with others. Even the social bond is regarded as a contract, an agreement among business partners, the most bourgeois of social institutions. Unlike the natural man, who thinks only of himself, or the classical citizen, who thinks only of his city, the bourgeois inhabits a kind of moral half-way house and is capable neither of natural pity nor political heroism. Such a person is duplicitous, hypocritical, and false. Perpetually torn between his duties and his inclinations, the bourgeois leads a frenzied and agitated existence. It is this condition of perpetual restlessness—later described by Tocqueville as the characteristic state of democratic man—goaded on by amour propre, that is the particular form of misery that civilization has bequeathed to us.

What to do about this? To be sure, Rousseau is deeply impressed with stories of the dignity and independence of native peoples—Icelanders, Greenlanders, Hottentots—and their proud refusal to assimilate to European customs and manners. They prefer their personal independence to all the comforts and luxuries of modern civilization. Consider the following wonderful observation in a footnote to the *Second Discourse:*

> On a number of occasions, savages have been brought to Paris, London, and other cities; people have scurried to spread out before them our luxury, our wealth, and all of our most useful and most interesting arts; all this never excited in them anything other than a stupid admiration, without the slightest stirring of covetousness. I remember, among others, the story of a chief of some North Americans who was brought to the Court of England about thirty years ago. He was shown a thousand things in search of some present he might like, without anything being found that he seemed to care for. Our weapons seemed to him heavy and clumsy, our shoes hurt his feet, he found our clothes cumbersome, he rejected everything; finally it was noticed that, having picked up a wool blanket, he seemed to take pleasure in wrapping it around his shoulders; you will at least allow, someone straightaway said to him, the usefulness of this furnishing? Yes, he answered, it seems to me almost as good as an animal skin. He would not even have said that, if he had worn them both in the rain. (219–20)

Did Rousseau believe it possible or desirable to return to the state of nature? He has frequently been read that way. In a letter to Rousseau, Voltaire wrote that never has so much intelligence been spent in the attempt to turn us into brutes. This is clever, but not right. Voltaire surely knew that 150 years before Rousseau's praise of the natural savage, Michel de Montaigne had written his important essay "Of Cannibals," describing the Indian tribes off the coast of Brazil, whom he praised against the true savagery and barbarism of their European conquerors. Montaigne's dislike of cruelty and his demand for compassion were an important influence on Rousseau's account of natural man.[6]

In any case, Rousseau makes plain that a return to the state of nature is no longer an option. In one of his footnotes Rousseau asks: "What, then? Must societies be destroyed, thine and mine annihilated, and men return to live in the forests with the bears? A conclusion in the style of my adversaries, which I would rather anticipate than leave them the shame of drawing it" (203). In other words: no. A return to the state of nature is impossible, for it would be like returning domesticated animals to the wild: they would not last a single day because their instinct for preservation is dulled by continual association with and dependence upon others. If a return to nature is impossible, the only alternative is to live in society.

Here is where the *Second Discourse* falls short. The book ends on a note of the utmost despair. It offers no positive answer by which to cure the problems of civilization but merely hints at two possible solutions. One is suggested in his dedicatory letter to the city of Geneva. Perhaps the closest approximation to the early stage of primitive society lauded by Rousseau is the small, isolated rural republic where simple patriotism and love of country have not been completely obliterated by the agitations of amour propre. Only in a "wisely tempered democracy" like Geneva is it still possible for citizens to enjoy some of the equality of the natural condition (115). Democracy is the social condition that most closely approximates the state of nature. This is a theme that Rousseau will develop at length in *The Social Contract*.

But Rousseau hints at another solution to the problem of civilization. The *Second Discourse* leads us to believe that all society is bondage and alienation from nature, from our true being. The answer to the problem of society is to return to the root of society. The root of society is the need for self-preservation, but self-preservation is only necessary to maintain the feeling of existence, "the sentiment of his own existence," as Rousseau says above. By giving oneself to the sole feeling of existence without a thought of the future, without care or fear, the individual has in a sense returned to nature in this way. Only a very few people are capable of finding their way back to nature. The type of human being who can do so is no longer a philosopher but an artist and poet. He is one of the rare, the few, one of nature's true aristocrats. His claim to special treatment is based less on superior understanding than on superior sensitivity, less on wisdom than on compassion. Rousseau considered himself one of these people. Are you perhaps another?

The Social Contract

The modern discipline of political science has become the study of democracy, what it is, what types there are, what causes democracies to come into being, what sustains and preserves them. Modern democracy is unthinkable without Rousseau. Whoever holds *The Social Contract* in his or her hands holds the key to modern democracy. Rousseau remains the sine qua non of democratic political theory. This does not mean, of course, that all modern democracies are Rousseauean democracies. Far from it. What I mean is that all later democratic theorists, from Madison to Tocqueville to contemporary advocates of "market theories" of democracy with its "rational voter paradox," have had to confront the challenge of Rousseau and to justify their departures from him.[7]

The Social Contract begins with one of the most famous sentences in all of political philosophy: "Man is born free and everywhere he is in chains" (I, 1). In a single sentence Rousseau delegitimizes every existing government and perhaps every government that has ever existed. The phrase seems perfectly in keeping with the teachings of the *Second Discourse*. In the state of nature we are born free, equal, and independent; only in society do we become weak, dependent, and enslaved. It is what follows from this sentence that is the shocker. "How did this change come about? I do not know. What can make it legitimate? I believe I can solve this question" (I, 1). While in the *Second Discourse* Rousseau attempted to delegitimize the bonds of society, in *The Social Contract* he now sets out to give them a moral legitimacy. What has happened? Has he undergone a massive change in the seven years separating the publication of the *Second Discourse* and *The Social Contract*?

Before answering this question, consider some of the differences between the two books. The *Second Discourse* is a hypothetical history of human development from the state of nature to the civil condition. It is written in a vivid, bold, and colorful language drawing on the biological sciences and their knowledge of newly discovered animal species like orangutans and their anthropological investigations of the Caribs and other North American peoples. *The Social Contract*, by contrast, is written in the dry, even bloodless, language of a legal document. It carries the subtitle *Principles of Political Right*. It is a work of considerable philosophical abstraction whose leading actors are concepts like the social contract and the general will. The book, Rousseau tells us, was originally part of a longer investigation of politics that has since been lost.

The Social Contract presents itself in the first instance as a utopia, an ideal city, much like Plato's *Republic*. And yet this is not quite true. Early in the work we find a phrase that comes directly out of Machiavelli's *Prince*. "Taking men as they are and laws as they can be, in this inquiry I shall try always to combine what right permits with what interest prescribes" (I, Introduction). Taking men as they are, that is, Rousseau will not begin by making any heroic assumptions about human nature, taking metaphysical flights of fancy, but rather stay on the low but solid ground of recognized fact. But what are these facts of human nature that Rousseau says describe men "as they are"?

The basic premise from which the whole of *The Social Contract* unfolds is the claim that man is born free. All subsequent relations of hierarchy, obligation, and authority are the result not of nature but of agreement or convention. Society and the moral ties that constitute it are conventional all the way down. *The Social Contract* as a whole is an attempt to work out a system of justice, "the principles of political right," that are appropriate to human beings understood entirely as free agents responsible to themselves alone. Rousseau's political philosophy begins, then, from the realistic or empirical belief that each of us has a deep-rooted interest in securing the conditions of his or her own liberty. Rousseau does not presuppose altruism or any other-regarding characteristics. Each of us has a selfish desire to preserve his or her own freedom, and a social order will be rational or just when it allows us to persevere in our freedom.

The problem is that in the state of nature my selfish desire to preserve my own freedom comes into conflict with your selfish desire for preserving yours. The state of nature quickly becomes a state of war based on conflicting desires. How, then, do we preserve our own freedom without lapsing into the anarchy that is the state of war? This is Rousseau's question, to which his doctrine of the social contract is the answer.

The General Will

The social contract is Rousseau's famous answer to the problem of natural freedom. This is so because nature provides no standards or guidelines for determining who should rule. Notice that when Rousseau speaks of the social contract as the foundation of all legitimate authority, he means literally that all standards of justice and right have their origin in the will. It is this liberation of the will from all transcendent guidance that forms the moral center of his philosophy. Rousseau most fully speaks in his own voice when he is dismissing all rival sources of authority—nature, custom, revelation—that would inhibit or usurp the primacy of the will.

Given Rousseau's libertarian conception of human nature, his description of the actual mechanism of the social contract comes as a surprise. The problem to which the formula of the social contract is the answer is stated succinctly in book 1, chapter 6: " 'To find a form of association that will defend and protect the person and goods of each associate with the full common force, and by means of which each, uniting with all, nevertheless obey only himself and remain as free as before.' This is the fundamental problem to which the social contract provides the solution."

This formula contains two clauses that merit close attention. The first clause says that the aim of the social contract is to protect and defend with the common force the goods and person of each member. So far this is thoroughly consistent with Locke's claims that government must protect everyone's life, liberty, and estate. Yet Rousseau adds to this Lockean liberal clause a second, more distinctively Rousseauean claim, namely, that the contract must not only ensure the conditions for mutual protection but also ensure that in uniting with others each person obeys only himself and therefore remains as free as before. But how is this possible? Is it not the essence of the contract that we give up some part of our natural freedom for the benefits of mutual peace and security? How can we remain as free as before, much less obey only ourselves?

Rousseau answers as follows: "These clauses, rightly understood, all come down to just one, namely the total alienation of each associate with all of his rights to the whole community" (I, 6). The two phrases "total alienation" and "entire community" are obviously central here. In the first place, all persons must give themselves over entirely to the social contract so as to guarantee that the terms of agreement are equal for all. The total alienation clause is Rousseau's manner of ensuring that the terms of the contract are the same for everyone.

Second, it is only when we alienate ourselves from the entire community that the individual is beholden not to the private will of some particular person but to the general will of all. The social contract is the foundation of the general will, which is the only legitimate sovereign (II, 1). Not kings, not parliaments, not representative assemblies, but the general will of the entire community is the only genuine sovereign. Since everyone combines to make up this general will, when we give ourselves over to it, we do nothing more than obey ourselves. The sovereign is not some third party, distinct from the people; it is merely the people acting in its collective capacity.

Arguably something seems amiss. From a set of highly individualistic premises where each person is concerned to protect his freedom alone, Rousseau appears to be heading toward a highly regimented and collectivized conclusion where the individual has given over his entire being to the will of the community. Does this foretell the condition of the tyranny of the majority later analyzed by Tocqueville? Is the general will a formula for totalitarianism?[8]

Rousseau's answer, paradoxical as it sounds, is that only when every person gives himself over entirely to society as a whole can the conditions of mutual freedom be achieved. Why is this? Because then no one is dependent upon the will of another person, as he would be if a king, president, or assembly were made sovereign. The people establish a new kind of sovereign—the general will—which is not, strictly speaking, the sum total of individual wills but more like the general interest or the rational will of a community. Since we all contribute to shaping this will, when we obey its laws, we are doing no more than obeying ourselves.

Rousseau describes the transformation that takes place when we legislate as members of the general will. The freedom of the citizen under the general will is not the freedom of the state of nature to do anything that our will and power allow us to; it is a new kind of moral freedom to do only what the law commands: "The transition from the state of nature to the civil state produces most remarkable change in man," Rousseau writes, "by substituting justice for instinct in his conduct and endowing his actions with the morality they previously lacked" (I, 8).

Rousseau continues as follows: "What man loses by the social contract is his natural freedom and an unlimited right to everything that tempts him and he can reach; what he gains is civil freedom and property in everything he possesses. . . . To the preceding one might add to the credit of the civil state moral freedom, which alone makes man truly the master of himself; for the impulsion of mere appetite is slavery, and obedience to the law one has prescribed to oneself is freedom" (I, 8).

The implications of this passage are massive. It is here where Rousseau departs most dramatically from his early modern predecessors. For Hobbes and Locke, liberty meant the sphere of human conduct that is unregulated by law. Where the law is silent—"praetermitted," in Hobbes's term—the citizen is free to do or not to do as he or she chooses. But for Rousseau the law is where our freedom begins. We are free to the extent that we participate in the making of laws that we in turn obey. Freedom means acting in conformity with the laws we have helped to shape. Only then does one become—as Rousseau says in the passage above—master of oneself.

At bottom is a dispute over two conceptions of liberty that could be called liberal and republican respectively. For liberals, freedom has always meant a sphere of privacy where the laws do not intrude. The separation of the private and the public sphere has always been sacred to liberalism, for it is only in the private sphere of civil society that the individual is free. For the republican theory of liberty, however, this separation is only an excuse for the exercise of private selfishness. The task is rather to create a community where the individual and the public interest are not in conflict, where the individual does not think of himself apart from the social body. This is the freedom of the citizen who takes an active role in the determination of the laws of his own community.

Rousseau's purpose is to bring back to life a concept that he believes has been dormant for centuries: the citizen. In a footnote to book 1, chapter 6, he writes that the true meaning of this word is lost on modern man. "Most [modern men]," he writes, "mistake a town for a city and a bourgeois for a citizen." The modern world furnishes almost no examples of the citizen. Like Machiavelli before him, Rousseau finds it is necessary to go back to the histories of antiquity, especially Rome and Sparta, to find a model of what citizenship meant. Only there can the spirit of self-sacrifice and devotion to the city be found. The modern world has no example of this spirit. Even the American founders must have felt this to some degree, which is why the three authors of the *Federalist Papers* adopted as their pen name the Roman Publius.

Does Rousseau's conception of citizen freedom lead to a higher form of nobility—higher than the pursuit of one's individual self-interest—or does it result in a new despotism? Underlying the sinister reading is Rousseau's famous (or infamous) statement that the general will is the source of freedom and that citizens who refuse to obey it may be "forced to be free" (I, 7). Does this combination of force and freedom suggest a new kind of tyranny, the tyranny of mind control, a tutelary despotism of the kind Tocqueville feared, where people are made to love their captivity?

Rousseau's language is extreme and clearly intended to shock. He is a lover of paradox. At the basis of the debate are two radically different ideas about the importance of political participation in law making. For Rousseau, laws are only legitimate if everyone has had a direct share in making them. For Hobbes—as for Locke and his heirs, the authors of the *Federalist Papers*—the value of direct citizen involvement is only a subordinate or secondary good. Legislation is better handled by persons chosen from the populace who serve as their agents or representatives of the people. It is far more important that laws be generally known and applied by impartial judges than that they be the direct expression of the popular will. Underlying this view is a general distrust of the people, but also a concern for the energy and efficiency of government. It is simply too cumbersome a mechanism to call the people together to decide on matters of public concern.

Rousseau would obviously disagree. It is often said that Rousseau makes heroic or unreasonable assumptions about human nature. Most people do not want to engage in endless debate with others over the public good, they simply want to be left alone. But Rousseau will tell you this is not idealistic at all. Unless everyone is engaged in the process of legislation there is no way to guarantee that the laws will actually be an expression of the general will. You will find yourself in a condition of dependence on the will of others or, what is really at issue, on the will of some faction, interest, or association that has come to control political power. Rousseau's appeal is not to our altruism but to our desire to preserve our freedom and resist the willful domination of others.

Rousseau's Sociology

So far this is very abstract, but Rousseau goes out of his way to specify the conditions under which the general will is possible. We might call this Rousseau's sociology. In the first place he emphasizes that the general will is only possible in a small, polis-like state. It is simply not conceivable in the large monarchical states of modern Europe, where class divisions and inequalities have been so deeply embedded that people are no longer able to conceive of a common good. Morals, manners, and habits have simply become too corrupt to create a sense of peoplehood. This is why Rousseau tends to favor rustic people over city dwellers. The society envisaged by *The Social Contract* will be an agrarian democracy, perhaps like a community of Jeffersonian yeoman farmers or an Israeli kibbutz. Of all the places in Europe, Rousseau mentions Corsica as the only example of where a general will may be possible (II, 10).

At the same time, one might get the impression that only a direct democracy would satisfy Rousseau's stern requirements for the general will. But this is not the case. In book 3 of *The Social Contract* Rousseau shows surprising flexibility about the kinds of government appropriate to different physical and moral climates. In the chapter "On Democracy" he remarks,

"If there were a people of gods, they would govern themselves democratically" and then adds, "So perfect a government is not suited to men" (III, 4). Democracies are possible only under very special circumstances; otherwise aristocracy and even monarchy are legitimate choices for people to make. Rousseau insists on the separation of powers for reasons very similar to those offered by Locke. The people who make the laws should not be the same as those responsible for executing them. Throughout this part of the book Rousseau is in dialogue with an unnamed rival, whom he sometimes refers to as a "famous author." This is, of course, the Baron de Montesquieu, whom he reads as suggesting that different kinds of government may be equally legitimate under different circumstances. He introduces an element of what appears to be very un-Rousseauean prudence and moderation to qualify the dogmatic claims of the first two books of *The Social Contract*.

Most important of all, however, Rousseau insists that legislative authority in whatever kind of constitution is adopted must always be held by the people. The offices of government may legitimately be held by a monarch or an aristocracy, but the people alone are sovereign. No one or no thing should ever be allowed to interfere with their law-making capacity. In book 3, chapter 15, entitled "On Deputies or Representatives," Rousseau denies the legitimacy of representative government. "Sovereignty cannot be represented," he says, "for the same reason that it cannot be alienated." The general will can only be expressed, never represented. Representative government is necessarily government by what we would call special interests and Rousseau calls factions. This in broad outline is his critique of the American Constitution that set up a complex system of representation precisely to avoid the problems associated with direct popular rule.

Rousseau's repudiation of representation extends to his skepticism of the role of intermediary associations. Partial associations can only advance their own group interests, never the general will. Instead of regarding legislation as the outcome of parliamentary give-and-take among competing factions, Rousseau offers his own theory of citizen deliberation: "If, when an adequately informed people deliberates, the citizens had no communication among themselves, the general will would always result" (II, 3). In what way, though, can citizens deliberate when there is "no communication" among them? Rousseau's answer is through voting in assembly: "When a law is proposed in the people's assembly," Rousseau writes, " what they are being asked is not exactly whether they approve the proposal or reject it, but whether it does or does not conform to the general will, which is theirs; everyone states his opinion about this by casting his ballot, and the tally of the votes yields the declaration of the general will" (IV, 2).

Rousseau's idea seems akin to the famous "miracle of aggregation" proposed by his French contemporary Condorcet. The idea is that when individuals make independent judgments, looking inward before voting rather than taking their cues from other parties attempting to influence the outcome, the result will favor the general will. The process of voting is thus seen not as a means of balancing competing interests but as a way of discovering a true judgment of what constitutes the people's rational will.

Perhaps the most difficult problem Rousseau had to face is how to establish the general will or, more precisely, how to establish a people capable of determining the general will for themselves. Here is where his doctrine of the Legislator kicks in (II, 7). Rousseau's Legislator is his answer to Machiavelli's prince. He speaks of the Legislator as a founding genius capable of "changing human nature" and capable of "beholding all the passions of men without feeling any of them." His examples, like Machiavelli's, are drawn from the annals of ancient history: Lycurgus, Romulus, Moses. Such Legislators are the true founders of a people—the fathers of a constitution—who establish the framework for all later statesmen and citizens to operate within. This is clearly Rousseau at his most Machiavellian, calling on some future Washington or Robespierre to remake a people from the ground up. Rousseau seems to believe that in the corrupt times in which we live, nothing short of a person of extraordinary power is needed to reinvigorate a taste for freedom.

Legacies

Rousseau's legacies—and I use the term in the plural—are as diverse as his writings. His description of the Legislator as a new kind of political founder was not lost on the French revolutionaries who disinterred Rousseau's body and in 1794 moved it to the National Pantheon in Paris as a hero of the new republic. Consider the words of Robespierre's *Dedication to Rousseau*, written in 1791: "Divine man, you taught me to know myself; while I was still young you made me appreciate the dignity of my nature and reflect upon the great principles of the social order. The old edifice is crumbling; the portico of a new edifice is rising up upon its ruins, and, thanks to you, I have brought my stone to it. Receive my homage, as weak as it is, it must please you. I wish to follow your venerable footsteps ... happy if, in the perilous career that an unprecedented revolution just opened before us, I remain constantly faithful to the inspirations that I found in your text."[9]

Rousseau has often been regarded as the forerunner of the French Revolution, and *The Social Contract* has been called the Revolution's "book of law." Even so, the influence of Rousseau's ideas on the French Revolution must be treated with care. Prior to the Revolution, Rousseau's influence was felt mainly through *Emile* and his novel *La nouvelle Héloïse* rather than *The Social Contract.* If anything, these works tended to caution against the possibility of large-scale social change, focusing instead on the more intimate and sentimental themes of love, marriage, and family. Rousseau's readers came mainly from the aristocracy, who endorsed his pastoral vision of childhood and "natural" parenting. It seems that it was only after the radical phase of the Revolution had run its course that writers seeking to explain where things had gone terribly wrong fixated on Rousseau's *Social Contract* as the source of the problem.

It was not only the revolutionary left but also the counterrevolutionary right who saw Rousseau as a major influence on the Revolution. A year after completing his *Reflections on the Revolution in France* in 1790, Edmund Burke wrote a kind of sequel entitled *Letter to a Member of the National Assembly.* Here he specifically singled out Rousseau—"the insane Socrates of the National Assembly"—as the proximate cause of the revolutionary turmoil: "The Assembly recommends to its youth a study of the bold experimenters in morality. Everybody knows that there is a great dispute amongst their leaders [as to] which of them is the best resemblance to Rousseau. His blood they transfuse into their minds and into their manners. Him they study; him they meditate; him they turn over in all the time they can spare from the laborious mischief of the day and the debauches of the night. Rousseau is their holy writ . . . their standard figure of perfection."[10]

It is common practice to conclude with Rousseau's influence on the French Revolution as if this were the end of the matter. In fact it is only the beginning. Rousseau's influence extended far beyond France and the immediate circumstances of his age. It is still felt in a number of areas, from philosophy to politics to popular culture. I want to mention only two.

The first and most decisive influence of Rousseau was on Kant. On the surface Rousseau and Kant could not have been more different. Kant was a man of extremely steady habits, so much so that the citizens of the town of Königsberg could set their clocks by his afternoon walks. It was said that the only day Kant missed his walk was when he began reading Rousseau's *Emile.* But there is more than anecdotal evidence for Rousseau's influence on Kant.

Kant may have said that it was Hume who awoke him from his "dogmatic slumber," but it was Rousseau who provided him with affirmative inspiration. Kant provides his own witness. In his *Observations on the Feeling of the Beautiful and Sublime*—written just two years after the publication of *The Social Contract*—Kant could write: "I myself am a researcher by inclination. I feel the entire thirst for knowledge and the eager restlessness to proceed further in it, as well as the satisfaction at every acquisition. There was a time when I believed this alone could constitute the honor of humankind, and I despised the rabble who know nothing. Rousseau has set me right."[11] By this Kant meant it was Rousseau who first alerted him to the rights of man.

What Kant discovered in Rousseau was above all a new formula for the sublimity of morality. The basis of morality, Kant argued, was to be found not in nature, custom, or history but in the self-given laws inherent in reason. The starry skies above and the moral law within are the two things, Kant wrote, that filled him with perpetual awe. Kant's criteria for a moral rule must possess two apparently contradictory features: they must be objective, that is, valid without reference to particular persons, and they must be self-imposed. Just as Rousseau had insisted that the criterion for the general will is a law that can withstand the test of generalization, Kant maintains that a moral law is one that should hold true for any person at any place at any time similarly situated. Do you want to know whether you should tell the truth in a given circumstance? Ask yourself what if everyone in your situation told a lie, and you know the answer. An action that can withstand the test of universalization Kant calls a Categorical Imperative because it is one that binds categorically, absolutely, and is not just a prudential maxim that can be adjusted to changing circumstances.

But Rousseau's influence on Kant goes beyond Kant's universalization of maxims. Just as Rousseau had argued that obedience to the general will makes us free because only then do we obey laws that we have prescribed for ourselves, so Kant argues that only when one is enacting universal moral laws does one become an autonomous moral agent. A moral law is one that I can fully accept as my own. Kant's formula for self-legislation provides the moral basis for what he calls the "rights of man." Kant radicalized Rousseau's teaching by making politics subordinate to morality and by endowing morality with a kind of sacred dignity and absoluteness that it had never assumed before. Henceforward every polity would need to justify itself before the bar of human rights. Under Kant's tutelage it would no longer be sufficient for politics to seek to secure the more modest ends of security and property, or even the pursuit of happiness; politics must be concerned with ensuring the more elevated conditions of human dignity and respect for persons as such. The peculiar idealism, moralism, and intransigence of Kantian politics that we find in a modern-day Kantian philosopher like John Rawls is the direct inheritance of Rousseau.

But Rousseau's influence went far beyond Kant. In the generation after the French Revolution a young Frenchman would make a trip to America and go on to pen the most important book about democracy ever written. One would search the seven hundred pages of Tocqueville's *Democracy in America* in vain for so much as a single reference to Rousseau, yet Rousseau's influence is manifest on virtually every page. Once again Tocqueville himself provides the evidence for the connection. In a letter to his closest friend, Louis de Kergolay, Tocqueville wrote: "There are three men with whom I spend some time every day; they are Pascal, Montesquieu, and Rousseau."[12] Taking him at his word—and leaving Pascal and Montesquieu aside—what did Tocqueville learn from Rousseau?

This will be taken up in the next chapter, but for now let me broadly suggest some areas of similarity between them. Although seventy-five years before Tocqueville Rousseau had taken the doctrine of popular sovereignty to be an ideal to be worked for, Tocqueville regards it as having come of age in the backwoods of Jacksonian America. His depiction of the self-governing townships of New England was a direct transposition of Rousseau's theory of the general will at work. The emphasis not just on laws and institutions but on habits and manners likewise shows the marks of Rousseau. Tocqueville's respectful treatment of the American founders (above all Jefferson) exhibits some of the earmarks of Rousseau's awe at the great lawgivers who put their distinctive stamp on a people, and Tocqueville's romantic depiction of native peoples includes something of Rousseau's noble savage. His treatment of American religion as a prophylactic against the tendency toward materialism, an ethic of self-interest, and the dangers of social isolation brings to light several of the features of Rousseau's civil religion discussed at the end of *The Social Contract*. And Tocqueville's treatment of compassion as the core of democratic morality brings to mind Rousseau's treatment of the same theme in his *Second Discourse* and *Emile*.

Even where Tocqueville seems to depart most visibly from Rousseau, one can see the marks of an internal dialogue. Tocqueville's fears about the danger of the "tyranny of the majority" and what he calls "democratic despotism" can be seen as an internal critique of Rousseau's claims about men being forced to be free under the rule of the general will. The defense of civil associations can be seen as a rejoinder to Rousseau's critique of the same as engendering partial group interests that distort the general will. Tocqueville's looking back with a certain fondness to the age of aristocracy as one of taste, manners, and true independence of spirit is in part an answer to Rousseau's idealization of Sparta and Rome as golden ages of political virtue when giants walked the earth. In short, Tocqueville's America is in many ways Rousseau's *Social Contract* come of age.

Rousseau's legacy is not confined to his specific political projects. Some of his proposals seem either reactionary or obsolete: his celebration of small, polis-like societies, his general lack of interest in the workings of modern economics, his preference for agrarian over commercial republics. But Rousseau shaped our modern sensibilities to a degree unmatched by any other thinker. Our love of equality, our peculiar deference to the will of the majority, our singular belief that democracy is not just one kind of regime among others but the only just or legitimate regime, all provide testimony to the continuing influence of Rousseau. Anyone who does not like Rousseau does not like democracy.

CHAPTER 11

Tocqueville and the Dilemmas of Democracy

Charles Alexis Henri Clerel de Tocqueville, 1805–1859. 1850.
Oil on canvas. Photo credit: The Art Gallery Collection / Alamy

In the seventeenth and eighteenth centuries the ideas of freedom and equality walked confidently hand in hand. Hobbes, Locke, and Rousseau all believed that in the state of nature men were born free and equal. As long as the enemy appeared to be entrenched hierarchies of power and privilege, freedom and equality were taken as mutually reinforcing aspects of the emergent democratic order.

It was not until the new democracies or proto-democracies began to take shape at the beginning of the nineteenth century that political philosophers began to wonder whether equality and liberty did not in fact pull in different directions. Tocqueville in particular—although we could add the names of Benjamin Constant and John Stuart Mill—saw the new democratic societies as creating new forms of power, new types of rule that represented organized threats to human liberty. These were the middle-class or bourgeois democracies emerging in France, England, and, of course, the United States. The question for Tocqueville was how to mitigate the effects of this new form of political power.

A standard answer to this question, taken up by the American constitutional framers, was to divide and separate powers. Tocqueville was less certain that this institutional device of checks and balances would be an effective safeguard in a democratic age where the people as a whole had become king. As I mentioned toward the end of the previous chapter, while seventy-five years before him Rousseau had taken the doctrine of popular sovereignty to be an ideal to be worked for, Tocqueville considers it to have come of age in the era of Jacksonian America:

> In the United States, the dogma of the sovereignty of the people is not an isolated doctrine that is joined neither to habits nor to the sum of dominant ideas; on the contrary, one can view it as the last link in a chain of opinions that envelops the Anglo-American world as a whole. Providence has given to each individual, whosoever he may be, the degree of reason necessary for him to be able to direct himself in things that interest him exclusively. Such is the great maxim on which civil and political society in the United States rests: the father of a family applies it to his children, the master to his servants, the township to those under its administration, the province to the townships, the state to the provinces, the Union to the states. Extended to the entirety of the nation, it becomes the dogma of the sovereignty of the people. (I.ii.10 [381])

For Tocqueville, there was no reason to believe that the new democratic states ruled by the people will be more just, or less arbitrary, than any other previous form of rule. No one—no person or body—can be safely entrusted with power, and the united power of the people is no more reliable as a guarantee of freedom than any other regime. The problem of politics in an age of democracy is how to control the sovereign power of the people. Who can do this?

In aristocratic ages, Tocqueville believed, there had always been countervailing centers of power. Kings had to deal with an often fractious nobility. But who or what can exercise this role in a world where the people in their collective capacity are sovereign? Who or what has the power to check the popular will? This is the problem that Tocqueville's political science—"a new political science for a world itself quite new"—set out to answer. To this extent we are all Tocqueville's children, insofar as we are all dealing with the problem of the guidance and control of democratic government, of how to combine popular government with political judgment.[1]

Who Was Alexis de Tocqueville?

Alexis de Tocqueville was born in 1805 to a Norman family with an ancient lineage. The Tocqueville estate still exists and is still owned by members of the family. Tocqueville was deeply attached to his ancestral home and in 1828 wrote: "Here I am finally at Tocqueville in my old family ruin. A league away is the harbor from which William set out to conquer England. I am surrounded by Normans whose names figure in the list of the conquerors. All of this, I must admit, flatters the proud weakness of my heart."[2] Tocqueville's parents had been arrested during the French Revolution and were held in prison for almost a year. Only the fall of Robespierre in 1794 saved them from execution. The young Tocqueville was born under the Napoleonic dynasty and spent his formative years in what might be called the most conservative, if not reactionary, circles of postrevolutionary France.

Tocqueville studied law in Paris and sometime during the late 1820s made the acquaintance of another young aristocrat by the name of Gustave de Beaumont. In 1830 the two men received a commission from the new government of King Louis Philippe to go to the United States in order to study the prison system there. Tocqueville's journey to America, which has been extensively documented, lasted for a little over nine months, from May 1831 to February 1832.[3] During that time he traveled as far north as

New England, south to New Orleans, and west to the outer banks of Lake Michigan. The result of this visit was, of course, two large volumes that he called *Democracy in America*. The first volume appeared in 1835, when its author was only thirty years of age, and the second volume five years later, in 1840. A few years ago another Frenchman, Bernard-Henri Lévy, toured America and hit all the high spots—Las Vegas, evangelical churches—in order to do an update of Tocqueville in his book *American Vertigo*.[4] The most charitable comparison one could make between Tocqueville and Lévy would be to say that there is no comparison.

Democracy in America is, to put it simply, the most important work about democracy ever written. To compound the irony, the most famous book on American democracy was written by a French aristocrat. From the time of its first publication, the book was hailed by no less an authority than John Stuart Mill as a masterpiece, "the first analytical inquiry into the influence of democracy" and the beginning of "a new era in the scientific study of politics."[5] Tocqueville has virtually taken a place alongside Washington, Jefferson, and Madison as an honorary American, and, as if this were not enough, his book was recently inducted into the prestigious Library of America series, setting upon it the mark of naturalization.

There is a textbook image of Tocqueville according to which the young aristocrat came to America as a kind of blank slate and was profoundly transformed by his experience of American democracy. Nothing could be farther from the truth. In a letter to his best friend, Louis de Kergolay, written just before the publication of the first volume of *Democracy*, Tocqueville describes his purpose in writing the book as follows:

> It is not without having carefully reflected that I decided to write the book I am just now publishing. I do not hide from myself what is annoying in my position: it is bound to attract active sympathy from no one. Some will find that at bottom I do not like democracy and I am severe toward it; others will think I favor its development imprudently. It would be most fortunate for me if the book were not read, and that is a piece of good fortune that may perhaps come to pass. I know all that, but this is my response: nearly ten years ago I was already thinking about parts of the things I have just now set forth. I was in America only to become clear on this point. The penitentiary system was a pretext.[6]

Two points about this letter bear comment. First, Tocqueville indicates that his idea for the book had already begun to germinate five years before his trip to America—he was hardly a blank slate. If you consider that he was only thirty when the first volume was published, that means that parts of the book had already become clear to him when he was only about twenty years old—the age of a college undergraduate! He came to America to confirm what he had already begun to suspect.

Second, Tocqueville was writing the book not for the benefit of Americans, who he thought had little taste for philosophy, but for Frenchmen. In particular he was hoping to persuade his fellow countrymen who were still devoted to the restoration of the monarchy that the democratic social revolution he had witnessed in America represented the future of France. If John Locke had said that "in the beginning all the world was America," Tocqueville's point was that in the future all the world will be America. His attitude toward what he saw was one of cautious skepticism mixed with hope. "I confess that in America I saw more than America; I sought there an image of democracy itself, of its penchants, its character, its prejudices, its passions; I wanted to become acquainted with it if only to know at least what we ought to hope or fear from it" (Preface [13]).

There are two questions that *Democracy* sets out to answer. The first concerns the gradual replacement of the ancien régime, the French term for the old aristocratic regime based on the principles of hierarchy, deference, and inequality, with a new democratic society based on equality. How did this happen, and what brought it about? The second, not explicitly asked but present on virtually every page of the book, concerns the difference between the form democracy had taken in America and the form it took in France during the revolutionary period. Why has American democracy been relatively gentle or mild—what we might call a liberal democracy—and why did democracy in France veer dangerously toward terror and despotism? Tocqueville believed it to be virtually a providential fact of history that society was becoming increasingly democratic. What is not certain is what form this democracy will take. Whether democracy will be compatible with liberty or whether it will issue in a new kind of despotism remains a question that only the statesmen of the future will be able to answer.

From these two questions we can see that Tocqueville wrote his book as a political educator. More than a mere chronicler of American manners and customs, he was a teacher of future European statesmen hoping to steer their countries between the shoals of revolution and reaction. Let us see further exactly what Tocqueville hoped to teach.

The Age of Equality

Near the end of the Introduction to the first volume of *Democracy* Tocqueville writes: "I think those who want to regard it closely will find, in the entire work, a mother thought that, so to speak, links all its parts" (14). What is this "mother thought" or mother idea to which Tocqueville refers? The most likely candidate is the idea of equality. The opening sentence of the book reads: "Among the new objects that attracted my attention during my stay in the United States, none struck my eye more vividly than the equality of conditions" (3). What does Tocqueville mean here by equality?

Note that Tocqueville speaks of equality as a social state ("equality of conditions") rather than a form of government. This is in part an expression of Tocqueville's sociological imagination. Equality of conditions precedes democratic government. It is the cause from which democratic government arises. Equality of conditions was planted in both Europe and America long before democratic governments arose in either place. Democratic governments are only as old as the American and French revolutions, but equality of conditions had been prepared by deep-rooted historical processes long before the modern age came into being.

In the Introduction Tocqueville gives a brief—very brief—history of equality, taking it back to the heart of the medieval world seven hundred years before. Unlike Hobbes or Rousseau, he does not invoke a state of nature as a way of grounding equality. In fact, while Hobbes and Rousseau believed that we are by nature free and equal and that only over time were social hierarchies and inequalities introduced, Tocqueville argues the opposite. The historical process has been moving away from inequality and toward greater and greater equality of social conditions. Equality is a historical force, something that has been working itself out in history over a vast stretch of time. Tocqueville often writes of equality not just as a "fact" but as a "generative fact" from which everything else derives: "As I studied America, more and more I saw in the equality of conditions the generative fact from which each particular fact seemed to issue," he writes in the third paragraph of the book (3).

Tocqueville writes about equality as a historical fact that has come to acquire almost providential force. He uses the term "providence" to describe a universal historical process that is constantly working, so to speak, even against the intentions of individual actors. The kings of France, for example, who struggled to subdue the power of the nobility were working—unbeknownst to them—to hasten the equality of social conditions. The

gradual spread of conditions of equality has two characteristics of providence: it is universal, and it always escapes the powers of human control. It
is the very power of equality that makes it seem an irresistible force. Tocqueville shows that rather than being the product of the modern age alone, the
steady emergence of equality has been at the heart of European history for
centuries.

It is in order to understand the advance of equality that Tocqueville
turns to America of the 1830s. "There is only one country in the world," he
writes, "where the great social revolution I am speaking of seems nearly to
have attained its natural limits" (12). That country is, of course, America. In
this context it is revealing that he chose to call his book *Democracy in
America* and not *American Democracy*. His point is not that democracy is a
peculiarly American phenomenon; far from it. His point is to show the
form that the democratic revolution has taken in America. What form it
will take elsewhere is by no means predetermined. Democracy is not a condition but a process. It has the quality that Rousseau described as *perfect-
ibilité*, an almost infinite elasticity and openness to change. It is less a
determinate regime than a perpetual work in progress.

This is an extremely astute observation. Democracy is the only regime
form that has become a verb. We do not know where the process of demo-
cratization will end or what form it will take elsewhere. Will future democratic regimes be liberal and freedom loving or harsh and rebarbative? This
question is at least as important for us as it was for Tocqueville. What Tocqueville is sure about is that the fate of America is the fate of Europe and maybe
the fate of the rest of the world. "It appears to me beyond doubt that sooner
or later we shall arrive, like the Americans, at an almost complete equality
of conditions," he remarks (12). Do you like what you see? he seems to ask
his readers. What form democracy will take elsewhere will be dependent
on circumstances and statesmanship. His is an attempt to educate the
statesmen of the future.

Democracy American Style

It is important to remember that *Democracy in America* was published in two
volumes, five years apart. Some interpreters of the work have even taken to
referring to them as *Democracy* I and *Democracy* II. *Democracy* I deals far
more with American materials; *Democracy* II with the problems of democracy in general. *Democracy* I is also more optimistic about the structure of
democracy; *Democracy* II is characterized by a far deeper pessimism about

democracy's fate. How to account for these differences? Let us consider first, however, Tocqueville's account of American democracy in *Democracy* I.

There are three features of American democracy that Tocqueville isolates and that account for what contributes to a flourishing democratic state. These are: local government, civil associations, and what he calls the spirit of religion. I will consider these in order.

The first and perhaps most fundamental feature of American democracy is the importance given to local government and local institutions. The importance of localism—and the spirit that emanates from it—is the key to the whole. The cradle of democracy is to be found in what Tocqueville calls the *commune* or the township. "It is nonetheless in the township that the force of free peoples resides. The institutions of a township are to freedom what primary schools are to science; they put it within reach of the people; they make them taste its peaceful employ and habituate them to making use of it. Without the institutions of a township a nation can give itself a free government, but it does not have the spirit of freedom" (I.i.5 [57–58]).

Does this sound familiar? It should. Tocqueville's description of the New England township breathes the spirit of Rousseau's general will. It is the people organizing, legislating, and deliberating over their common interests that is the core of liberty. This coincidence is hardly fortuitous. In the letter to Kergolay cited in the previous chapter, Tocqueville admitted that Rousseau was one of three writers with whom he spent time every day. It is Rousseau more than any other writer who crafted the lenses through which Tocqueville observed democracy.

Yet Tocqueville combines Rousseau with an Aristotelian twist: "The township," he continues, "is the sole association that is so much *in nature* that everywhere men are gathered a township forms by itself" (I.i.5 [57]; emphasis added). The township is said to be a product of nature, it "eludes, so to speak, the effort of man." The township exists by nature, but its existence, far from being guaranteed, is fragile and uncertain. It is continually threatened by invasions, not by foreign powers, but from larger forms of government. The township is continually threatened by federal or national authority, and Tocqueville adds, with a definite hint of Rousseau, that the more "enlightened" a people are, the more difficult it is to retain the spirit of the town. The spirit of local freedom goes hand in hand with rustic, even primitive, manners and customs. For this very reason, he laments, the spirit of the township no longer exists in Europe, where the process of political centralization and the progress of enlightenment have destroyed the conditions for local self-government.

Tocqueville's celebration of the township form of government is supported by another pillar of democracy: civil associations. This is the part of
Democracy in America that has received the most attention in recent years.
"In democratic countries," Tocqueville writes in one of the most famous
sentences in his book, "the science of association is the mother science; the
progress of all the others depends on the progress of that one" (II.ii. 5 [492]).

It is through uniting and joining together in common endeavors that
people develop a taste for liberty. "In America I encountered sorts of associations of which, I confess, I had no idea, and I often admired the infinite
art with which the inhabitants of the United States managed to fix a common goal to the efforts of many men and to get them to advance to it freely"
(II.ii.5 [489]).

It is in the importance he attributes to local voluntary groups and
associations that Tocqueville seems to depart most widely from Rousseau.
Rousseau, recall, had warned against "partial associations" for their tendency to frustrate the general will. Tocqueville, on the other hand, regards
voluntary associations of all sorts—interest groups, as we might call them—as
the place where we learn habits of initiative, cooperation, and responsibility. By taking care of our own interests, we learn to take care of others.
"Sentiments and ideas renew themselves," Tocqueville writes, "the heart is
enlarged and the human mind is developed" (II.ii.5 [491]). It is through free
associations—volunteer groups, PTAs, churches, synagogues, unions, and
other parts of civil society—that institutions are formed that can resist the
power of centralized authority. It is in such associations that we learn how to
become democratic citizens.

The argument about the necessity of civil association has been taken
up recently by political scientist Robert Putnam in his book *Bowling Alone*.[7]
Here Putnam speaks about "human capital"—what Tocqueville called *mores* or the habits of mind and heart—that is developed through civic association. Putnam's chief example is the bowling league. He is concerned
with the decline of such associations in contemporary America. More and
more, Putnam complains, people choose to bowl alone, and this tendency
toward isolation represents a danger to our civic capacities. Have our capacities for joining with others been eroded by forces of modern society and
technology? Are we becoming more and more a nation of solitaries and
couch potatoes?

These are serious questions, and a large literature has grown up
around them. Some of this literature suggests that Putnam's findings are
overdrawn and that he exaggerates the decline of membership in civic or-

ganizations like Rotary Clubs and bowling leagues. Still others suggest that he overstates the relation between civic organizations and democracy. Many voluntary associations are exclusionary, whether along racial, ethnic, or gender lines. The Ku Klux Klan and the Aryan Nation are voluntary groups, but they are hardly teaching the lessons in democracy that either Tocqueville or Putnam would want us to learn. Is it even clear that clubs like bowling leagues make good citizens? Consider the Coen brothers' great film *The Big Lebowski.* In the movie the Dude, Walter, and Donny are avid bowlers, and their great ambition is to enter the finals. The Dude is a stoned hippie, Walter a psychologically damaged Vietnam vet, and Donny a lost waif. Standing in their way is Jesus Quintana, a convicted sex offender ("That creep can roll," Walter says). These men are all members of the same bowling league. Are they Putnam's ideal democratic citizens? Is their team a model of civil association?

The third and final leg of the stool on which American democracy rests is what Tocqueville calls "the spirit of religion." "On my arrival in the United States," he observes, "it was the religious aspect of the country that first struck my eye" (I.ii.9 [282]). Like other European observers, then as well as now, Tocqueville was perplexed by the fact that in America the spirit of democracy and the spirit of religion have worked hand in hand. This is virtually the exact opposite from what has occurred in Europe, where religion and democracy have generally been on a collision course. What accounts for this peculiarity of American democratic life?

In the first instance Tocqueville notes that America is a uniquely Puritan democracy. "I see the whole destiny of America contained in the first Puritan who landed on its shores, like the whole human race in the first man" (I.ii.9 [267]). America was created by a people with strong religious habits who brought to the New World a suspicion of government and a strong desire for independence. This contributed to the separation of church and state that has done so much to promote both religious and political liberty.

Tocqueville drew two important theoretical conclusions from the fact of religious life in America. First, the thesis propounded by the philosophers of the Enlightenment that religion would wither away with the advancement of modernity is demonstrably false. "The philosophers of the eighteenth century," he writes, "explained the gradual weakening of beliefs in an altogether simple fashion. Religious zeal, they said, will be extinguished as freedom and enlightenment increase. It is unfortunate that the facts do not accord with this theory" (I.ii.9 [282]).

Second, Tocqueville regarded it as a terrible mistake to attempt to eliminate religion or to secularize society altogether. It was his belief—as it was for Rousseau as well—that free societies rest on public morality and that morality cannot be effective without religion. Individuals may be able to derive moral guidance from reason alone, but societies cannot. The danger of attempting to eliminate religion from public life is that the need or will to believe will find other outlets. "Despotism can do without faith," Tocqueville remarks in an arresting sentence, "but freedom cannot. Religion is much more necessary in a republic and in a democratic republic more than all others" (I.ii.9 [282]). But why is religion so necessary to a republic?

Tocqueville gives a variety of answers. One persistent theme of *Democracy* is that only religion can resist the tendency toward materialism and a kind of low self-interest that is intrinsic to democracies. "The principal business of religions [in a democracy] is to purify, regulate, and restrain the too ardent and too exclusive taste for well-being that men in times of equality feel" (II.i.5 [422]).

Tocqueville also operates with a kind of metaphysics of faith that regards religious belief as necessary for the efficacy of human action. "When religion is destroyed in a people," he writes, "doubt takes hold of the highest portions of the intellect and half paralyzes all the others" (II.i.5 [418]). This paralysis of the will is a condition that later writers would diagnose as nihilism. Faith is a necessary component for our belief that we are free agents and not simply the playthings of a blind and random fate. "Such a state [of disbelief]," Tocqueville asserts, "cannot fail to enervate souls; it slackens the springs of the will and prepares citizens for servitude" (II.i.5 [418]). Our beliefs about the freedom and dignity of the individual are inseparable from religious faith, and it is unlikely that these beliefs could survive without religion to support them. "As for me," Tocqueville writes, "I am brought to think that if he has no faith he must serve, and if he is free, he must believe" (II.i.5 [418–19]). No more powerful challenge to the Enlightenment has ever been uttered.

One final issue remains. Tocqueville often writes as if religion is valuable only for the social function it serves. This is surely consistent with the sociological interpretation of his thought, and Tocqueville often writes as though he is concerned only with the social and political consequences of religion rather than with the truth of religious beliefs. "I view religions only from a purely human point of view," he says (II.i.5 [419]). How accurate is this view?

The sociological or functionalist reading of Tocqueville only captures a part of his complex attitude toward religion. Tocqueville was a student not only of Rousseau but also of Blaise Pascal, the seventeenth-century religious philosopher who more than any other philosopher saw the emptiness of knowledge without faith. Man may be the rational animal, but our reason is as nothing before the unfathomable depths of the universe. "A vapor, a drop of water, is enough to kill him," Pascal wrote. "Man is but a reed, the weakest in nature. But he is a thinking reed."[8]

Tocqueville discovered in Pascal a sense of the existential emptiness and incompleteness of life that cannot be explained in rational terms alone. His fear was that of an individual cast adrift in the vast, infinite space of the universe. Furthermore, there is something about the equality of conditions that fosters an ominous sense of the loneliness of humanity cut off from grace and true communion with others. Tocqueville sought the limits of reason precisely to leave room for faith. "The short space of sixty years," he writes almost as an aside, "will never confine the whole imagination of man; the incomplete joys of this world will never suffice for his heart" (I.ii.9 [283]). In other words, there is something we desire beyond the here and now that only faith can supply. The soul exhibits a longing, a desire, for eternity and a certain disgust with the limits of physical existence: "Religion is therefore only a particular form of hope and it is as natural to the human heart as hope itself. Only by a kind of aberration of the intellect and with the aid of a sort of moral violence exercised on their own nature do men stray from religious beliefs; an invincible inclination leads them back to them. Disbelief is an accident; faith alone is the permanent state of humanity" (I.ii.9 [284]). This passage shows that Tocqueville was more—much more—than a sociologist of religion. It addresses the metaphysical side of his thought and shows him to be a writer of great psychological depth and insight.

The Tyranny of the Majority

Although there was much in American democracy to admire—its town meetings, its spirit of civil association, its religious commitments, and so on—Tocqueville also identified in it dangerous tendencies toward democratic tyranny. He in fact offered two quite distinct analyses of this problem, one in volume 1 and the other in volume 2 of *Democracy*. What was the problem of democratic tyranny that Tocqueville feared?

In *Democracy* I he treated the problem of "tyranny of the majority" largely in terms inherited from Aristotle and the *Federalist Papers*. In the

Politics Aristotle had associated democracy with the rule of the many, generally the poor, in their own interests. The danger of democracy was precisely that it represented the self-interested rule of one class of the community, the largest class, over the minority. Democracy was thus always potentially a form of class struggle exercised by the poor over the rich, often egged on by populist demagogues. This theme was considered by the *Federalist* authors. Their solution to the problem of majority faction was to "enlarge the orbit" of government in order to prevent the creation of a permanent majority faction. The greater the number of factions, the less likely any one of them would be able to exercise despotic power over national politics.

The chapter of *Democracy* entitled "On the Omnipotence of the Majority in the United States and Its Effects" should be read as a direct reply to the *Federalist*. The U.S. Constitution enshrined the majority ("We the People") even as it sought to limit its power. Although Tocqueville devoted a lengthy chapter to the federal structure of the Constitution, he was less convinced than Madison that the problem of majority faction had been solved. In particular he was skeptical that the Constitution's plan for a system of representation and checks and balances could serve as an effective check on "the empire of the majority," a term that has clear theological evocations of the doctrine of divine omnipotence (I.ii.7 [235]). Rather than regarding the people in Madisonian terms as a shifting coalition of interest groups, Tocqueville tended to regard the power of the majority as unlimited and unstoppable. Legal guarantees of minority rights were not likely to be effective in the face of mobilized opinion.

Tocqueville's image of majority tyranny was inseparable from the threats of revolutionary violence fueled by "charismatic" military leaders like Andrew Jackson and Napoleon capable of mobilizing the masses in fits of patriotic zeal. Jacksonianism was the American equivalent of Bonapartism in France, a military commander riding to power on the wings of popular support (I.ii.9 [265]). More than anything, Tocqueville feared this militarism combined with a kind of unlimited patriotic fervor. It is in America that one can begin to see the ennobling qualities of equality of conditions and also the more ominous possibilities of democratic tyranny.

The power of the majority makes itself felt first of all through the dominance of the legislature. "Of all political powers," Tocqueville writes, "the legislature is the one that obeys the majority most willingly" (I.ii.7 [236]). In a dramatic moment in the text he cites Jefferson's warning to Madison: "The tyranny of the legislature is the most formidable dread at present and will be for long years." Tocqueville regards this warning as especially ominous because in Jefferson he finds "the most powerful apostle that democracy has ever had" (I.ii.7 [249]).

What is it about legislative tyranny that Tocqueville fears? As the title of the chapter indicates, it is not the causes of tyranny but its effects that is Tocqueville's main concern. In the first place, Tocqueville takes issue with the belief that there is necessarily more wisdom in the many than the few. He describes this as "the theory of equality applied to brains" (I.ii.7 [236]). There may be strength in numbers, but not necessarily truth. And second, Tocqueville questions the idea that in matters of policy the interests of the many must always take precedence over the few. It is precisely the "omnipotence" of the majority, not any particular policy, that Tocqueville finds "dire and dangerous for the future" (I.ii.7 [237]).

Tocqueville cites two examples of how intolerant local majorities can violate the rights of individuals and minorities. In a footnote he recalls the story of two antiwar journalists in Baltimore during the War of 1812 when pro-war sentiment was running high. The two journalists were arrested for their opinions, taken to prison, and under cover of darkness murdered by a mob. Those who participated in the crime were later exonerated by a jury of their peers. Tocqueville then tells a story of how even in Quaker Pennsylvania freed blacks were unable to exercise their right to vote because of popular prejudice against them. He sums up this situation with the following barb: "What! The majority that has the privilege of making the law still wants to have that of disobeying it" (I.ii.7 [242]).

It is, however, in the realm of thought and opinion that Tocqueville believes the empire of the majority makes itself especially felt. In an always startling passage Tocqueville remarks: "I do not know any country where in general less independence of mind and genuine freedom of discussion reign than in America" (I.ii.7 [244]). The dangers to freedom of thought do not come from the fear of an inquisition, they come in the more subtle forms of exclusion and social ostracism. Tocqueville is perhaps the first and still one of the most perceptive analysts of what today would be called the power of "political correctness" to stifle thought, to render "unthinkable" that of which the majority does not approve.

Tocqueville's statement that there is less freedom of discussion in America than in any other country known to him is clearly an overstatement intended to shock the complacent. His point is that persecution can take many forms, from the cruelest to the mildest. It is the very mildness—a term that Tocqueville uses throughout *Democracy*—of democratic exclusion that he regards as exercising a profound, chilling effect on the free expression of unpopular beliefs: "Chains and executioners are the coarse instruments that tyranny formerly employed; but in our day civilization has perfected even despotism itself which seemed, indeed, to have nothing more to learn. . . . Under the absolute government of one alone, despotism struck the body crudely, so as to reach the soul; and the soul, escaping from those blows rose gloriously above it; but in democratic republics, tyranny does not proceed in this way; it leaves the body and goes straight for the soul" (I.ii.7 [244]).

The Centralization of Power

Tocqueville's account of the tyranny of the majority in the first volume of *Democracy* remained tied to a fear of mob rule and general lawlessness. The danger of "mobocracy" (as Abraham Lincoln called it) combined with the ambitions of popular demagogues was very real. For Tocqueville and those of his generation, the images of the mob were invariably tied to the memory of the National Assembly during the French Revolution. Revolution and tyranny were virtually synonymous for a range of postrevolutionary writers. But by the time Tocqueville wrote his second account of democratic despotism in the second volume of *Democracy* either the memory or the fear of revolution had begun to wane. What might account for this change of mind?

As the images of revolutionary violence began to recede in Tocqueville's mind, a new threat arose to take its place. This was the danger of centralization. Tocqueville is often read as a critic of the centralization of power and a defender of local self-government, and this is more or less correct, but it only grasps a piece of the picture. Tocqueville was not opposed to the growth of state power per se; he was opposed to the rise of bureaucracy and with it the growth of the centralizing spirit as the most serious threat to political liberty.

The theme of centralization is a constant in Tocqueville's thought, linking not only the two volumes of *Democracy* but also *Democracy* and his other great work, *The Old Regime and the Revolution*. The issue of centralization emerges early in *Democracy* I with Tocqueville's distinction between political and administrative centralization (I.i.5). Political or governmental centralization Tocqueville regards as a good thing. The idea of a uniform center of legislation is greatly to be preferred to any system of competing or overlapping sovereignties such as existed in France under the old regime. Political centralization has made significant progress in the United States in part due to supremacy of the legislature.

The danger is not with centralization of the law-making function but with what Tocqueville calls "administrative centralization." What does this distinction amount to? Tocqueville regards a centralized sovereign as necessary for the promulgation of common laws that pertain equally and equitably to all. Governmental centralization is required to ensure that equal justice is afforded to all citizens. Administrative centralization is another matter. The science of administration concerns not the establishment of common laws but the oversight of the details of conduct and the direction of the everyday affairs of citizens. It represents the slow and insidious penetration of the bureaucracy into every aspect of daily affairs. While governmental centralization is needed for the purpose of making laws and national defense, centralized administration is mainly preventative and produces nothing but languid and apathetic citizens who are unable to look after themselves.

Administrative centralization carries with it the germ of what today is called the regulatory state. It is the spirit of regulation that Tocqueville regards as enervating the initiative of citizens to act for themselves. This kind of regulation, he writes, "succeeds without difficulty in impressing a regular style of current affairs, in skillfully regimenting the details of social orderliness [and] in keeping in the social body a sort of administrative somnolence that administrators are accustomed to calling good order and public tranquility" (I.i.5 [86]). It is clear that what Tocqueville is anticipating here is the rise of what we would call the administrative state.

What led Tocqueville to focus on administrative centralization as a peculiar threat to liberty? In many ways this expresses a peculiarly French view of the world. When Tocqueville was writing in the first third of the nineteenth century, the development of the great regulatory agencies that we associate with the Progressive movement was still at least half a century away. Only in France did the centralization of administrative power go back deep into the heart of the old regime.

Tocqueville's interest in the theory and history of the administrative state grew out of his reading of the dynamics of French history. The last twenty years of his life were devoted to the examination of French municipal archives to find the earliest evidence of the growth of centralized administrative power. Fully consistent with his Introduction to *Democracy*, he found that the emergence of a central bureaucracy was not a new development but went at least as far back as the reign of Louis XIV. The administrative conquests of the French kings did the most to produce the coming age of equality and the democratic revolutions. In his paradoxical formulation the Revolution merely completed what had been set in motion during the ancien régime. The broad tendency of history was toward the greater and greater concentration of administrative power, and this is what deeply worried Tocqueville.

Democratic Despotism

It is only at the very end of *Democracy* II that Tocqueville provides his final reflection on the administrative state, in a chapter ominously entitled "What Kind of Despotism Democratic Nations Have to Fear" (II.iv.6). Here we see him abandon his earlier concerns with the tyranny of the majority and the danger of mob rule for a new kind of power, the outlines of which are only now becoming legible. Tocqueville gives some indication of his change of perspective when he remarks near the outset of the chapter that "five years of new meditations have not diminished my fears but they have changed their object" (II.iv.6 [661]).

Tocqueville seems at first reluctant to define this new power. "I think that the kind of oppression with which democratic peoples are threatened," he writes, "will resemble nothing that has preceded it in the world." No longer is he concerned with the emergence of a revolutionary charismatic leader, the prototype of the military despot. Instead there will be no image for this new despotism in our memories. Even our language is inadequate to define it; "the old words 'despotism' and 'tyranny' are not suitable" (II.iv.6 [662]. What, then, is it?

One feature of Tocqueville's new despotism that distinguishes it from tyrannies of the past is its very mildness or "sweetness" (*douceur*) (II.iii.1). The mildness of democratic habits and manners is a theme that runs throughout both volumes of *Democracy*. The equality of conditions has rendered men gentler and more considerate with respect to one another. Being more alike, we have, in the words of a recent American president, an enhanced ability to feel one another's pain. "Do we have more sensitivity than our fathers?" Tocqueville asks with apparent incredulity. "I do not know, but surely our sensitivity bears on more objects" (II.iii.1 [538]).

The word *douceur* is, of course, a term that Tocqueville's readers would have associated with Montesquieu's description of commerce in his book *The Spirit of the Laws*. Commerce was seen by many of the great eighteenth-century writers—Montesquieu, Hume, Kant—as exercising a pacifying and purifying effect on a fierce and warlike people. Commerce makes people less harsh toward one another and more tolerant toward strangers. It is the cause of a new, more cosmopolitan ethic of *l'humanité*. Montesquieu regarded the transition from the feudal warrior ethic to the modern bourgeois commercial ethic as a marker of progress; Tocqueville, while also appreciating the contrast, drew less optimistic conclusions.

The fact that democracy has rendered people gentler in their habits and practices, Tocqueville writes, is no doubt preferable to the kind of deliberate cruelty and indifference to human suffering quoted in the letters of Madame de Sévigné to her daughter (II.iii.1 [537]). It has also, Tocqueville believes, rendered us more pliant and subject to manipulation. It is here that he coins the term "democratic despotism" for this new species of power that has so far defied definition. He describes this despotism as "an immense tutelary power" (*un pouvoir immense et tutélaire*) that keeps its subjects in a state of perpetual political adolescence (II.iv.6 [663]). It is, above all, the paternalism of the new administrative state that elicits his strongest reaction. "It was not tyranny, but rather being held in tutelage by government that has made us what we are," Tocqueville writes in a marginal comment in volume 2 of *The Old Regime*. "Under tyranny, liberty can take root and grow; under administrative despotism, liberty cannot be born, much less develop. Tyranny can create liberal nations; administrative despotism, only revolutionary and servile peoples."[9]

Tocqueville is clearly concerned with the effects of this new kind of soft despotism on the character of its citizens. It is not revolutionary outbreaks of uncontrollable passion that will characterize the democratic social order but rather an extreme form of docility and apathy, a quality that he terms "individualism" (II.ii.2 [482–84]). For Tocqueville individualism is not a term of praise but the name for a pathology unique to democratic times. It points to a condition of extreme isolation, anomie, and alienation. He defines it as "a reflective and peaceable sentiment [*un sentiment réfléchi et paisible*] that disposes each citizen to cut himself off from the mass of his fellow men and to withdraw into the circle of family and friends" (II.ii.2 [482]). The isolated individual was not the village eccentric or nonconformist—someone whom Tocqueville might have admired—but the eremite, the solitary, cut off from society altogether, and is in Tocqueville's chilling phrase confined in "the solitude of his own heart" (*la solitude de son propre coeur*) (II.ii.2 [484]).

The fact that equality renders us alike also renders us indifferent to one another and our common fate. The democracy of the future is less likely to be a land of rugged individualists and freethinkers than of couch potatoes:

Thus after taking each individual by turns in its powerful hands and kneading him as it likes, the sovereign extends its arms over society as a whole; it covers its surface with a network of small, complicated painstaking uniform rules through which the most original minds and the most vigorous souls cannot clear a way to surpass the crowd; it does not break wills, but it softens them, bends them, and directs them; it rarely forces one to act, but it constantly opposes itself to one's acting; it does not destroy, it prevents things from being born; it does not tyrannize, it hinders, compromises, enervates, extinguishes, dazes, and finally reduces each nation to being nothing more than a herd of timid and industrious animals of which the government is its shepherd. (II.iv.6 [663])

Has there ever been a more powerful and prescient description of the modern administrative state?

Tocqueville came to regard the rise of this soft despotism as ultimately more dangerous to liberty than his early concerns about majority tyranny. The image of this new kind of tutelary despotism anticipates what the English call the nanny state or what is sometimes called the therapeutic state. This state, in the words of Michael Oakeshott, "is understood to be an association of invalids, all victims of the same disease and incorporated in seeking relief from their common ailment; and the office of government is a remedial engagement. Rulers are *therapeutae*, the directors of a sanatorium from which no patient may discharge himself by a choice of his own."[10] While Montesquieu had located the principle of despotism in fear, Tocqueville sees it as acquiescence. With all countervailing powers under the administrative control of the state, citizens have no choice but to become its wards. "They console themselves for being in tutelage [*en tutelle*] by thinking they have chosen their schoolmasters [*tuteurs*]" (II.iv.6 [664]).

The Democratic Soul

It would be misleading to conclude a consideration of Tocqueville with his account of democratic tyranny. A brief perusal of the section headings of *Democracy* II shows that his deepest concerns were not just with the institutions of democracy but with the ideas, sentiments, and habits that form democratic life. Following Plato, one could say that Tocqueville's most profound reflections concern the state of the democratic soul. What indeed are the traits and characteristics of democratic man described in *Democracy*?

There are three features of the democratic soul on which I would like to spend some time: compassion, restiveness, and self-interest. Taken together these features constitute the psychology, the moral scope, of the democratic state. In describing these character traits Tocqueville is providing a moral phenomenology of democratic life, one into which we are invited to look and ask whether we see ourselves and whether we like what we see.

The first and most important moral effect that democracy has on its citizens is its constant tendency to make us gentler toward one another. This is an old eighteenth-century theme. Montesquieu had argued that it was commerce that made manners milder, but it was Rousseau who made pity or compassion—a repugnance to view the suffering of others—a fundamental feature of natural man. Compassion remains a remnant of our natural goodness even amid the growth of more powerful and noisier passions. For Tocqueville, however, compassion is a feature not of natural man but of democratic man. It is not nature but democracy that has rendered us gentler, and led to the softening of mores and manners.

In a chapter entitled "How Mores Become Milder as Conditions Are Equalized" (II.iii.1 [535–39]), Tocqueville describes the moral and psychological consequences of the transition from an age of aristocracy to the age of democracy. Under aristocratic times, individuals inhabited a world where members of one class or tribe may have been like one another but regarded themselves as different from members of any other class. This did not make them cruel so much as indifferent to the pain and suffering of others outside their group. Under democracy, where all people are equal, "all men think and feel in nearly the same manner." The moral imagination of the democratic citizen is able to transport itself into the position of others more easily than in aristocratic ages. All become alike—or at least are perceived as being alike—in their range of emotions, sensibilities, and capacities for moral sympathy. "As peoples become more like one another," Tocqueville remarks, "they show themselves reciprocally more compassionate regarding their miseries, and the law of nations becomes milder" (II.iii.1 [539]).

This transformation of morality has had different but profound effects. It has certainly made people gentler and more civil toward one another. Torture, deliberate cruelty, and spectacles of pain and humiliation that were once so much a part of everyday life have been largely eliminated from the world. Just think of the torture and execution of Damien so graphically described in the opening pages of Michel Foucault's *Discipline and*

Punish, or of William Wallace in the film *Braveheart,* to get a sense of how far we have moved from the world of the ancien régime.[11] We more readily identify with those in pain or those who are suffering, even in distant parts of the world. Consider our responses to victims of the tsunami in Indonesia or to the genocide in Darfur. All of these events affecting people and places where we may never go have a claim on our moral sympathies. President Bill Clinton profoundly captured this point of view when he told his audiences, "I feel your pain"; when George W. Bush was running for president he referred to himself as a "compassionate conservative." Compassion, it seems, is the moral marker of our time.

Tocqueville clearly believes that this represents a moral progress of sorts, especially in our unwillingness to tolerate policies of deliberate cruelty—note his statement that Americans, of all peoples, have almost succeeded in abolishing the death penalty (II.iii.1 [538])—but still, the advance of compassion comes at a price. "In democratic centuries," Tocqueville writes, "men rarely devote themselves to one another, but they show a general compassion for all members of the human species" (II.iii.1 [538]). This generalized sympathy is genuine but soft; my ability to feel your pain does not require me to do very much about it. Compassion is a rather easy virtue, so to speak. It suggests sensitivity and openness; it implies caring without being judgmental; it is not exactly relativistic, but it refrains from imposing one's own morals on others.

Does Tocqueville believe that democratic peoples are in danger of becoming too soft, too morally sensitive, and thus incapable of exhibiting the kind of manly virtues of nobility, self-sacrifice, and love of honor that formed the core of the aristocratic moral code? Yes. Compassion is an admirable sentiment and one likely to expand our range of moral sympathies, but there is also a kind of misplaced compassion that Tocqueville fears. Compassion is a virtue, but it carries with it its own form of misuse when, for example, it becomes a standard by which to express our moral superiority. To be accused of "insensitivity" is in many places today, especially college campuses, the worst moral crime imaginable. We must all care—or at least pretend as if we all care—about the plight of others worse off than ourselves. The result is to create new hierarchies of compassion where one's superiority is demonstrated by a heightened sensitivity and feeling for others. It is precisely the fallacy of misplaced compassion that is at the root of contemporary forms of "political correctness"—who is the most sensitive among us?—and other moral idiocies of our age.

Compassion is not the only psychological trait of the democratic soul. At the core of the democratic character is a profound sense of uneasiness, of anxiety, which Tocqueville designates by the French word *inquiétude*. The term has been translated sometimes as "restlessness," sometimes as "restiveness," to indicate the perpetually dissatisfied character of the democratic soul. The democratic soul, like democracy itself, is never complete but is always a work in progress.

This feeling of perpetual restlessness is usually tied by Tocqueville to the desire for well-being, by which he always understands *material* well-being. It is the desire for happiness measured in terms of material happiness that is the dominant drive of the democratic soul. Tocqueville brings to his analysis of democratic restiveness something of the aristocrat's disdain for the acquisition of mere material goods for which other people have had to work their whole lives. Perhaps this more than anything else is what perplexes him about democracy. Democracy meant for Tocqueville predominantly the middle-class or bourgeois democracies made up of people who are constantly in pursuit of some obscure object of desire.

Consider the following passage from a chapter entitled "Why the Americans Show Themselves so Restive in the Midst of Their Well-Being" (II.ii.13):

In the United States, a man carefully builds a dwelling in which to pass his declining years, and he sells it while the roof is being laid; he plants a garden and he rents it out just as he was going to taste its fruits; he clears a field and he leaves to others the care of harvesting its crops. He embraces a profession and quits it. He settles in a place from which he departs soon after so as to take his changing desires elsewhere. Should his private affairs give him some respite, he immediately plunges into the whirlwind of politics. And when toward the end of a year filled with work some leisure still remains to him, he carries his restive curiosity here and there within the vast limits of the United States. He will thus go five hundred leagues in a few days in order better to distract himself from his happiness. Death finally comes, and it stops him before he has grown weary of this useless pursuit of a complete felicity that always flees from him. (II.ii.13 [512]; see also I.ii.9 [271–72])

Tocqueville's account here of the restlessness of the democratic soul sounds as if it could have come directly out of book 8 of the *Republic,* where Plato similarly describes democratic life as continually tempted by various curiosities, hobbies, and stimulants of all kinds, making it always more difficult to concentrate on those few things on which our wholeness entirely depends.

Tocqueville writes here with a kind of disdain for a life understood as a constant—and self-defeating—pursuit of happiness. The desire for well-being becomes the right of the democrat, but the more one desires it, the more it eludes one's grasp. Thus in the sentence after the passage I have just quoted, Tocqueville says: "One is at first astonished to contemplate the singular agitation displayed by so many happy men in the very midst of their abundance" (II.ii.13 [512]).

There is a world of social commentary condensed into these sentences. Tocqueville's combination of the words "agitation" and "abundance" in the same passage conveys his sense that the pursuit of happiness is more likely to bring frustration and anxiety than satisfaction and repose. He speculates in the same chapter that while in France there are more suicides than in America, in America there is more insanity. He attributes this ceaseless restlessness and anxiety to the virtual obligation to be happy. He notes "the singular melancholy that the inhabitants of democratic lands often display amid their abundance" (II.ii.13 [514]). Life, liberty, and the pursuit of happiness have become once more the joyless quest for joy.

The third and final aspect of Tocqueville's democratic psychology is the doctrine of self-interest or "self-interest well understood." The doctrine of self-interest well understood is the kind of everyday, practical utilitarianism with which we are instinctively familiar when we are told things like "honesty is the best policy." It seems simple and obvious enough, but it has a complex history. By the time Tocqueville wrote *Democracy,* theories of self-interest had long been a staple of European moral philosophers. Already in the seventeenth century, the concept of interest was put forward as a kind of talisman by which to explain all kinds of human behavior.[12]

What work was the concept of self-interest intended to do? In the first place we often think of self-interest in contrast to altruism. Although interest is an inherently self-regarding disposition, altruism is an inherently other-regarding disposition. But at the time that Tocqueville wrote, self-interested behavior was put forward as a comprehensive antonym to behavior motivated by fame, honor, and, above all, glory. While glory was associated with war and warlike pursuits, interest was invariably associated with commerce and peaceful competition. In contrast to the aristocratic concern with fame and glory, interest was regarded as a relatively peaceful or harmless passion leading men to cooperate with one another for the sake of common ends. The pursuit of self-interest also had an unmistakably democratic and egalitarian impulse. It was something *everyone* could follow, while such things as honor and glory were by their nature unequally available.

Into this debate between honor and self-interest enters Tocqueville. He begins his chapter entitled "How the Americans Combat Individualism by the Doctrine of Self-Interest Well Understood" (II.ii.8) with the following observation: "When the world was led by a few wealthy and powerful individuals, these liked to form for themselves a sublime idea of the duties of man; they were pleased to profess that it is glorious to forget oneself and that it is fitting to do good without self-interest like God himself. This was the official doctrine of the time in the matter of morality. I doubt that men were more virtuous in aristocratic centuries than in others, but it is certain that the beauties of virtue were constantly spoken of; only in secret did they study their utility" (II.ii.8 [500–501]).

Note that Tocqueville adds to the concept of self-interest the modifier "well understood" (*bien entendu*). What does this add? Self-interest well understood is not the same thing as egoism or what Rousseau called *amour propre*. It is not the desire to be talked about, to be looked at, to be first in the race of life. Rather, self-interest is connected to the passion for well-being and the desire to improve one's condition, which remain for Tocqueville important wellsprings of human action. But it is important to remember that these are not the only motives for action. Tocqueville is not a moral or psychological reductionist. He is not saying that *all* behavior is self-interested, in the way that some economists and political scientists today assert. In the same chapter Tocqueville cites an essay by Montaigne, significantly entitled "Of Glory," to remind the reader that the desire for fame and honor will always contend with the desire for well-being and happiness as the principal motives of human behavior.

What did Tocqueville hope that this new ethic of self-interest well understood would bring about? First, it is important to note that he was not recommending the doctrine of self-interest as a universal antidote to the older aristocratic ethos of honor and glory. In a later chapter he laments the decline of the older aristocratic codes of honor and chivalry (II.iii.17). By contrast the doctrine of self-interest well understood may not seem lofty, but it is "clear and sure." It has the characteristics of reliability and predictability. Self-interest is not itself a virtue, but it can form people who are "regulated, temperate, moderate, farsighted, masters of themselves" (II.ii.8 [502]). These are the virtues of the modern democratic republic: safe, predictable, and bourgeois. Such qualities may not be heroic or extraordinary, but they are within the reach of most.

Tocqueville notes, somewhat ambiguously, that of all "philosophical theories" the doctrine of self-interest well understood is "the most appropriate to the needs of men in our time." He does not regard self-interest as the key to all human behavior. In that case it would simply be a tautology. It is a guarantee against egoism or selfishness; yet it is also a barrier to the excessive love of glory and honor. Like democracy itself, it addresses "the ordinary level of humanity" (II.ii.8 [502–3]).

Democratic Statecraft

What, finally, is the task of statesmanship in a democratic age? *Democracy in America* is—as mentioned earlier—a work of political education addressed to leaders (or potential leaders) in Tocqueville's time and the future. The possibilities of statecraft are themselves dependent on what we understand by political science. In the Introduction to the book Tocqueville states in one of his characteristically epigrammatic sentences that "a new political science is needed for a world altogether new" (7). He clearly believes that his political science departs not only from the ancients but also from some of his modern predecessors, like Locke and Rousseau. What, then, is the distinguishing feature of Tocquevillian political science?

Tocqueville's new political science, I want to suggest, is based on a novel appreciation of the relation between history or historical forces and human agency. Almost any reader of *Democracy* quickly notes that Tocqueville attributes to history a kind of providential power that we do not find in earlier writers. The immense, centuries-long transition from the aristocratic to the democratic age seems almost to be an act of divine providence. Tocqueville warns his readers that to try to resist this movement would be not only futile but also impious—to go against the will of God, as it were. He no doubt deliberately overstates his case, but he does so to make a point. Our politics are deeply embedded within long structures of human history, the *longue durée*, that we can do little to alter or escape. We seem to be deeply embedded within these structures that modern political scientists sometimes call "path development."

Indeed, Tocqueville sometimes writes as a historical or sociological determinist who allows little room for human initiative and individual agency. Words like "fate," "destiny," and "tendency" are used frequently throughout his book to underscore the limits of political action. Tocqueville frequently offers predictions on the basis of underlying trends or causes. Much of this seems, again, to deny the role of independent human initiative or statecraft in history. Consider the following passage from *Democracy* I: "Sometimes after a thousand efforts, the legislator succeeds in exerting an indirect influence on the destiny of nations, and then one celebrates his genius—whereas often the geographical position of the country, about which he can do nothing, a social state that was created without his concurrence, mores and ideas of whose origin he is ignorant, a point of departure unknown to him, impart irresistible movements to society against which he struggles in vain and which carry him along in turn" (I.i.8 [154–55]).

This passage almost seems to be mocking the claims of writers like Plato, Machiavelli, and Rousseau, who saw the ability of a new prince or Legislator to literally found new peoples and institutions. Tocqueville seems to think that the statesman can do relatively little on his own, that he is strongly circumscribed by a host of factors—geographical, social, moral— over which he can exercise little influence. In Tocqueville's language, these factors impart "irresistible movements" which simply "carry him along." The statesman is more like a ship's captain, dependent on the external circumstances that control the fate of the ship. "The legislator," he continues, "resembles a man who plots his course in the middle of the sea. Thus he can direct the vessel that carries him, but he cannot change its structure, create winds, or prevent the ocean from rising under his feet" (I.i.8 [155]).

Yet if Tocqueville often writes as if the statesman is hemmed in by a host of external circumstances that constrain his powers of initiation, he also strongly opposes all systems of historical determinism that deny the powers of human agency. While he sometimes writes to shame or humble the pretentions of human greatness, he is just as concerned about the tendency toward self-abnegation that denies the role of the individual. He frequently writes as if this is a peculiarity of democratic times, when all people are considered equal, and therefore each is equally powerless to effect anything. Who has not felt this way?

Consider the often-neglected two-page chapter entitled "What Makes the Mind of Democratic Peoples Lean Toward Pantheism" (II.i.7). On the surface this seems like an odd worry. Pantheism today is regarded as a somewhat benign cult of nature worship of the kind often ascribed to American writers like Emerson and Thoreau. Tocqueville, however, looks at pantheism as an all-embracing form of determinism that is in fact fostered by the equality of conditions. It is an illusion peculiar to democratic times that we are governed by large impersonal forces over which we have no control, and a dangerous illusion at that: "As conditions become more equal and each man in particular becomes more like all the others, weaker and smaller, one gets used to no longer viewing citizens so as to consider only the people; one forgets individuals so as to think only of the species. . . . I shall have no trouble concluding that such a system, although it destroys human individuality, or rather because it destroys it, will have secret charms for men who live in democracy" (II.i.7 [426]).

Tocqueville returns to this theme fifty pages or so later in a chapter entitled "On Some Tendencies Particular to Historians in Democratic Times" (II.i.20). Here he observes that if ancient historians—think here of Herodotus, Thucydides, Livy—made all events dependent on the actions and dispositions of a few great individuals, modern historians (today we would call them social scientists) do precisely the reverse—they deny altogether the role of the individual in history:

> Historians who live in democratic times not only deny to a few citizens the power to act on the destiny of a people, they also take away from peoples themselves the ability to modify their own fate, and they subject them either to an inflexible providence or to a sort of blind fatality. According to them, each nation is invincibly attached, by its position, its origin, its antecedents, its nature, to a certain destiny that all its efforts cannot change. They render generations interdependent on one another, and thus going back from age to age and from necessary events to necessary events up to the origin of the world, they make a tight and immense chain that envelopes the whole human race and binds it. (II.i.20 [471–72])

Note that Tocqueville considers this conception of history a peculiarity of historians in democratic ages. It is not necessarily true. But—and here is Tocqueville's point—it will *become* true if we continue to think of it as such. There is a self-fulfilling element to these theories of historical necessity. It is a doctrine that must be resisted, if only because the future of human freedom may be at stake. "I shall say," Tocqueville continues, "that such a doctrine is particularly dangerous in the period we are in; our contemporaries are only too inclined to doubt free will because each of them feels himself limited on all sides by his weakness, but they will still willingly grant force and independence to men united in a social body. One must guard against this idea, for it is a question of elevating souls and not completing their prostration" (II.i.20 [472]). In other words, the kind of history or political science we adopt is always a kind of moral choice; it will determine to some degree what kind of people we are, whether dependent or free.

Tocqueville is certainly correct in his evaluation of his contemporaries. His was the age of different schemes of historical determinism. Marx was simply the best known of the socialist thinkers who offered a sweeping view of all history as determined by economic factors and class struggle. No less important was the emerging doctrine, just beginning to be enunciated by Tocqueville's contemporary Arthur de Gobineau, that all history is governed by racial genetics. It is worth noting that Tocqueville carried out a lengthy but respectful correspondence with Gobineau in which he vehemently resists Gobineau's reductionism that regards all differences between peoples and nations as reducible to racial (including ethnic) features.[13]

Tocqueville certainly did not discount the importance of race as a factor in history. The longest chapter in either volume of *Democracy* is called "Some Considerations on the Present State and the Probable Future of the Three Races That Inhabit the Territory of the United States," where he discusses whites, blacks, and native Americans (I.ii.10 [302–96]). But for Tocqueville race was merely one factor in social explanation. If history is a science—and Tocqueville believes it is—it is not a science that requires a single all-determining cause, whether class, race, or (as might be added today) gender. History is characterized by complexity; there are many sources of causation—physical causes, moral causes, ideas, and sentiments. All of these may be sources of historical change. What Tocqueville wants to resist is the spirit of a system that would reduce all of these to a single factor.

So what, then, is Tocqueville's teaching, and more specifically what is his advice for the statecraft of the future? Tocqueville is walking a very narrow tightrope. He wishes to convince his contemporaries that the democratic age is upon us, that the transition from aristocracy to democracy is irreversible, and that what he calls the "democratic revolution" is an accomplished fact. Yet, at the same time, he wants to instruct us that what form democracy takes will very much depend on will, intelligence—what he often calls "enlightenment"—and individual human agency. Democracy may be inevitable, but democracy is not all of a piece. It depends not just on impersonal historical forces but also on active virtue and intelligence, ranging from self-interest well understood to ambition and honor. Democracy can still take many forms, and whether it will favor liberty or some kind of collectivist tyranny is very much an open question.

Tocqueville returns to this theme in the final paragraphs of his book. "I am not unaware," he writes, "that several of my contemporaries have thought that peoples are never masters of themselves here below, and that they necessarily obey I do not know which insurmountable and unintelligent force born of previous events, the race, the soil, or the climate. Those are false and cowardly doctrines that can never produce any but weak men and pusillanimous nations." And yet he continues: "Providence has not created the human race either entirely independent or perfectly slave. It traces, it is true, a fatal circle around each man that he cannot leave; but within its vast limits man is powerful and free; so too with peoples" (II.iv.8 [675–76]).

Tocqueville leaves us not with a solution but with a paradox or, more precisely, a challenge. We are determined, but not altogether so. The statesman must know how to navigate the shoals between the historical, social, and cultural forces over which we have no say, and the matters of institutional design and moral suasion that are within our power. Politics, as intelligent people have always known, is a medium that takes place within language; it is a matter of providing people with the linguistic and rhetorical abilities both to construct their past and imagine their future. It is language that gives us a latitude, an ability, to adapt to changing circumstances and create new ones. Tocqueville provides us living in a democratic age with the language to shape the democratic statecraft of the future. What we do with that language, how we apply it to new circumstances and conditions that Tocqueville could never have imagined, will be entirely up to us.

CHAPTER 12

In Defense of Patriotism

The great tradition of political philosophy regarded patriotism as an ennobling sentiment. It was often thought to be the task of political philosophy to
teach or to give reasons for the love of country. Consider just a few of the
following thoughts from different writers in different historical periods:

Hillel: "If I am not for myself, who will be for me? And being for
myself, what am I? And if not now, when?" (first century B.C.E.).[1]

Cicero: "Why am I speaking of Greek examples? Somehow our
own give me more pleasure" (44 B.C.E.).[2]

Machiavelli: "I love my country [*mia patria*] more than my soul"
(1527).[3]

Rousseau: "Whenever I meditate upon government, I always
find new reasons to love my own country" (1762).[4]

Burke: "To make us love our country, our country ought to be
lovely" (1790).[5]

Lincoln: "He [Henry Clay] loved his country partly because it
was his own country, but mostly because it was a free country" (1852).[6]

Today the idea of patriotism has fallen on hard times, at least among
philosophers. This is not to say that patriotism is on the verge of disappear-
ance. It is only in educated circles that patriotism has come to appear as
morally questionable. Patriotism is widely taken to be a kind of primitive,

atavistic sentiment that demonstrates an unenlightened preference for what is one's own and for one's own ways at the expense of a more universal or enlightened point of view. Furthermore, patriotism is frequently tied to other sentiments, like nationalism and chauvinism, that are said to reveal an aggressive, militaristic attitude. These go hand in hand with a desire to dominate other people or at least to proclaim the superiority of one's own ways at the expense of others. Notice the squeamishness that many people felt after 9/11 with the public demonstrations of flag waving and other patriotic displays.

Raise the issue of patriotism on a college campus and one is likely to hear Samuel Johnson's barb "patriotism is the last refuge of a scoundrel."[7] Or one might hear E. M. Forster's wish that if he had to betray either his country or his friend, he would hope to have the courage to betray his country.[8] Forster presents the choice of friendship over country, of private over public goods, as a tragic, even a noble, decision. But this way of posing the problem is false. Loyalty is a moral virtue, just as betrayal is a moral vice. People who practice one are less likely to indulge the other. No doubt influenced by thoughts like these, three young Cambridge undergraduates in the 1930s—Kim Philby, Donald Maclean, and Guy Burgess—chose to betray their country. They became Soviet agents and for years passed on vital secrets to Moscow as they ascended the ladder of the British intelligence services, until they were finally exposed in the 1950s and '60s. Before long the three began to betray one another. Loyalty, like betrayal, is not a bus that one can get off at will. People who betray in one area of life are more likely to do so in others.

A better way to think about patriotism would be to follow Aristotle. In the *Politics* he famously posed the question whether a good citizen is the same as a good human being. Can we be loyal members of a particular city, nation, or state and at the same time fulfill our larger moral obligations to humanity? Is there a conflict between a commitment to intellectual inquiry and the free exchange of ideas, wherever that might lead, and the offices of citizenship that require loyalty to a particular set of institutions and beliefs? In short, is patriotism a virtue, and, if so, what kind of virtue is it?[9]

Nationalism and Cosmopolitanism

Following Aristotle, the best way of thinking about any virtue is as a mean point along a continuum of excess and deficiency. "Virtue or excellence," he writes, "is a characteristic involving choice that consists in observing the mean relative to us, a mean which is defined by a rational principle such as a man of practical wisdom would use to determine it."[10] The mean, as he understands it, is not a quantitative measure but something closer to the fitting or the appropriate, knowing the right thing to do in particular situations. It might be useful to think of patriotism in this light. If patriotism is a virtue requiring deliberation over competing choices, it must be located at a midpoint between two contending vices—between an excess and a deficiency. What might these look like?

The excess of patriotism would be a kind of partisan zeal that holds absolute attachment to one's own way of life—one's country, one's cause, one's nation—as unconditionally good. This is the kind of loyalty expressed in sentiments like "my country right or wrong" and that once-popular bumper sticker urging, "My country: love it or leave it." The most lethal expression of this attitude was given by the German legal philosopher Carl Schmitt in his short and incendiary 1927 book, *The Concept of the Political.*[11] Schmitt drew extensively on Thomas Hobbes, but rather than tying the state of war to a prepolitical state of nature, Schmitt viewed war—and the constant preparation for war—as the inescapable condition of political life. Man, Schmitt says, is the dangerous animal because he can kill; individuals, then, are always in a state of virtual war with one another, or at least of constant preparation for war.

Schmitt believed Hobbes had concluded correctly that war is the natural condition of human beings; he thought Hobbes was wrong, however, to believe that the social contract could create a sovereign that could put an end to war. There is no way of putting an end to war, and therefore the inescapable political fact is the distinction between friend and enemy—those who are with us and those who are against us. Rather than putting an end to war, the social contract intensifies it—creating a new grouping of friends who then owe one another their loyalty, drawing yet another line of distinction by which all others may be classified as enemies. "The political," Schmitt wrote, "is the most intense and extreme antagonism, and every concrete antagonism becomes that much more political the closer it approaches the most extreme point, that of the friend-enemy grouping."[12] All humanitarian appeals to human rights or free trade or democracy are attempts to evade the fundamental fact of conflict and the need for a politics of group solidarity, to stand with others on our side. For Schmitt, only partisanship and war are real; consensus and peace are phony. The politics of the future will be determined by those who have the courage to recognize this fact and act upon it.

At the other end of the continuum, the deficiency of patriotism involves a kind of transpolitical cosmopolitanism. The cosmopolitan idea runs deep within the Western tradition. It was very much present in Plato's *Apology of Socrates,* where the first political philosopher was accused of treason for not believing in the gods of the city and for corrupting the young. But ancient cosmopolitanism was given its canonical expression by the Stoics, who lived in the first and second centuries C.E. Their doctrine of world citizenship came of age at a time when Rome exerted a kind of global hegemony, and its universal empire was seen as having replaced the smaller parochial political units like the free city-state. To be sure, the Stoics were a small philosophical sect and never believed for an instant that their austere teachings about moral autonomy and independence could become a recipe for humanity as a whole. The task of becoming a citizen of the world is no easy business. It requires a kind of abstraction from the comfort and security of the familiar.

Present-day cosmopolitanism has been shaped decisively by another German thinker: Immanuel Kant. Kant stressed that our moral duties and obligations respect no national boundaries or other parochial attachments such as race, class, and ethnicity. In this view, we owe no greater moral obligations to fellow citizens than to any other human beings on the planet. Citizenship is an arbitrary fact, generally conferred through the accident of birth. And since birthright citizenship is an artifact of the genetic lottery, there are no moral obligations attached to it. The Kantian emphasis on universality—that a moral law is one that holds for all human beings, however situated—stresses that we are all members of a "kingdom of ends," one where every individual is due equal moral value and respect simply by virtue of reason and humanity alone.

The idea of a cosmopolitan ethic of humanity, Kant thought, could be realized only in a republican form of government or, more precisely, in a confederation of republics overseen by international law. In his pathbreaking essay "Perpetual Peace," Kant proposed a league of nations to put an end to war between states for the sake of achieving a perpetual peace. Only by eliminating the threat of war would it be possible to remove obstacles to the full and free recognition of human rights. Kant thought that Hobbes and Locke were wrong in attributing sovereignty to the individual nation-state; for him, the state was a mere developmental stage along the path to a world republic of states organized around the idea of peace. Only in a league of republics would the prophet Isaiah's dream of peace among the nations finally be realized. Kant's plans for an international league of states eventually came to fruition more than a century after his death, in Woodrow Wilson's Fourteen Points, in the creation of the United Nations, and in the Universal Declaration of Human Rights of 1948.[13]

Kant's belief in the pacific nature of republican government was based on a combination of blindness and optimism. He was blind to the historical record of republics, which has been anything but peaceful. Sparta, Athens, Rome, and Florence were armed camps that celebrated martial vigor and war. Montesquieu famously compared the harshness and moral asceticism of the ancient republics to life under a medieval monastic order.[14] No doubt, however, Kant was thinking of the modern commercial republic, where trade and commerce serve as a surrogate for war. Kant hoped, as we all do, that increased commerce and communication between people would dampen the flames of nationalist, religious, and other enthusiasms, but even here the record has been spotty at best. Increase of acquaintance does not necessarily improve feeling. Most of the wars of the twentieth century would not have been possible had not the nations of all sides received the full support of their respective populations. This became especially clear during World War I, when the socialist workers chose to go with their own countries. Kant dramatically underestimated the pull of nationalism, a vital power in both the past and the present.

The Good European

Neither Schmitt's view nor Kant's view—neither the excess nor the deficiency of politics—captures the specificity of patriotism. Schmitt's view is, to be sure, rooted in an important truth: the world is a dangerous place. Like Machiavelli and Hobbes, Schmitt takes the extreme situation—the situation of war or of mobilization for war—and turns it into the normal situation. An extreme situation is one in which the very survival, the very independence, of society is at stake. It is an existential condition. For Schmitt, every situation is potentially a life-and-death situation in which one must choose between friends and enemies. Politics, in this account, is an endless struggle for power guided exclusively by national interest. And yet a politics of unremitting war would have to be self-defeating even in Schmitt's own terms. Why should war be something that takes place only *between* states and not *within* them, as the logic of bitter rivalry and partisanship cuts all the way down into our domestic affairs? The logic of Schmitt's argument points not only to wars between states but also to ongoing civil wars or civil conflicts between rival groups within states. The result of such a logic of conflict would, ironically, be the negation of politics—the destruction of the regime as the locus of organized political power.

If the effect of Schmitt's distinction between friend and enemy is to reduce politics to war, the effect of Kantian cosmopolitanism is to confuse politics with morality. Kant and his followers (like John Rawls and Jürgen Habermas) have been eager to transcend the sovereign state and replace it with international rules of justice. If for Schmitt man is the dangerous animal, for Kant man is the rule-following animal. But the Kantian desire to transcend the state with an international forum of jurists is naïve and antipolitical. If, as Hobbes said, "covenants without the sword are but words," who will enforce these international norms of justice? The Kantian ideal of global justice yearns for a world without states, a world without national boundaries, a world, in short, without patriotism or politics. International bodies like the United Nations have been notoriously ineffective in curbing or restraining aggressive behavior. International courts like that at The Hague are often quick to condemn but slow to act in bringing criminals to justice, and may do so in selective and arbitrary ways. Cosmopolitans may feel themselves attached to such global causes as Green Peace and Amnesty International but never to their own country. When America or any other nation fails the test of living up to the impossibly high moral standards that such groups set, the result is a morbidly self-hating form of disillusionment that can often lead to nihilistic fits of rage and contempt.[15]

The question is to what degree cosmopolitanism is compatible with the patriotic sentiment. Does it require the abolition of the state or the creation of some form of world government? Even Kant admitted that a world state would be a "soulless despotism."[16] It is worth remembering that the twentieth century—perhaps the most violent in world history—saw the passing away of another kind of cosmopolitanism that promised the "withering away of the state."[17] I refer, of course, to Marxian communism, which similarly regarded classes, ethnicities, nationalism, and the like as doomed to be replaced by a universal classless society. The idea underlying the cosmopolitan ideal is that life itself, regardless of the kind of life one leads, is the highest and most absolute good. Such an ideal can lead only to moral decay, an inability or unwillingness to dedicate one's life to ideals, to the relatively few things that matter and that give life wholeness and meaning. The cosmopolitan state would be a world where nothing really matters, where there is nothing left worth struggling for—a world of entertainment, of fun, of shopping, a world void of moral seriousness.[18] It is perhaps no coincidence that the television show *Sex and the City* popularized a drink by the name of—you guessed it—the Cosmopolitan.

Too often, of course, the new cosmopolitanism is not cosmopolitan at all but a specifically culture-bound idea expressing the values of one part—and maybe only a very small part—of humanity. It seems to run contrary to the virtually universal experience of humankind. The idea of the citizen of the world is often aloof and detached, as if staring down on human affairs from a distant planet. Although its defenders are quick to present it as something heroic, cosmopolitanism seems to lack passion and intensity. It is a peculiarly austere and loveless disposition. The world citizen is, above all, "cool," that is, someone who embodies the common features of humanity and not any individual nation, tribe, or state. Cool is above all an aesthetic pose, one of increasingly postnational appeal as embodied in dress, cuisine, language, and shopping. While cool originally grew out of the African American experience—think of Miles Davis's *Birth of the Cool*—it has increasingly become mainstream, moving from the outside to the inside.

The embodiment of cool is Rick Blaine, the character played by Humphrey Bogart in the great film *Casablanca*. At the beginning of the film we learn that Rick was previously a committed partisan; he ran guns to Ethiopia and fought for the loyalists in Spain, but has since dropped out and now runs the most popular bar and casino (Rick's Café Américain) in the cosmopolitan city of Casablanca. Here his friend Louis Renault, the corrupt prefect of police, warns him not to interfere with the efforts of the Germans to detain Victor Laszlo, a famous anti-Nazi agitator. In order to recoup losses from his roulette wheel, Rick bets Louis ten thousand francs that Laszlo will escape. Rick's coolness is expressed in the following bit of dialogue when he is being interrogated by a Nazi officer:

MAJOR STRASSER:	Do you mind if I ask you a few questions, unofficially of course.
RICK:	Make it official if you like.
MAJOR STRASSER:	What is your nationality?
RICK:	I'm a drunkard.
CAPTAIN RENAULT:	And that makes Rick a citizen of the world.[19]

Of course, by the end of the film we discover that Rick has always been a romantic and idealist at heart. He drops his aloof demeanor and helps Laszlo and his great love, Ilsa Lund, escape. Laszlo's last words to Rick as he prepares to board the flight for Lisbon are revealing: "Welcome back to the fight. This time I know our side will win."

The model for contemporary cosmopolitanism is often drawn from Europe, where the European Union is taken by many to represent a new type of "transnational" citizenship. This development was brilliantly predicted more than a century ago by Friedrich Nietzsche, who described the emergence of a new phenomenon, the "good European," who would be someone beyond nationalities and even beyond politics: "The Europeans are becoming more similar to each other; they become more and more detached from the conditions in which races originate that are tied to some climate or class; they become increasingly independent of any *determinate* milieu that would like to inscribe itself for centuries in body and soul with the same demands. Thus an essentially supra-national and nomadic type of man is gradually coming up, a type that possesses, physiologically speaking, a maximum of the art and power of adaptation as its typical distinction."[20]

Nietzsche's description of this nomadic individual, essentially adaptive to new and changing environments with no ties to place, has certainly come to pass in the contemporary European world, with its common currency, open borders, and increasingly stateless existence. Such a vision is notably different from an older conservative model of *l'Europe des parties,* a Europe characterized by political diversity and rooted in particular nation-states with their distinct and healthily competing traditions. This older perspective is apt to look askance on a single union of states made possible only by certain economic, scientific, and technological developments. The new cosmopolitanism with its indifference to all traditions, especially religion, entails not only a soft version of the Marxian dream of a world in which politics has withered away; it would also have to be coupled with Max Weber's fear of a world governed by narrow-minded specialists and technocrats, a world of "specialists without spirit, sensualists without heart."[21]

Nationalism and cosmopolitanism are today often thought of as the only two political options available to us, but in fact they both tend to obscure the true nature of patriotism. Each contains at best a part of the truth. The nationalist is correct to see that politics is a matter of the particular— particular states, particular nations, particular peoples and traditions. For the nationalist, the particular—*this* people, *this* culture, *this* state—stands for something higher, more noble, than the cosmopolitan idea. Everything great derives from something rooted and particular. We enter the world as members of a particular family, in a particular neighborhood, in a particular state, in a particular part of the country. Each of us is a composite of particularities. These attachments are not something extraneous to our identities; they make us who we are. The demand that we give up our particular identities and assume a new and artificial cosmopolitan identity would be like asking us to stop speaking our native languages and embrace Esperanto. Who is the Shakespeare of Esperanto?[22]

The fact is, we learn to care about others by caring about those who are closest to us. Cosmopolitan internationalism has the disadvantage of uprooting people from their traditions and from the local arrangements that most people find worthy of reverence. There seems to be little room for a sense of awe or for the sacred in the cosmopolitan ideal. The ancient historian Herodotus tells the following story about the Persians: "Most of all they held in honor themselves, then those who dwell next to themselves, and then those next to them, and so on, so there is a progression in honor in relation to the distance. This is because they think themselves to be the best of mankind in everything and that others have a hold on virtue in proportion to their nearness; those that live furthest away are the most base."[23]

What Herodotus attributes to the Persians is closer to the universal experience of all humankind. We care about those things that are closest to us and have weaker ties of attachment to things the farther away they seem to our moral dispositions and sympathies. Herodotus did not write this to condemn Persian parochialism. To the contrary. We live in a series of concentric circles in which those who dwell with us are held in high esteem. This is the core belief, the basic disposition, underlying patriotism. It indicates that patriotism—love of one's own—is not a sign of narrow-mindedness or bigotry, it is the near-universal experience of all peoples. Patriotism is not necessarily a mark of prejudice or insularity but can be generous and ennobling, open to all people who share a common set of beliefs, values, and way of life.

But there is truth also on the cosmopolitan side. Are we condemned by the accident of birth to live by the traditions of the particular nation into which we happen to be born? Doesn't this deny what is highest in us: our capacity for choice, to detach ourselves from our surroundings, to determine for ourselves how we will live and who we will be? This idea of choice is at the core of our experience of human dignity. We often experience our moral worth through our ability to choose how we will live, with whom, and under what conditions. This kind of cosmopolitan ethic has the virtue of allowing us to stand imaginatively outside of our particular situation and to view ourselves from a universal point of view, from the standpoint of a disinterested spectator. Clearly such critical distance can help us to judge ourselves and our societies. We must view them as we would view anyone else—neutrally, objectively, disinterestedly. This is the morality of cosmopolitanism, and while it cannot stand alone, it does have some virtues to recommend it.

"Tact of the Heart"

Each of these components—let us call them the national and the cosmopolitan ideals—has a certain place in a properly constituted patriotism. Consider, for instance, the case of the American regime. In one respect, America is the first truly modern nation—a nation founded upon the principles of modern philosophy. Our founding document, the Declaration of Independence, is dedicated to the proposition that all men are created equal. The principle of equality is the foundation for certain rights to life, liberty, and the pursuit of happiness. From this it is said to follow that all legitimate government is based upon the consent of the governed, and when government fails to protect our rights it may be overturned and begun anew. These principles were (and are) said to hold true not for Americans alone but for all human beings always and everywhere. Far from suggesting a traditional form of customary morality, American patriotism requires a commitment to the highest, most universal moral principles. A cosmopolitan dimension is built into the very nature of American patriotism.

At the same time, American patriotism requires more than devotion to a set of formal principles. It consists of the entire way of life—that mix of moral and religious practices, habits, customs, and sentiments—that makes a people who they are. The regime is in Aristotle's sense an *ethos,* a distinctive character that nurtures distinctive human types. The ethos describes the tone of a regime, what it finds most worthy of admiration, what it looks up to. Thus when Tocqueville studied the American regime in *Democracy in America,* he started first with our formal political institutions as enumerated in the Constitution (the separation of powers, the division between state and federal authority, and so on) but then went on to look at such informal practices as American manners and morals, our tendency to form small civic associations, our religious life, as well as our peculiar defensiveness and tendency to bombastic moralism. It was this last quality that led Tocqueville to complain that there was "nothing more irritating in the habits of life than this irritable patriotism of the Americans."[24]

Ours is a patriotism that contains elements of both moral universalism and a robust commitment to a specific way of life. It is not just a way of knowing but also a manner of feeling. Patriotism is a moral sentiment, or what Tocqueville called a "habit of the heart."[25] This is all a way of saying that patriotism requires an understanding and appreciation of not only a set of abstract ideas but also a particular history and tradition. To love one's country well is to love something particular. I may admire France's language, its food, its countryside, and its culture, but I cannot love France the way a Frenchman does. I can never feel the way a French person feels when he or she hears the "Marseillaise." We love best what is our own. This is what I think Burke meant when he said that the British constitution and way of life are "an entailed inheritance derived to us from our forefathers and to be transmitted to posterity."[26]

Patriotism, then, is a particular species of love. But love of what? How can one feel love or gratitude to millions of people one cannot even know? This issue was at the core of the debate between Gershom Scholem and Hannah Arendt over the publication of her book *Eichmann in Jerusalem*.[27] In covering the Eichmann trial for the *New Yorker* magazine, Arendt had submitted the Israeli tribunal and even the testimony of eyewitnesses to withering criticism. Scholem could not but regard this degree of detachment as a betrayal, expressed as it was at a time when the wounds of the Holocaust (he always preferred to call it the Catastrophe) were still fresh. Under the circumstances, he wondered, would it not have been proper to show a little more sympathy? To this Arendt loftily replied that she could not love an abstraction like a people, only individual persons. It was here that Scholem accused her of lacking *Ahavat Yisrael* or a proper love of the Jewish people, her own people. "In you, dear Hannah, as in so many intellectuals who come from the German Left, I find little trace of this," he wrote. "In circumstances such as these, would there not have been a place for what I can only describe with that modest German word—*Herzenstakt* [tact of the heart]?"[28]

There is no good idea that cannot be abused, and this is especially true of patriotism. Patriotism seems to bring out both the best and the worst in people. If critics on the left have routinely disparaged any display of patriotism as tantamount to warmongering and nationalistic chauvinism, bullies on the right have been quick to depict any questioning of America as somehow un-American and therefore not patriotic. America is, I believe, the only country in the world where there are words like "Americanization" and "un-American." To the best of my knowledge, there are no words in any European language to denote similar phenomena. But if patriotism can be harsh and punitive, it can also be elevating and ennobling. American patriotism at its best is not just indoctrination but also a form of moral education in the virtues of civility, law-abidingness, respect for others, responsibility, love of honor, courage, loyalty, and leadership.

Political Education

Patriotism is not just a moral but also an intellectual virtue. The proper love of country is not something we inherit, it must be taught. Man may be the political animal, but this does not mean that politics is encoded in our DNA. Politics is an art and, like all arts, it must be taught. But teaching requires teachers, and where are the teachers of this art to be found?

Not, it appears, in departments of history, political science, or economics. Modern professors of history often appear to teach everything but a proper respect for their political tradition. One often gets the impression that America alone among the nations of the world is responsible for racism, homophobia, and the despoliation of the planet. In my own field of political science—the field that once designated the skill or art possessed by the statesman and citizen—civic education has been replaced by something called "game theory," which regards politics merely as a marketplace in which individual preferences are formed and utilities maximized. Rather than teaching students to think of themselves as citizens, the new political science treats us as "rational actors" who exist simply to exercise preferences. But what should we have a preference for? How should choice be exercised? On these most fundamental questions, our political science is silent. It has nothing to offer. By reducing all politics to choice and all choices to preferences, the new political science is forced to accord legitimacy to every preference—however vile, base, or indecent—that an individual or group may express. In such a nihilistic view, there is no room for political judgment.

But the very possibility of politics assumes the primacy of political judgment. By judgment I mean the art of practical reason as practiced by members of a jury, a political assembly, or a civic association, anywhere deliberation takes place. Politics is a practical art in precisely the manner intended by Aristotle. It is oriented not only toward knowledge but also toward action, where action involves deliberation, foresight, and prudence. Political judgment entails know-how or savvy of the kind exhibited by the statesman. It is both an intellectual and a moral quality. It requires knowledge of political facts, but it is not essentially empirical.

Political judgment should be distinguished from technical know-how—the kind of expertise required for administrative work. But it also needs to be distinguished from theoretical knowledge—the search for universal laws governing human behavior. Political judgment, by contrast, is knowledge of the fitting or the appropriate, requiring an attention to the nuances or particularities of a situation. Such knowledge will always be provisional; it will be true only for the most part and will always admit of exceptions. The person who possesses this kind of knowledge will have that special quality of insight or discrimination that distinguishes him or her from persons of a purely theoretical or speculative cast of mind.

The faculty of judgment is something that requires experience. Judgment is not simply a technique that can be learned by heart, repeated by rote, and applied mechanically. It is something akin to the capacity to learn a language; it is not just a matter of memorizing grammar and syntax but requires immersion in the language itself. It entails a capacity for synthesis rather than analysis. It is not necessarily a matter of having more information or access to a larger body of facts. Rather, it requires the ability to see something before others do, to know what to do and when to do it. It is the ability to adapt to new and often unforeseen situations, in order to keep the ship of state afloat.

Winston Churchill best described this capacity for political judgment in his classic essay "Consistency in Politics." I will only say that it is one of the greatest political essays in the English language. Churchill argues there that there are two kinds of consistency. One connotes absolute commitment to a rule or principle (never lie, never cheat, and so on). But consistency in politics is more complicated. It involves knowing how to adapt principles to changing circumstances and to adjust them as the situation warrants. This may sound like opportunism or flip-flopping, but it amounts in fact to the oldest of all policies: keeping the ship on an even keel. Listen to Churchill on this theme:

> A distinction should be drawn between two kinds of political inconsistency. First, a statesman in contact with the moving current of events and anxious to keep the ship on an even keel and steer a steady course may lean all his weight now on one side and now on the other. His arguments in each case when

contrasted can be shown to be not only very different in character, but contradictory in spirit and opposite in direction; yet his
object will throughout have remained the same. His resolves,
his wishes, his outlook may have been unchanged; his methods
may be verbally irreconcilable. We cannot call this inconsis-
tency. In fact it may be claimed to be the truest consistency.[29]

Churchill's point is that the world of moral and political experience is
too complex to be reduced to a single rule or principle, whether this be
Thomas Aquinas's natural law, Immanuel Kant's Categorical Imperative, or
the Utilitarian's principle of the greatest happiness for the greatest number.
Just as there is no single wine that goes equally well with all foods, so there
is no single moral rule that can be used for all cases. The principle of practical judgment should be thought of not as an inflexible moral imperative but
as a rule of thumb, that is, a useful but nevertheless inexact standard that
will have to be continually modified to fit the circumstances. In each new
case the standard will be determined by the person best capable of captur-
ing the nuance, color, or texture of the particular situation.

Much of modern-day political science has neglected the role of political judgment precisely because it appears too "subjective" and resists or
stands outside the realm of quantification. In place of the faculty of judgment, our political science has stressed a narrow-minded focus on
"methodology"—often at the expense of the life-and-death issues that make
up the substance of politics. This attempt to turn the study of politics into a
science like physics, or into social sciences like economics or psychology, is
to lose sight of its original purpose. The purpose of political science is not
to stand above or outside the political community, like an entomologist
observing ant behavior, but to serve as a civic-minded guardian of disputes
in order to restore peace and stability to conflict-ridden situations.

So what should the study of political science be now? To ask a question once posed by Karl Marx: Who will educate the educators? How can
we reintroduce the art of political judgment, and who is equipped to do so?
The best answer is through the study of old books, often very old ones.
These are our best teachers in a world where real teachers are in short supply. In addition to the works covered in this book, let me mention works
like Plato's *Laws*, Tacitus's *Annals*, Montesquieu's *Spirit of the Laws*, and the
Federalist Papers. To read these books in the spirit in which they were written is to acquire an education in political responsibility.

But the works of our greatest political philosophers need to be supplemented by the works of our most astute psychological novelists. A great novel contains instances of moral reasoning, persuasion, and deliberation equal to the theories of the greatest philosophers; the novels of Leo Tolstoy, Henry James, and Jane Austen are only the most obvious. A dozen pages of Austen's *Persuasion* will teach more about the delicate art of judgment than a shelf full of contemporary books claiming to study conflict resolution. These in turn should be supplemented by the deeds and writings of the most important statesmen from around the world, from Pericles, Bismarck, and Disraeli to Jefferson, Madison, Lincoln, Wilson, both Roosevelts, Churchill, and Mandela. Their works are a virtual education in how to negotiate affairs in times of crisis.

Once you have read these works—and only when you have done that—can you say that you are living up to the highest offices of a Yale student summarized on Memorial Gate at Branford College: "For God, for Country, and for Yale."[30]

Notes

CHAPTER 1
Why Political Philosophy?

1. John Maynard Keynes, *The General Theory of Employment, Interest, and Money* (New York: Harcourt, Brace and World, 1964), 383.
2. Alexander Hamilton, *The Federalist Papers,* ed. Clinton Rossiter (New York: Signet, 1961), 33.
3. Abraham Lincoln, "Eulogy on Henry Clay," in *The Writings of Abraham Lincoln,* ed. Steven B. Smith (New Haven: Yale University Press, 2012), 48.

CHAPTER 2
Antigone and the Politics of Conflict

1. James Madison, *The Federalist Papers,* ed. Clinton Rossiter (New York: Signet, 1961), 322.
2. On this point see Peter Ahrensdorf, *Greek Tragedy and Political Philosophy: Rationalism and Religion in Sophocles' Three Theban Plays* (New York: Cambridge University Press, 2009); for other works that have proved useful, see Bernard Knox, *The Heroic Temper: Studies in Sophoclean Tragedy* (Berkeley: University of California Press, 1964); Seth Benardete, "A Reading of Sophocles' *Antigone*," *Interpretation* 4 (1975): 148–96; 5 (1975): 1–55, 148–84; Arlene Saxonhouse, "From Tragedy to Hierarchy and Back Again: Women in Greek Political Thought," *American Political Science Review* 80 (1986): 403–18; Warren J. Lane and Anne M. Lane, "The Politics of *Antigone*," in *Greek Tragedy and Political Theory,* ed. J. Peter Euben (Berkeley: University of California Press, 1986), 162–82.
3. Leo Strauss, "Preface to Spinoza's Critique of Religion," in *Liberalism Ancient and Modern* (New York: Basic Books, 1968), 224.
4. Knox, *The Heroic Temper,* 84.
5. G. W. F. Hegel, *Lectures on the Philosophy of Religion,* trans. E. B. Speirs and J. B. Sanderson (London: Routledge and Kegan Paul, 1962), II:264–65.
6. See Martin Heidegger, *An Introduction to Metaphysics,* trans. Ralph Manheim (New Haven: Yale University Press, 1959), 146–65.
7. Numa Denis Fustel de Coulanges, *The Ancient City* (Baltimore: Johns Hopkins University Press, 1980), 34.
8. Fustel de Coulanges, *The Ancient City,* 381.

CHAPTER 3
Socrates and the Examined Life

1. For useful studies on the trial of Socrates, see I. F. Stone, *The Trial of Socrates* (New York: Little, Brown, 1988); Thomas C. Brickhouse and Nicholas D. Smith, *Socrates on Trial* (Princeton: Princeton University Press, 1989); Mogens Herman Hansen, *The Trial of Socrates from the Athenian Point of View* (Copenhagen. Royal Danish Academy of Sciences and Letters, 1995); Joseph Cropsey, *Plato's World: Man's Place in the Cosmos* (Chicago: University of Chicago Press, 1995); Arlene Saxonhouse, *Free Speech and Democracy in Ancient Athens* (Cambridge: Cambridge University Press, 2006); Robin Waterfield, *Why Socrates Died: Dispelling the Myths* (New York: W. W. Norton, 2009).
2. John Stuart Mill, *On Liberty*, ed. David Spitz (New York: W. W. Norton, 1975), 24.
3. Thucydides, *The Peloponnesian War*, Crawley translation (New York: Modern Library, 1982), II.37
4. Thucydides, *Peloponnesian War*, II.39.
5. Thucydides, *Peloponnesian War*, II.40.
6. For an account of the Thirty, see Aristotle, *The Athenian Constitution*, XXXV.1–4.
7. For those who have argued for Socrates as a kind of conscientious objector from politics, see Hannah Arendt, "Philosophy and Politics," *Social Research* 57 (1990): 73–103; Dana Villa, *Socratic Citizenship* (Princeton: Princeton University Press, 2001); George Kateb, "Socratic Integrity," in *Patriotism and Other Mistakes* (Princeton: Princeton University Press, 2006), 215–44.
8. Socrates is referring to an actual historical event in the year 406, when the Assembly illegally voted to try the Arginusae generals; see Xenophon, *Memorabilia*, trans. Amy L. Bonnette (Ithaca: Cornell University Press, 1994), I.i.18.

CHAPTER 4
Plato on Justice and the Human Good

1. The work devoted to Plato in general and the *Republic* in particular is staggering, but among the works from which I have learned the most I would include Leo Strauss, "On Plato's *Republic*," in *The City and Man* (Chicago: University of Chicago Press, 1964), 50–138; Danielle S. Allen, *Why Plato Wrote* (Malden, MA: Wiley-Blackwell, 2010); Seth Benardete, *Socrates' Second Sailing: On Plato's "Republic"* (Chicago: University of Chicago Press, 1989); Eva Brann, *The Music of the Republic: Essays on Socrates's Conversations and Plato's Writings* (Philadelphia: Paul Dry Books, 2004); G. R. F. Ferrari, *City and Soul in Plato's "Republic"* (Chicago: University of Chicago Press, 2005); Iris Murdoch, *The Fire and the Sun: Why Plato Banished the Poets* (Oxford: Oxford University Press, 1977); Stanley Rosen, *Plato's "Republic": A Study* (New Haven: Yale University Press, 2005); Bernard Williams, "The Analogy of City and Soul in Plato's *Republic*," in *Exegesis and Argument: Studies in Greek Philosophy Presented to Gregory Vlastos*, ed. E. N. Lee, A. P. D. Mourelatos, and R. M. Rorty (Assen: Van Gorcum, 1973), 196–206.
2. The claim that the *Republic* should be read as a satire has been argued provocatively by Allan Bloom, "Interpretive Essay" in Plato, *Republic* (New York: Basic Books, 1968), 409–11.

3.   Plato, *Seventh Letter,* in *Plato: Complete Works,* ed. John M. Cooper (Indianapolis: Hackett, 1997), 324b–36b; translation slightly modified.

4.   The debate over the totalitarian aspects of Plato was raised most prominently in Karl Popper, *The Open Society and Its Enemies,* 2 vols. (New York: Harper and Row, 1963); for similar charges, see R. H. S. Crossman, *Plato Today* (London: George Allen and Unwin, 1959); see also Mark Lilla, *The Reckless Mind: Intellectuals in Politics* (New York: NYRB, 2001), 193–216.

5.   Jean-Jacques Rousseau, *Emile or On Education,* trans. Allan Bloom (New York: Basic Books, 1979), 40.

6.   The story is first told in Herodotus, *The History,* trans. David Grene (Chicago: University of Chicago Press, 1987), I.8–15 (pp. 36–39).

7.   Simone de Beauvoir, *Force of Circumstance,* trans. Richard Howard (New York: Putnam, 1965), 34–35.

8.   Paul Shorey, *The Republic,* in the Loeb Classical Library (Cambridge, MA: Harvard University Press, 1937), 5:489.

CHAPTER 5
Aristotle's Science of Regime Politics

1.   For works on Aristotle's *Politics* from which I have benefited, see Carnes Lord, *Education and Culture in the Political Thought of Aristotle* (Ithaca: Cornell University Press, 1982); Stephen Salkever, *Finding the Mean: Theory and Practice in Aristotelian Political Philosophy* (Princeton: Princeton University Press, 1990); Carnes Lord and David K. O'Connor, eds., *Essays on the Foundations of Aristotelian Political Science* (Berkeley: University of California Press, 1991); David Keyt and Fred D. Miller, eds., *A Companion to Aristotle's "Politics"* (Oxford: Basil Blackwell, 1991); Judith A. Swanson, *The Public and the Private in Aristotle's Political Philosophy* (Ithaca: Cornell University Press, 1992); Bernard Yack, *The Problems of a Political Animal: Community, Justice, and Conflict in Aristotelian Political Thought* (Berkeley: University of California Press, 1993); Clifford Angell Bates Jr, *Aristotle's "Best Regime": Kingship, Democracy, and the Rule of Law* (Baton Rouge: Louisiana State University Press, 2003); Jill Frank, *A Democracy of Distinction: Aristotle and the Work of Politics* (Chicago: University of Chicago Press, 2005).

2.   Stuart Hampshire, "Two Theories of Morality," in *Morality and Conflict* (Cambridge, MA: Harvard University Press, 1983), 10.

3.   Thomas Jefferson to John Adams, October 28, 1813, in *The Adams-Jefferson Letters: The Complete Correspondence Between Thomas Jefferson and Abigail and John Adams,* ed. Lester J. Cappon (Chapel Hill: University of North Carolina Press, 1987), 388–89.

4.   John Stuart Mill, *Considerations on Representative Government,* ed. Currin V. Shields (Indianapolis: Bobbs-Merrill, 1958), 114–16.

5.   For the claim that the principle of election was designed to introduce oligarchic elements into popular government, see Bernard Manin, *The Principles of Representative Government* (New York: Cambridge University Press, 1997).

6.   Isaiah Berlin, "Political Judgment," in *The Sense of Reality: Studies in Ideas and Their History,* ed. Henry Hardy (New York: Farrar, Straus and Giroux, 1997), 47.

7.   Berlin, "Political Judgment," 47.

CHAPTER 6
The Politics of the Bible

1. See Leo Strauss, "Jerusalem and Athens: Some Preliminary Reflections," in *Studies in Platonic Political Philosophy,* ed. Thomas Pangle (Chicago: University of Chicago Press, 1983), 147–73; Leo Strauss, "Progress or Return," in *The Rebirth of Classical Political Rationalism,* ed. Thomas Pangle (Chicago: University of Chicago Press, 1989), 227–70; see also Lev Shestov, *Athens and Jerusalem,* trans. Bernard Martin (Athens: Ohio University Press, 1966).

2. For a modern philosopher's attempt to wrestle with the Abraham story, see Soren Kierkegaard, *Fear and Trembling: A Dialectical Lyric,* in *Fear and Trembling and Sickness unto Death,* trans. Walter Lowrie (Princeton: Princeton University Press, 1974); see also Emil L. Fackenheim, "Abraham and the Kantians," in *Encounters Between Judaism and Modern Philosophy* (New York: Schocken, 1973), 33–77.

3. My own reflections on Genesis are indebted to Leo Strauss, "On the Interpretation of Genesis," in *Jewish Philosophy and the Crisis of Modernity,* ed. Kenneth Hart Green (Albany: SUNY Press, 1997), 359–76; see also Umberto Cassuto, *A Commentary on the Book of Genesis* (Jerusalem: Judah Magnes Press, 1964); Robert Alter, *Genesis: Translation and Commentary* (New York: W. W. Norton, 1996); Leon Kass, *The Beginning of Wisdom: Reading Genesis* (New York: Free Press, 2003).

4. John Milton, *Paradise Lost,* ed. David Scott Kastan (Indianapolis: Hackett, 2005), XII (p. 406).

5. Fackenheim, "Idolatry as a Modern Possibility," in *Encounters Between Judaism and Modern Philosophy,* 185–86.

6. My reading of the story of David owes much to Robert Alter, *The David Story: A Translation and Commentary of 1 and 2 Samuel* (New York: W. W. Norton, 1999); Robert Pinsky, *The Life of David* (New York: Schocken, 2005); Israel Finkelstein and Neil Asher Silberman, *David and Solomon: In Search of the Bible's Sacred Kings and the Roots of the Western Tradition* (New York: Free Press, 2007).

7. Larry McMurtry and Diana Ossana, *Brokeback Mountain: A Screenplay,* based on a short story by Annie Proulx, in Annie Proulx, Larry McMurtry, and Diana Ossana, *Brokeback Mountain: Story to Screenplay* (New York: Scribner, 2005), 83.

CHAPTER 7
Machiavelli and the Art of Political Founding

1. Among the most important recent works on Machiavelli are Leo Strauss, *Thoughts on Machiavelli* (Seattle: University of Washington Press, 1958); Isaiah Berlin, "The Originality of Machiavelli," in *Against the Current: Essays in the History of Ideas* (New York: Viking, 1980), 25–79; Vickie B. Sullivan, *Machiavelli's Three Romes: Religion, Human Liberty, and Politics Reformed* (DeKalb: Northern Illinois University Press, 1996); Harvey C. Mansfield, *Machiavelli's Virtue* (Chicago: University of Chicago Press, 1996); Louis Althusser, *Machiavelli and Us,* trans. Gregory Elliott (London: Verso, 1999); Mikael Hörnqvist, *Machiavelli and Empire* (Cambridge: Cambridge University Press, 2004); John P. McCormick, *Machiavellian Democracy* (Cambridge: Cambridge University Press, 2011).

2. For the best biography of Machiavelli, see Roberto Ridolfi, *The Life of Niccolò Machiavelli,* trans. Cecil Grayson (Chicago: University of Chicago Press, 1963); for a more recent work see Maurizio Viroli, *Niccolò's Smile: A Biography of Machiavelli,* trans. Anthony Shuggar (London: I. B. Tauris, 2001); and more recently still, see Miles Unger, *Machiavelli: A Biography* (New York: Simon and Schuster, 2011).

3. Machiavelli to Francesco Vettori, December 10, 1513, in *Machiavelli and His Friends: Their Personal Correspondence,* trans. and ed. James B. Atkinson and David Sices (DeKalb: Northern Illinois University Press, 1996), no. 224 (p. 264).

4. The classic study is Friedrich Meinecke, *The Doctrine of Raison d'État and Its Place in Modern History,* trans. Werner Stark (New Brunswick, NJ: Transaction, 1998); see also Ernst Cassirer, *The Myth of the State* (New Haven: Yale University Press, 1946); Maurizio Viroli, *From Politics to Reason of State: The Acquisition and Transformation of the Language of Politics* (Cambridge: Cambridge University Press, 1992).

5. Strauss, *Thoughts on Machiavelli,* 9.

6. Jean-Paul Sartre, *Dirty Hands,* in *No Exit and Three Other Plays* (New York: Vintage International, 1989), act V (p. 218); for a philosophical treatment of this problem, see Michael Walzer, "Political Action: The Problem of Dirty Hands," *Philosophy and Public Affairs* 2 (1973): 160–80.

7. Graham Greene, *The Third Man,* www.dailyscript.com/scripts/the_third_man .html.

8. John Le Carré, *The Spy Who Came in from the Cold* (New York: Coward-McCann, 1964), 246.

9. Sheldon Wolin, *Politics and Vision: Continuity and Innovation in Western Political Thought* (Boston: Little, Brown, 1960), 223.

10. Baruch Spinoza, *The Political Treatise,* in *The Political Works,* ed. and trans. A. G. Wernham (Oxford: Clarendon Press, 1958), V, 7 (p. 313).

11. Jean-Jacques Rousseau, *On the Social Contract,* in *The Social Contract and Other Later Political Writings,* trans. Victor Gourevitch (Cambridge: Cambridge University Press, 1997), III, vi, 95.

12. For the debate over the dating of the final chapter, see John M. Najemy, *Between Friends: Discourses on Power and Desire in the Machiavelli-Vettori Letters of 1513–1515* (Princeton: Princeton University Press, 1993), 177–84.

13. Machiavelli to Francesco Vettori, August 26, 1513, in *Machiavelli and His Friends,* no. 222 (pp. 259–60).

14. For the social circles of Machiavelli's dedicatees, the so-called *Ottimati,* see J. G. A. Pocock, *The Machiavellian Moment: Florentine Political Thought and the Atlantic Republican Tradition* (Princeton: Princeton University Press, 1975), 114–55, 185–86.

15. For Machiavelli's democratic or plebian propensities, see John P. McCormick, *Machiavellian Democracy* (Cambridge: Cambridge University Press, 2011).

16. For the classic account of Numa, see Livy, *The Rise of Rome: Books 1–5,* trans. T. J. Luce (New York: Oxford University Press, 1998), I.18–21/23–27; see Mark Silk, "Numa Pompilius and the Idea of Civil Religion in the West," *Journal of the American Academy of Religion* 72 (2004): 863–96.

17. Robert Bellah, "Civil Religion in America," *American Civil Religion,* ed. Russell Richey and Donald Jones (New York: Harper and Row, 1974), 21–44.

18. Bellah, "Civil Religion," 29.

19. Bellah, "Civil Religion," 34–35.
20. Abraham Lincoln, "Address to the Young Men's Lyceum of Springfield, Illinois," in *The Writings of Abraham Lincoln,* ed. Steven B. Smith (New Haven: Yale University Press, 2012), 10–11.

CHAPTER 8

Hobbes's New Science of Politics

1. For some important studies of Hobbes, see Leo Strauss, *The Political Philosophy of Hobbes: Its Basis and Its Genesis,* trans. Elsa M. Sinclair (Chicago: University of Chicago Press, 1966); Michael Oakeshott, *Hobbes on Civil Association* (Berkeley: University of California Press, 1975); Richard Tuck, *Hobbes* (New York: Oxford University Press, 1989); Norbert Bobbio, *Thomas Hobbes and the Natural Law Tradition,* trans. Daniela Gobetti (Chicago: University of Chicago Press, 1993); Quentin Skinner, *Reason and Rhetoric in the Philosophy of Hobbes* (Cambridge: Cambridge University Press, 1996); Noel Malcolm, *Aspects of Hobbes* (Oxford: Clarendon Press, 2002).
2. Thomas Hobbes, *De Corpore,* in *The English Works of Thomas Hobbes,* ed. Thomas Molesworth (London: Bohn, 1839–1845), vol. 1, p. ix; see also Strauss, *The Political Philosophy of Hobbes,* 1–2.
3. Alexis de Tocqueville, *Democracy in America,* trans. Harvey C. Mansfield and Delba Winthrop (Chicago: University of Chicago Press, 2000), II, ii, 2 (p. 482); for the rise of individualism in the Renaissance, see Ian Watt, *Myths of Modern Individualism: Faust, Don Quixote, Don Juan, Robinson Crusoe* (Cambridge: Cambridge University Press, 1996).
4. In Fred R. Shapiro, ed., *The Yale Book of Quotations* (New Haven: Yale University Press, 2006), 790. Vidal was quoted in the *Newport Daily News,* 3 November, 1978.
5. For the claim that Hobbes establishes the foundations of liberalism, see Leo Strauss, *Natural Right and History* (Chicago: University of Chicago Press, 1971), 181–82; Pierre Manent, *The Intellectual History of Liberalism,* trans. Rebecca Balinski (Princeton: Princeton University Press, 1994), 25–26; for a contrary view, see Judith Shklar, "The Liberalism of Fear," in *Political Thought and Political Thinkers,* ed. Stanley Hoffman (Chicago: University of Chicago Press, 1998), 6.
6. For a reflection on this problem, see Francis Fukuyama, *The End of History and the Last Man* (New York: Free Press, 1992).
7. Pierre Hassner, "The Bourgeois and the Barbarian," in *The Future of War,* ed. Gwyn Prins and Hylke Tromp (The Hague: Kluwer, 2000).
8. James Bowman, *Honor: A History* (New York: Encounter, 2006).

CHAPTER 9

Locke and the Art of Constitutional Government

1. For the connection between Locke and liberal politics, see Martin Seliger, *The Liberal Politics of John Locke* (New York: Praeger, 1968); Ruth Grant, *John Locke's Liberalism* (Chicago: University of Chicago Press, 1984); Nathan Tarcov, *Locke's Education for Liberty* (Chicago: University of Chicago Press, 1984); Thomas L. Pangle, *The Spirit of Modern Republicanism: The Moral Vision of the American*

Founders and the Philosophy of Locke (Chicago: University of Chicago Press, 1988); Michael Zuckert, *Launching Liberalism: On Lockean Political Philosophy* (Lawrence: University Press of Kansas, 2002).

2. Jeremy Waldron, *God, Locke, and Equality: Christian Foundations of Locke's Political Thought* (New York: Cambridge University Press, 2002); see also John Dunn, *The Political Thought of Jock Locke: An Historical Account of the Argument of the "Two Treatises of Government"* (Cambridge: Cambridge University Press, 1969). Dunn has also insisted on the theological origins of Locke's thought but concludes with the melancholy reflection that this is what renders Locke completely irrelevant today.

3. The role of Locke as a defender of capitalism has been argued by C. B. Macpherson, *The Political Theory of Possessive Individualism: Hobbes to Locke* (Oxford: Clarendon Press, 1962); see also Joyce Appleby, *Economic Thought and Ideology in Seventeenth-Century England* (Princeton: Princeton University Press, 1978).

4. James Madison, *The Federalist Papers,* ed. Clinton Rossiter (New York: Signet, 1961), 78.

5. Michael Oakeshott, "Rationalism in Politics," in *Rationalism in Politics and Other Essays* (Indianapolis: Liberty Press, 1991), 30.

6. Karl Marx, *Capital,* trans. Samuel Moore and Edward Aveling (London: Lawrence and Wishart, 1970), 76–77.

7. Max Weber, *The Protestant Ethic and the Spirit of Capitalism,* trans. Talcott Parsons (New York: Charles Scribner's Sons, 1958), 53.

8. Leo Strauss, *Natural Right and History* (Chicago: University of Chicago Press, 1971), 251.

9. Daniel Bell, *The Cultural Contradictions of Capitalism* (New York: Basic Books, 1978).

10. For the claim that Locke was a populist democrat, see Willmore Kendall, *John Locke and the Doctrine of Majority Rule* (Urbana: University of Illinois Press, 1941).

11. David Hume, "Of the Original Contract," in *Essays: Moral, Political, and Literary,* ed. Eugene F. Miller (Indianapolis: Liberty Press, 1987), 465–88.

12. Abraham Lincoln, "Speech on the Kansas-Nebraska Act," in *The Writings of Abraham Lincoln,* ed. Steven B. Smith (New Haven: Yale University Press, 2012), 76.

13. See Harvey C. Mansfield, *Taming the Prince: The Ambivalence of Modern Executive Power* (New York: Free Press, 1989), 181–211.

14. U. S. Constitution, Article 1, Section 9; Abraham Lincoln, "To Erastus Corning and Others," in *The Writings of Abraham Lincoln,* 402.

15. See Louis Hartz, *The Liberal Tradition in America: An Interpretation of American Political Thought Since the Revolution* (New York: Harcourt, 1955); the attempt to decouple Locke from the American founding was given an early salvo in John Dunn, *The Political Thought of Jock Locke;* here Dunn asserts—he does nothing more than this—that the claim that Locke's *Second Treatise* was "causally responsible" for the direction of American thought is "largely false," although later in the work, he discerns a "mildly fortuitous relationship" between Locke's book and the American revolution (7, 204). More recently numerous attempts have been made to minimize Locke's role or even read Locke out of the American founding by emphasizing instead the republican or civic humanist tradition of

Machiavelli—see, for example, J. G. A. Pocock, *The Machiavellian Moment: Florentine Political Thought and the Atlantic Republican Tradition* (Princeton: Princeton University Press, 1978)—and sometimes the Scottish Enlightenment tradition, as in Garry Wills, *Explaining America: The Federalist* (New York: Penguin, 1982); for an attempt to update the older view about Locke's influence on the American framers, see Michael Zuckert, *Natural Rights and the New Republicanism* (Princeton: Princeton University Press, 1994).

16. John Rawls, *A Theory of Justice* (Cambridge, MA: Harvard University Press, 1971).
17. Rawls, *A Theory of Justice*, 3–4.
18. Rawls, *A Theory of Justice*, 101.
19. Joseph Cropsey, "The United States as Regime and the Sources of the American Way of Life," in *Political Philosophy and the Issues of Politics* (Chicago: University of Chicago Press, 1977), 7.

CHAPTER 10

Rousseau on Civilization and Its Discontents

1. There are so many wonderful books on Rousseau, one hardly knows where to begin; just a few from which I have learned are Judith Shklar, *Men and Citizens: A Study of Rousseau's Social Theory* (Cambridge: Cambridge University Press, 1969); Hilail Gildin, *Rousseau's "Social Contract": The Design of the Argument* (Chicago: University of Chicago Press, 1983); Jean Starobinski, *Jean-Jacques Rousseau: Transparency and Obstruction,* trans. Arthur Goldhammer (Chicago: University of Chicago Press, 1988); Arthur Melzer, *The Natural Goodness of Man: On the System of Rousseau* (Chicago: University of Chicago Press, 1990).
2. The best guide to Rousseau's life is still Rousseau himself; see Jean-Jacques Rousseau, *The Confessions and Correspondence, Including the Letters to Malesherbes,* trans. Christopher Kelly, ed. Christopher Kelly, Roger D. Masters, and Peter G. Stillman (Hanover, NH: University Press of New England, 1995); a good contemporary biography is Maurice Cranston, *Jean-Jacques: The Early Life and Work of Jean-Jacques Rousseau, 1712–1754* (Chicago: University of Chicago Press, 1990) and *The Noble Savage: Jean-Jacques Rousseau, 1754–1762* (Chicago: University of Chicago Press, 1991); see also Christopher Kelly, *Rousseau's Exemplary Life: The "Confessions" as Political Philosophy* (Ithaca: Cornell University Press, 1987).
3. Jean-Jacques Rousseau, *Emile, or On Education,* trans. Allan Bloom (New York: Basic Books, 1979), 37.
4. For some highly suggestive Marxified readings of Rousseau, see Louis Althusser, *Politics and History: Montesquieu, Rousseau, Hegel, and Marx,* trans. Ben Brewster (London: Verso, 1972); Lucio Colletti, *From Rousseau to Lenin: Studies in Ideology and Society,* trans. John Merrington and Judith White (London: Verso, 1972); Andrew Levine, *The General Will: Rousseau, Marx, Communism* (Cambridge: Cambridge University Press, 1993).
5. Alexandre Kojève, *Introduction to the Reading of Hegel,* trans. James H. Nichols (New York: Basic Books, 1969).
6. See Michel de Montaigne, "Of Cannibals," in *The Complete Essays of Montaigne,* trans. Donald Frame (Stanford: Stanford University Press, 1976), 150–59; this essay

became the basis for Judith Shklar's "Putting Cruelty First," in *Ordinary Vices* (Cambridge, MA: Harvard University Press, 1984), 7–44.

7. For some of the recent attempts to deny the coherence of the Rousseauean notion of a general will, see Anthony Downs, *An Economic Theory of Democracy* (New York: Harper, 1957); William H. Riker, *Liberalism against Populism: A Confrontation between the Theory of Democracy and the Theory of Social Choice* (San Francisco: W. H. Freeman, 1982); for an insightful critique of this literature, see Brian Barry, *Economists, Sociologists, and Democracy* (Chicago: University of Chicago Press, 1978).

8. For the "totalitarian" reading of Rousseau, see Jacob Talmon, *The Rise of Totalitarian Democracy* (Boston: Beacon, 1952); see also Lester Crocker, *Rousseau's Social Contract: An Interpretive Essay* (Cleveland: Case Western Reserve University Press, 1968).

9. Robespierre, cited in Carol Blum, *Rousseau and the Republic of Virtue: The Language of Politics in the French Revolution* (Ithaca: Cornell University Press, 1986), 156–57; see also Bernard Manin, "Rousseau," in *A Critical Dictionary of the French Revolution,* ed. François Furet and Mona Ozouf, trans. Arthur Goldhammer (Cambridge, MA: Harvard University Press, 1989), 829–41.

10. Edmund Burke, "A Letter to a Member of the National Assembly," in *Further Reflections on the Revolution in France,* ed. Daniel E. Ritchie (Indianapolis: Liberty Press, 1992), 47.

11. Immanuel Kant, *Observations on the Feeling of the Beautiful and Sublime and Other Writings,* trans. Paul Guyer and Patrick Frierson (New York: Cambridge University Press, 2011), 96.

12. Tocqueville to Louis de Kergolay, November 12, 1836; cited in Harvey C. Mansfield and Delba Winthrop, "Editors' Introduction," in *Democracy in America,* (Chicago: University of Chicago Press, 2000), xxx.

CHAPTER 11
Tocqueville and the Dilemmas of Democracy

1. For some of the better attempts to understand Tocqueville's "new science," see Raymond Aron, *Main Currents of Sociological Thought,* vol. 1, trans. Richard Howard and Helen Weaver (New York: Doubleday, 1970); John Koritansky, *Alexis de Tocqueville and the New Science of Politics* (Durham, NC: Carolina Academic Press, 1986); Roger Boesche, *The Strange Liberalism of Alexis de Tocqueville* (Ithaca: Cornell University Press, 1987); Pierre Manent, *Tocqueville and the Nature of Democracy,* trans. John Waggoner (Lanham, MD: Rowman and Littlefield, 1996); for a strange effort to turn Tocqueville into a "rational choice" theorist, see Jon Elster, *Alexis de Tocqueville: The First Social Scientist* (Cambridge: Cambridge University Press, 2009).

2. Tocqueville to Louis de Kergolay, October 5, 1828, in *Journeys to England and Ireland,* ed. J. P. Mayer, trans. George Lawrence and K. P. Mayer (New Brunswick, NJ: Transaction, 1988), 21.

3. Tocqueville's American journey has been discussed in George Pierson, *Tocqueville in America* (New York: Oxford University Press, 1938); James Schleifer, *The Making*

of Tocqueville's "Democracy in America" (Chapel Hill: University of North Carolina Press, 1980).

4. Bernard-Henri Lévy, *American Vertigo: Traveling America in the Footsteps of Tocqueville* (New York: Random House, 2006).

5. John Stuart Mill, "De Tocqueville on Democracy in America," in *The Philosophy of John Stuart Mill: Ethical, Political, and Religious,* ed. Marshall Cohen (New York: Modern Library, 1961), 123.

6. Tocqueville to Louis de Kergolay, January 1835, in *Alexis de Tocqueville: Selected Letters on Politics and Society,* trans. Roger Boesche and James Toupin (Berkeley: University of California Press, 1985), 95

7. Robert D. Putnam, *Bowling Alone: The Collapse and Revival of American Community* (New York: Simon and Schuster, 2000). Putnam was not the first to use Tocqueville to reflect on the fate of community in America; see also Robert N. Bellah, Richard Madsen, William M. Sullivan, Anne Swidler, and Steven M. Tipton, *Habits of the Heart: Individualism and Commitment in American Life* (Berkeley: University of California Press, 1985).

8. Blaise Pascal, *Pensées,* trans. Roger Ariew (Indianapolis: Hackett, 2005), frag. 200 (p. 64); for some interesting thoughts on Pascal's influence on Tocqueville, see Peter Augustine Lawler, "The Human Condition: Tocqueville's Debt to Rousseau and Pascal," in *Liberty, Equality, Democracy* (New York: New York University Press, 1992), 1–20.

9. Alexis de Tocqueville, *The Old Regime and the Revolution, Volume II: Notes on the French Revolution and Napoleon,* ed. François Furet and Françoise Mélonio, trans. Alan S. Kahan (Chicago: University of Chicago Press, 2001), 296.

10. Michael Oakeshott, *On Human Conduct* (Oxford: Clarendon Press, 1975), 308.

11. Michel Foucault, *Discipline and Punish: The Birth of the Prison,* trans. Alan Sheridan (New York: Vintage Books, 1995), 3–6.

12. For some useful accounts of the concept of self-interest, see J. A. W. Gunn, *Politics and the Public Interest in the Seventeenth Century* (London: Routledge and Kegan Paul, 1969); Albert O. Hirschman, *The Passions and the Interests: Political Arguments for Capitalism before Its Triumph* (Princeton: Princeton University Press, 1977); Jane J. Mansbridge, ed., *Beyond Self-Interest* (Chicago: University of Chicago Press, 1990).

13. For a fascinating discussion of the Tocqueville-Gobineau correspondence on race, see James W. Ceaser, *Reconstructing America: The Symbol of America in Modern Thought* (New Haven: Yale University Press, 1997), 136–61.

CHAPTER 12
In Defense of Patriotism

1. *Sayings of the Fathers or Pirke Aboth,* trans. Joseph H. Hertz (New York: Behrman, 1945), I:14.

2. Cicero, *On Divination,* trans. David Wardle (Oxford: Oxford University Press, 2006), I, 55 (p. 63).

3. Machiavelli to Francesco Vettori, April 16, 1527, in *Machiavelli and His Friends: Their Personal Correspondence,* trans. and ed. James B. Atkinson and David Sices (DeKalb: Northern Illinois University Press, 1996), no. 331 (p. 416).

4. Jean-Jacques Rousseau, *The Social Contract and Other Later Political Writings,* trans. Victor Gourevitch (Cambridge: Cambridge University Press, 1997), book 1 (p. 41).

5. Edmund Burke, *Reflections on the Revolution in France,* ed. Connor Cruise O'Brien (New York: Viking, 1986), 172.

6. Abraham Lincoln, "Eulogy on Henry Clay," in *The Writings of Abraham Lincoln,* ed. Steven B. Smith (New Haven: Yale University Press, 2012), 48.

7. James Boswell, *The Life of Samuel Johnson,* ed. R. W. Chapman (London: Oxford University Press, 1957), 615; Boswell adds the following clarification: "He did not mean a real and generous love of country but that pretended patriotism which so many, in all ages and countries, have made a cloak for self-interest."

8. E. M. Forster, *Two Cheers for Democracy* (New York: Harcourt and Brace, 1951), 68–69.

9. For a recent collection that expresses a number of contemporary views, see *For Love of Country: Debating the Limits of Patriotism,* ed. Joshua Cohen (Boston: Beacon Press, 1996); see also George Kateb, *Patriotism and Other Mistakes* (New Haven: Yale University Press, 2006); for one of the very best, although frequently unacknowledged, discussions, see Alasdair MacIntyre, "Is Patriotism a Virtue?" (The Lindley Lecture, University of Kansas, 1984); for a defense of patriotism, see Walter Berns, *Making Patriots* (Chicago: University of Chicago Press, 2001).

10. Aristotle, *Nicomachean Ethics,* trans. Martin Ostwald (Indianapolis: Bobbs-Merrill, 1962), 1106b–7a (p. 43).

11. Carl Schmitt, *The Concept of the Political,* trans. George Schwab (New Brunswick, NJ: Rutgers University Press, 1976).

12. Schmitt, *The Concept of the Political,* 29.

13. Immanuel Kant, "Perpetual Peace: A Philosophical Sketch," in *Political Writings,* ed. Hans Reiss, trans. H. B. Nisbet (Cambridge: Cambridge University Press, 1970), 93–130.

14. Montesquieu, *The Spirit of the Laws,* trans. Anne Cohler, Basia Miller, and Harold Stone (Cambridge: Cambridge University Press, 1989), V, ii (pp. 42–43).

15. See Michael Ignatieff, "The Seductiveness of Moral Disgust," in *The Warrior's Honor: Ethnic War and the Modern Conscience* (New York: Henry Holt, 1997), 72–108.

16. See Kant, "Perpetual Peace," 113.

17. Frederick Engels, "Socialism: Utopian and Scientific," in Karl Marx and Frederick Engels, *Selected Works,* vol. 3 (Moscow: Progress, 1973), 147, 151.

18. See Francis Fukuyama, *The End of History and the Last Man* (New York: Free Press, 1992).

19. Screenplay by Julius J. Epstein, Philip G. Epstein, and Howard Koch, *Casablanca* (www.weeklyscript.com/casablanca.txt).

20. Friedrich Nietzsche, *Beyond Good and Evil,* trans. Walter Kaufmann (New York: Vintage, 1966), para. 242 (p. 176).

21. Max Weber, *The Protestant Ethic and the Spirit of Capitalism,* trans. Talcott Parsons (New York: Charles Scribner's Sons, 1958), 182.

22. See the lovely essay by Robert Pinsky, "Eros against Esperanto," in Cohen, ed., *For Love of Country,* 85–90.

23. Herodotus, *The History,* trans. David Grene (Chicago: University of Chicago Press, 1987), I.134 (p. 96).

24. Alexis de Tocqueville, *Democracy in America*, trans. Harvey C. Mansfield and Delba Winthrop (Chicago: University of Chicago Press, 2000), I.ii.6 (p. 227).

25. Tocqueville, *Democracy in America*, I.ii.9 (p. 275).

26. Burke, *Reflections on the Revolution in France*, 119.

27. Hannah Arendt, *Eichmann in Jerusalem: A Report on the Banality of Evil* (New York: Viking, 1963).

28. Gershom Scholem to Hannah Arendt, June 23, 1963, in *On Jews and Judaism in Crisis: Selected Essays*, ed. Werner J. Dannhauser (New York: Schocken, 1976), 302.

29. Winston Churchill, "Consistency in Politics," in *Thoughts and Adventures*, ed. James W. Muller (Wilmington: ISI Books, 2009), 35–36.

30. Some of the ideas contained in this chapter appeared in Steven B. Smith, "In Defense of Politics," *National Affairs* (Spring 2011): 131–43.

Index